My Wretched A

This Damn Puppeteer

Brian Charles Harding

Circaidy Gregory Press

Copyright information

Cover illustrations by Louise Hackman-Hexter

Paperback ISBN 978-1-910841-21-1
First published December 2015
ebook ISBN 978-1-910841-22-8
First published December 2015
Available in .mobi, ePub and .pdf formats from
Circaidy Gregory Press contact info@circaidygregory.co.uk

Printed in the UK by
Catford Print

Published by Circaidy Gregory Press
Creative Media Centre,
45 Robertson St, Hastings,
Sussex TN34 1HL

www.circaidygregory.co.uk

Acknowledgements

To my wife, Indra

Thank you from the bottom of my heart. You never stumbled; your confidence in us never faltered, and for that I am deeply indebted to you. There are people who advised you to leave me alone, but despite this, you persevered – you never gave up. Thank you, Indra.

To PC John Hearn, CA345

Thank you for not nicking me as often as you could. You told me once that the answer to a lot of our social ills is understanding and communication. I have to believe you. Thank you, John.

To Ms Fay Ritchie RON, RMN, Dip C, BA (Hons)

Thank you for everything. I often wonder whether you, like me, ever answer – when being questioned about who is on the outside loooking in, and who is on the inside looking out – I don't know. Thank you, Fay.

To Robyn Rimell

The Community Alcohol Team was formed in or around 1991. Robyn Rimell was a counsellor at that time. I was her first client. While I remember little of the counselling that took place during that period, because I was in such a mess, I never forgot Robyn.

Robyn had an insight that other people didn't have. It was another ten years or so before I met her again. I explained 1 was trying to put a book together, and whilst it was supposed to be a cathartic exercise, 1 had yet to experience any feelings of catharsis. Robyn's reply was short and to the point. 'It will be cathartic. I'll help you.' She would sit for hours with me, going over every little detail. Thank you, Robyn.

Foreword

Brian Charles Harding has been known to our agency (Action for Change) since 1993, and I have known Brian in my role as alcohol liaison nurse for the past 6 years.

My work with Brian has been frustrating, arduous, inspiring, humbling and complex. I have often found Brian to be enigmatic, making our contacts and interventions at times challenging, and our relationship provocative and inflammative.

Brian's feud with alcohol, himself and his past cannot easily be contextualised – however, Brian's journey with alcohol is presented here – for you, the reader – in an honest, frank and candid way.

Exposing the anguish, torment and wretchedness of his life and alcohol use in such a way was astounding to me – Why? A question I have asked myself many times – my answer – Brian's Journey was exactly that – his journey – not mine.

My need as a worker to attempt every intervention to 'help' Brian was – my need, not his. Brian's need was to drink alcohol – yet the severity of his consumption and the subsequent gravity of his ill-health meant he had no choice but to either make changes or face the reality of a premature death.

He chose to make changes, hence this book which lays bare the traumatic experiences of his life and relationships with alcohol and people. It has been the most cathartic intervention for his alcohol misuse of any I or our agency has been able to offer.

This accentuates Brian's inner strengths and his ability to dig deep past his alcohol use into his very soul to find a part of the person he still is. I would encourage every alcohol worker, alcohol user and lay person who reads this book to reflect profoundly on their own beliefs, understanding and assumed knowledge of alcohol and its cause and effect.

Although Brian is still drinking and his journey continues, we can all learn from his courage. This book is a poignant reminder that alcohol misuse is not a carefree or fun choice, but a protector and defender for many individuals.

So my journey continues with Brian, neither of us knowing where it will lead, but it is a journey I feel privileged to be witness to, and one which I hope concludes with some sense of conciliation for Brian.

Fay Ritchie, RGN, RMN, Dip C, BA (Hons)   Alcohol Liaison Nurse

Contents

1

An Open Letter to Alcoholism

Alcoholism,

As I stand before you, bloodied, shaken, and almost without resources, you know I'm still not bowed. For over forty years you've clawed at my very soul, but I'm still with you, and you now know I know you. After all this time I've finally recognised you; you have been exposed; my friends and neighbours recognise you also. They have seen at first hand what you've done to me.

I will tell everybody about you and, as I stand before them, sometimes incoherent, sometimes speaking gibberish, I will be all the evidence they need. You will be outed; you will have no invitations from any of these people who have been witness to my drunkenness; they will tell their friends about you, and their friends will tell their children.

Nobody will ever invite you in again; you will end up having to stand on the borders searching for your prey, and nobody will come to you. It will be you that is alone; you will have no secrets you can conceal. You will be openly exposed for what you are. There is a whole army of people that, after all this time, recognises you and is willing to take you on.

As you know, I live in Hastings, East Sussex. We have our own Community Alcohol Team. They are hard-working, diligent, and very knowledgeable people. They have seen at first hand the damage you cause, the heartache, the confusion, and, ultimately, death. They accept you are real and will no longer tolerate it. They recognise the damage you have caused, and have closed ranks to help us take up arms against you. You will not flourish, at least not in our town; we will kill you.

The Community Alcohol Team, myself, and any other drunk I know, will fight you on a daily basis. We have detox units, rehabilitation centres and halfway houses. They are full to the gunnels, but we will keep on and on and on, and between us we will do it. I'm afraid our government takes so much revenue from you that they can't just suddenly make you illegal, but they are slowly realising that a large chunk of this is being taken up by having to treat all the thousands upon thousands of people who you make ill, so ill in fact that a large proportion of these people are also unemployable, and will remain so until they die.

Also, a certain percentage among their ranks of government are suffering too, so beware alcoholism, we are on to you. You must be laughing your head off at our government's feeble attempt to stop our children from engaging in you until they are sixteen years of age. For we both know you can be bought anywhere by anyone at anytime. And, even as I write this letter, the government is pushing ahead with legislation to legalise longer licensing hours.

My contribution in our battle to have you destroyed is in the writing of this book. I will expose you for what you really are, to as many people, young or old, as I can. We are aware that you will get in where a virus wouldn't survive.

Yours sincerely,

You know my name

Introduction

I sat transfixed. It was 10am. I had just finished my fourth can. I had an empty stomach, having not eaten for several weeks. To have consumed four cans at this time of the day was normal. The lady in front of me was my doctor. I guess she was about forty, although she looked much younger. 'If you continue to drink,' she intoned, 'you will have no quality of life.'

A pearl of wisdom I had heard many times before. I was 56 years of age. I had my first taste of alcohol on the day of the Queen's Coronation in 1953. While I didn't then know what 'being drunk' meant, I now know that it's what it made me. A further six years were to pass before I started to use drink. The doctor I was listening to was allocated to me. All my previous doctors had struck me from their registers. I will explain more about this later. The doctor was kind. Despite my addled and disorientated brain, I was immediately impressed by her manner. In retrospect I know she had no first hand knowledge of alcoholism. I, at this point, knew everything – except how to stop. I've led a wretched life, never providing, producing, creating or contributing anything.

My affair with drink has rendered me, for the most part, incontinent, impotent, and without any real place in this society. I still manage to keep clean, although I don't feel it. My wife's friends treat me politely and with a respect that I feel is guarded, and with a false affinity. False, in that everyone is a "holic" of some sort or another. They have no idea.

I have no point of reference as to how life would be without drink. It seems I have always been steeped in drink. I am drunk now. I quite probably won't finish this diary.

I leave the doctor's surgery at 10.20am – we've spoken for 20 minutes. She gave me a prescription for some drug that will stop my arms from bleeding, caused by liver failure. My doctor's surgery, for the 20 minutes I was there, was safe, sanitary, efficient, warm and without time. How contrasting can one hour be? I am now cold, detached, isolated, but I am aware, very aware. The lady who passed me by didn't speak; the guy walking his dog changed his course to avoid me. Welcome, reality.

You can trust somebody your whole life until they ask you, 'Do you trust me?' And it is at that point that you question yourself. Not so with a bloke I met about 21 years ago. He, at that point, was a complete stranger. He asked me for 89 pence, with the promise that he would pay me back the very next day – I liked and trusted him immediately. My instinct proved me right. I still like him, as I know he does me. He still lives in Hastings and, although I haven't seen him for several months, I know via the grapevine that he is still alive. The reason I mentioned this gentleman is because there's a good chance I will see him this morning. I'm in a small park opposite where I live. I spoke with a girl I know, Sandra. She, like myself, is an alcoholic, and she told me that Ron, who is also an alcoholic, might be up today as another girl we know owes him some money: £5 in fact. I have been here an hour and have seen no-one except that lady who ignored me, and the chap who changed his course to avoid me. I don't think Ron will get his money.

I'm doing a stock-take; I have about one litre of cider left. In a minute I'll have to walk down to Fat Alan's – the off-licence. I'm powerless. Powerless, that is, until I reach a certain stage of drunkenness whereby I can sit down, read the latest headlines and feel unaffected. That to me is a little bit of power – albeit short-lived. There is no sign of Ron. I'm feeling centred, at one with the universe, bullet proof, so will I walk among my fellow men and feel normal, even superior?

Fat Alan's not serving; a new girl's on. I think that, by the way she looked at me, she must have a PhD in looking with disdain without speaking. 'I'm only an alcoholic and it isn't contagious.' That's what I wish I had said to her. Instead, I thanked her profusely and left.

At this point, I have a stagger. My addled mind tells me it must be around mid-day. I see the Community Sergeant whom I've known since he was just a PC and I was insane with drink. We greet each other with a handshake. He took stock of me in an instant. I must have appeared reasonably sober, as he allowed me to continue on towards the shopping centre. The journey between Fat Alan's and the shopping centre is about a quarter of a mile. It would take a normal person, walking purposefully, about five minutes. It took me 20.

I'm now sitting outside Marks & Spencer's. I have no fear, and want to be noticed. I am desperate for the milk of human kindness, although I know it will never be. For the people who find some sort of attraction in me instinctively know something is wrong. Perhaps I and my ilk send out signals subliminally. I've been here almost one hour, and drunk two litres. Security is watching me. Their uniforms are neatly pressed; they look clean and smart. They have obviously got up this morning in their own good time, had breakfast, showered and are ready to take on the low-life.

4

They target me immediately because they know me from old, and they know I will bite. I don't think it's in my favour that I am articulate; this un-nerves them. They flounder, they panic. They are not equipped to deal with polite reasoning. They are bullies with a basic fundamental flaw in their own characters, and I think they know it. They call the police. I am arrested. They said I wouldn't leave the shopping precinct; funnily enough I was just about ready to leave.

I am now in a cell, and a doctor has been called. He will administer 20 milligrams of Librium which will sedate me until I get home. They don't care where that is.

Three hours after my arrest and temporary confinement, I am staggering home. They have done their job: the police, the security guards and most members of the general public are suitably satisfied that justice has been done; so am I.

It's 6.20am. In seconds I will be sick, violently and seemingly without end. Today I have a free day: no doctor. Early morning sickness is all part and parcel of being an alcoholic; we accept it. I realise that this isn't attractive to a potential mate, and also understand that's why we're alone. After all, who wants to wake up with a bloke whom you think at any minute now is about to die? The kettle's turned itself off, and I have stopped being sick. I am now thinking about my supply. I have two litres of cider, £31, and it's Tuesday. I must be back in the precinct this morning, although I don't know why I have to be there.

I am now back in the shopping precinct. I'm sitting here thinking I'm doing a sentence, but I don't recall committing a crime. Experts say they can't help a drinker unless that drinker helps him or herself. I find that odd, as I would do anything for myself, even give my life. Perhaps that's what I *am* doing. I don't want to dwell on this.

Margaret, Head of Security, walks by; she asks how I got on yesterday. I don't think she's interested. I rather think she just has this fascination for, as she sees it, the seedier side of life. I nod, and gesture towards my drink, which says, 'I'm still free and still drinking.' She smiles knowingly, almost conspiratorially, and carries on walking, probably looking for someone seedier than me, for after all, apart from abusing myself, I still know what respect means. I envy her and her ilk. What a conflicting mess I'm in!

I've decanted my cider into a soft drinks container so as to avoid detection. How creepy this illness is, as if my fellow men don't know. My very demeanour screams I'm not right.

It is exactly four weeks to the day since I completed 24 days in a Detox Unit. I was pumped full of vitamins, and gained a stone in weight. I am now ten stone. My detox, after the first week, was for the following three weeks, heaven on earth. I actually became potent; a feeling void in almost all alcoholics. I say "almost" because I know a fellow alcoholic who raped someone. He was sentenced to five years, and yet recalls nothing of the event. The poor girl will have to live with that for the rest of her life. How sad!

A young woman has knelt before me to tend her child. There is a gap between the top of her trousers and the bottom of her sweat top. The small of her back is exposed; she has a small tattoo, and it's erotic. I have a twinge; it's sexual, and she is unaware. Is there a penalty for desire? She finishes tending the child, and turns to me and asks almost solicitously: 'Can I squeeze in there?' I reply, 'Yes, we're both only small.' She tells me her partner, the father of her child, is on drugs. I don't really know what to say, so I just say: 'It's a shame.' She says, 'A SHAME? It's a fucking LIBERTY. How dare he?' I think of her tattoo and why she thinks she had that done other than to be attractive to men. Think about it! Yes, it is a LIBERTY, but who's taking it? Her partner comes out of the store and says, 'I'll fucking kill them cunts.' Apparently they wouldn't give him a refund. 'Calm down,' she says.

'I'll kill 'em. Who's this cunt?' She says: 'He is just sitting here.' He responds: 'Let's fuck off.' They leave. I will probably never see them again. What a LIBERTY!

Being sober means you have to be able to speak in cold blood. It's difficult, but it can be achieved with practice; to be drunk and speak doesn't count. It's not allowed.

My wife stops by with her friend. They have been busy shopping; she tells me that there is a young couple at the entrance to the precinct, fighting. 'She was lying on the floor, crying and bleeding. He was standing over her with fists clenched.' My wife tells me that the girl had a tattoo on the small of her back; what a LIBERTY! My wife tells me she will see me later. I nod, and she leaves.

My mobile rings – it's a drinking companion of mine from way back. He asks if I have any tobacco. I tell him I have if he has the money – he says he has, and we arrange to meet in 30 minutes, in the park just opposite where I live.

The chap I'm about to meet is now dead. He died just ten days after our meeting; in the park, from hypothermia. He lived alone in a bedsit. I will talk more about this later.

6

As I approached the park, I could see Tony's back. He was talking to the lady who ignored me a couple of days previously, or even that same day – I am not sure. As I sat down, Tony turned to me and said, 'I love this man,' then he kissed me on the head. The lady looked at both of us and mused.

Tony had been drinking vodka and still had half a bottle left. I walked over to my flat and got Tony's tobacco. I returned; I had with me a two-litre plastic jug and a two-litre bottle of cider. We drank about a litre of cider, and then we poured the vodka and the remaining litre of cider into the plastic jug. Tony and I were now drinking.

The lady who had found us both amusing a few minutes ago now had a change of heart. I think she felt threatened, not from anything physical, but more by our raw, naked uninhibited state. She had never seen anything like it at first hand. She wished us 'Bon voyage', and then left.

Tony and I came to at dusk; we were both lying on the ground – a familiar position. We managed to sit upright on the bench. It's stock-taking time again. How much do we hurt? How much money do we have? Is there any drink left? Were we rude to that lady? Why hasn't my wife come to find me? We decide that I should go to the off-licence and get two litres of cider just to enable us to stay alive and get home.

I feel a sense of outrage, but I don't know at what. I can't blame my first drink at the Queen's Coronation, or my last drink with Tony, so the blame must lay with me. Damn these people. I, and I alone, own this problem: these people haven't even got part shares. We alcoholics are a bit like captive animals. We can be looked at, frowned upon, ridiculed, taken into custody and made to pay a penance. It really is a funny thing to have to command this amount of attention and yet have no power. I think it says more about sober people than it does about us alcoholics. What a LIBERTY!

It's morning, and I'm in bed. I have to be sick; that done, I can now concentrate on my DTs – *Delirium Tremens*. I know that this state will last for about thirty minutes. It's a good job that the lady in the park can't see me now. I absent-mindedly wonder about Tony. Today I am supposed to have a brain scan; my GP arranged it as my fits are becoming more frequent. I think I may have picked up Alcoholic Dementia – a term I picked up in Detox – and was beginning to think that I might be mental. Now that WOULD be a LIBERTY. It would mean I have no control over this illness. That means I would have to relinquish all responsibility, and I'm not going to do that! I want to stand responsible for how I've lived. Everybody I've ever known has suffered through my drinking. How can I hand this problem over to an expert? Experts don't lose control, drinkers do. That alone renders them unqualified. When I'm dead these people will become experts. They will tell you at what time I died, and exactly of what. But, do you know, while I'm alive, they won't do anything. That also is a LIBERTY!

I'm waiting outside my flat; it's 10.30am, my taxi is booked for 10.45am. I have no money except my taxi fare up there, and my bus fare for coming back. I do however have four litres of cider. My taxi arrives on time; we agree the destination, and exchange pleasantries. The journey takes twenty minutes, and neither the driver nor I speak. I just assume he knows me from old.

As I approached the main entrance to the hospital I saw the back of a figure that was familiar, but I didn't quite recognise. As I got closer, I saw it was Ron Milligan, the chap I mentioned earlier, who had been waiting in the park for the girl who owed him some money. I crept up behind him and stuck my fingers in his back; made out I was a policeman. His response was not to turn round, but just to say, 'Fuck Off!' That was Ronnie! He explained that he was there waiting for test results as he had been kicked senseless the previous night. He didn't know how he got there and he was worried; he had only one can. I put his mind at rest and said that he could share mine. Ronnie and I laughed and drank until it was time to keep my appointments.

I went via the lift and the labyrinth of corridors to the designated area where mental people have brain scans. I undressed and sat as instructed. The nurse who treated me was young and very pretty. She couldn't speak very good English. She was of Eastern origin, so she just kept repeating, 'Alcohol; Alcohol; Alcohol – you drink alcohol, yes?' I nodded in agreement, then she just walked away. On the floor next to my feet is my shoulder bag, which hides my cider. I know it will be just a matter of a few minutes before my name is called, and I think, even if I just have to enter the town of my birth, I want to be ready. *Glug, glug, glug* – let's do it! I'm called. I walk robotically, drunkenly to this machine. Then it's over. I feel nothing. My brain is now on a computer – I feel abused, and Ronnie is nowhere to be seen.

The bus takes me to St Leonards where I have lived and drunk for seventeen years. I decide to get off. I go to the off-licence, get some cider, and walk to Bottle Alley. My God! What a state these people are in. It brought me up with a start because I realised in an instant that in their ignorance they were a mirror image of myself. They were totally unaware. Where in God's name are the people who do the brain scans? If that nurse of this morning, who was so concerned about my drinking, could see these people, I think she would faint. I enter the group; my drink-ravaged face is my entry fee. I am automatically allowed a space on the bench. I am accepted. At least four of this small group of seven are comparative newcomers and don't actually know me. My drink-experienced outlook and the fact that I have my own drink is my acceptance to take a place on the bench. They tell me Ronnie had the shit kicked out of him last night; I tell them: 'I know, I saw him at the hospital this morning.'

My sudden arrival in this group generated a bit of anticipation until they all realised that I had no drugs, no tobacco, no drink and no hope. We then became one. What a peculiar thing this drinking is. Bottle Alley is – and I have to be graphic here, for this is how I saw it – almost purpose-built for drinkers. The open side faces east and as you would expect it is just like a wind tunnel in that the wind comes up from the south and heads out to the north.

The girl to my left is now talking to herself; it's not unusual in drinkers. The unusual thing is that she has a dress on. She pulls the dress up to her waist. She turns to Noble (we call him Noble as he has only one testicle) and asks, 'Do you want to fuck me?' He thinks about it for a while, then says, 'O.K. I'll try.' He kneels in front of her and takes his cock out; it is flaccid. He tries to masturbate himself into some sort of sexual state, but can't. She pulls her dress down and storms off into the corner where she urinates. If this sounds graphic, it's simply what I saw and what I heard.

The wind blows up the alley as I sit with the seven other drinkers and you can hear a pin drop; nobody has anything to say. I can't help but wonder what that brain scan has to say. I really wish someone could put some sort of value on that girl's life. I can't because I am involved. I drink. I've been away from this Bottle Alley for just over 17 years so, while I am accepted, I can't help but feel I am an imposition. 'Goodbye Noble.' Nobody speaks. They just stare blankly out to sea.

My journey home from Bottle Alley is uneventful. I walk in, undress and go to bed. I haven't eaten for 36 hours. It's 6.30am and I am being sick. I don't remember much about yesterday except that I had a brain scan and watched Noble try to have sex with this girl.

My doorbell rings; it's Sara the girl who supplies my tobacco. She asks if I am sober. 'No,' I reply. She says, 'OK, I'll come in.' She looks beautiful, and gushes. I wish I didn't drink.

It's 10.20pm the following day and I've just been released from police custody. I can't write any more. Gordon died last night.

It's now 7.00am and I've already been sick. I'm trying to concentrate on the events of yesterday that led up to my arrest. I know I had an appointment here at home with a young lady called Fay. That was at 11.00am. She is 17, a hard-working member of our local community alcohol team. It was a very good meeting, constructive; I find her very helpful.

Adrian rings my bell; it's now just about 12.30pm. We have a couple of glasses of cider. It was he who told me Gordon had died the previous evening in a mutual friend's flat. Quite simply, his cardiac was arrested. We walk towards the town centre. I take with me two litres of cider, a quarter of which is decanted into a soft drinks container. This is to avoid detection – it's an alcohol-free zone. Gordon came from the other part of town where I no longer live. I knew him almost from day one. He was more of a friend of Tony and Ronnie than he was of mine. We were later to spend time together in jail, for totally unrelated crimes, but in almost identical mitigating circumstances: drunk, steal something that is immediately saleable, sell it, buy drink, get arrested, and if you're unlucky on the day, get bird. And that's what we were on that particular day. Unlucky. That incident happened 21 years ago. It was the first of two sentences; the second came some five years later. And I know that's going to be the last.

We reach the shopping precinct and enter the enclosed part. It feels quite warm. I can sense Adrian is getting restless. He is 25 years my junior, and fit. His restlessness worries me, so when he gets up and says, 'I'll catch you later man,' I am actually relieved. I have this overwhelming feeling of having committed a crime again, and I feel I need to be punished. I take my sweat top off and sit in the centre of the enclosed part of the precinct. Other than attracting attention, I just don't know why I'm doing it. I feel I need to be locked up, and yet don't know why. The funny thing is that, once I've been arrested, processed and then locked up for a while, I feel better. In fact, once I'm released and get myself home, I have a strange feeling of contentment, calmness; at one with myself, I really am quite worried about this. I'm frightened where this could lead. And it's just occurred to me that this is my second arrest for D & D in as many months.

It's 8.00am, the day after my arrest. Adrian is ringing my bell; I let him in. Today I want to be quiet; we quickly talk about events that happened to us since last we spoke. Adrian said he wasn't surprised about my arrest as he recognised my mood, and that's the reason he left when he did.

10

My doorbell rings again; it's Sandra, her partner Steve, and friend Neil. Neil is 48 years of age, Scottish, totally bald and a chronic alcoholic. I've never had too much to do with him but have always liked his company. Steve, Sandra's partner, is not an alcoholic. In fact he works quite hard. It's an odd relationship, but does seem to work. They sit down and all have their own drinks except Steve, who, at this time of day, wouldn't dream of drinking; he prefers a cup of tea, which he proceeds to make himself. Sandra has her staple diet of strong, cheap cider, but also has her special half a bottle of brandy. We drink.

As Neil and I start a conversation, we realise we were in adjoining cells the previous day. Small world. He, like me, was charged with being drunk and disorderly. As we laugh and talk and drink, my doorbell goes again; it's Garry, my brother-in-law. I can tell instantly by his demeanour that he's drunk, lucid but drunk. We all re-introduce each other again and carry on where we left off I think the most apt description of Garry would be that of a bumbling professor. He really is quite clever, but you can't help thinking he's useless. I know it's a contradiction but that's how I see Garry. I like him. Neil has to leave; Sandra and Steve follow suit. I don't remember Garry leaving – I am by now quite drunk.

I wake up at 5.00am, almost totally dehydrated. I automatically put the kettle on, and before it switches itself off I am sick. I need a drink. My heart sinks; I'm beside myself with despair to think it was only as little as four weeks ago that I finished my detox and, while a little apprehensive, I felt really fit and quite confident. Now look at me – this is never going to end. I am no longer allowed in the shopping precinct as they have a banishment order against me. What a LIBERTY!

I now have to find a new venue. It's almost the end of January; soon it will be warm. Then I can sit anywhere and spectate. I have a job to take my trousers off. I've just left the Priory Meadow Shopping Precinct. I've been there specifically to see a Mr Steven Ball, who is Head of Security and also the man who authorised my expulsion from the warmth and safety of that very precinct.

I kiss my wife goodnight, but she doesn't respond, and I go to sleep. It's 3.30pm. I wake at 5.45pm and eat a piece of chicken my wife had roasted earlier. I think of my meeting with Mr Steven Ball. I can't help but wonder why he is afraid of me. I've never believed people who claim they are psychic and can foretell the future. But I am bound to say that I do believe in ESP (Extra Sensory Perception). I mention this purely because Mr Steven Ball and myself have actually only ever exchanged words

11

twice, the second time being this afternoon about my banishment from the Centre, but have always felt that we have been aware of each other.

I remember the last time I was in prison: I6 years ago. I was standing in a queue; I think it was for a kit change. I had my eyes squarely fixed on the back of the guy's head in front of me, neither looking to the right nor left. But I was I00% aware of everybody around me. I think it can only be an in-built safety mechanism that kicks in when we sense danger but don't necessarily see it. I think that's probably how Mr Ball sees me – a loose cannon, someone to be wary of. What a LIBERTY!

As I said earlier, I first got drunk at a party in our Council Estate's playground. That was 50 years ago. I was five, and I now know it was watered down wine I was drinking. I also now know it was watered down to save money. It's an all too popular myth in working class people of my age that in the old days we were poor but happy; that isn't true. We were poor but I just can't remember being happy. My mum and dad were forever skint, although I must say I can't ever remember my dad being out of work. He was a hard man, and still is to this day. He is now ninety years of age. I cannot think of one instance when my father showed me any love or affection. Not once. In fact it was the opposite; I do believe he hated me.

I've come to this conclusion by using the fathers of my peers as points of reference. For example, they would kiss, cuddle and praise their sons and daughters. My father though, (this is unbelievable, but quite true), when he had come home from work and eaten his dinner, would then sit in his chair positioned to the right hand side of the lounge door. I used to sit on the left hand side of the door. This seating arrangement for the evening was unwritten, unspoken and yet cast in stone. The reason my father sat on the right hand side of the door was because the door opened inwards and, when it was open, it blocked his view of me. He, for some reason at that point, just couldn't stand the sight of me. It's funny, because it was only a few years previously when he used to try and stick his fingers up my backside in front of my friends and the rest of the family; put them under his nose and say, 'Lovely grub.' It's only now I'm coming towards the latter part of my middle age that I realise that was out and out abuse. I wouldn't even do that to the girl I met in Bottle Alley; the one who asked Noble to have sex with her. Perhaps her father used to do the same thing to her; who knows?

I muddled through and managed to finish my apprenticeship. But at this point, whilst I had a lot of energy and even felt vital, I was completely at a loss as to what to do next. My father didn't like me, and this rubbed

12

off on to my brothers and sisters who, quite naturally, thought if their father didn't like me then something must be wrong.

At the time, the isolation I felt destroyed me. I am now what the more respected members of our society call an oddball. My whole family, myself included, know with experience, knowledge and hindsight, that I was at the very least, badly treated. I took a job at a dry cleaners, so that while I was thinking what to do with myself, I at least had an income.

It was while I was working there that an advert in the daily paper caught my eye. There was this beautiful picture of a modern day North Sea trawler. The advert read, *Be part of our modern day fishing fleet: must be aged between 18 and 21, fit, able-bodied and with a love of the sea. We will train you.* I couldn't believe it; it was almost as if it were written for me. I applied and got an interview; they would forward me a travel warrant for the seaport at Lowestoft.

It was at about this time that I was becoming really quite concerned about this damn drinking business. I think I realised then that I needed to have a drink inside me to be able to have any sort of social interaction with other people. It was a bloody nuisance. I remember so well this part of my life – it was the late '60s.

I arrived on time for my appointment in the shipping office. My actual interview was for the following day. I was given an introductory letter for a local B & B that would ensure that my stay for the night would be paid for. I was told that they did actually have a vacancy in the Seamen's Mission just two doors away but I declined and said the B&B would be fine. I had already noticed a very big sign in the window of the Mission saying, *Absolutely NO alcohol.*

The B&B was just around the corner from all the shipping offices. I rang the bell and was invited in. There were three other lads there, all about my age. I was later to realise that this particular B&B was almost entirely dependent for their income on the shipping company that I was later to be contracted to. In short, they would tolerate almost anything. That in itself meant I could drink. While it was very important for me to pass this exam of Basic Seamanship and become a Qualified Deck Hand, it was equally important for me to be able to drink.

I had a good feeling I could do both, which I did, with consequences that I still suffer from to this day. I soon found out that three other lads had travelled up the same day, from their respective home towns. We were given two rooms, and I shared a room with a bloke called Billy. I noticed he declined the offer of dinner, which was to be served at 6.00pm, saying that he had already eaten. I also declined; I had half a bottle of vodka I wanted to drink, and I didn't want dinner taking up any space. It seems that Billy had the same idea, for when I went to my room to drink my vodka, Billy was sitting by the window drinking from a bottle of whisky.

Apart from saying 'OK', neither of us spoke. We didn't have to, although we had never met before, we knew we were both alcoholics and were glad of each other's company, so this ritual took place in complete silence. I was aware of somebody knocking on the door; it was the other two lads asking us to join them for a night on the town. Billy and I readily agreed, for after all we were confident, happy, and by now bullet-proof 'Let's do it!' We entered this pub and, whilst I didn't know it at the time, it was to be my place of refuge for the next two years.

I did keep my appointment the following day, and was accepted. I did do my Observer trip for 21 days, and I did attend the Navigational College for eight weeks and, after just three trips as a Deckhand Learner, did get a Fully Qualified Deckhand's Certificate. I was on my way.

As soon as we entered the pub, I was struck by how friendly the girls were. There were also many of them, but what put me off a little bit was the fact that they did seem a bit old. At that point I was 20. Although by then I was drinking huge amounts of alcohol, I did also have a huge appetite for sex, and these women did look to me to be about 40. I was soon to learn that they were really just about my own age. I was also soon to learn that they were to become very important in my life for the next two years. They were commonly known as "dock girls". The pub was called *The Bank Stores*; the house next to it was where at least four of these girls lived permanently.

I never did know who the landlord was; I don't think they did. Between trips at sea and my run-ashore leave, this is where I spent most of my time. I always had money and, whilst ashore, the love of these girls.

When I look back on my life now, I realise I had opted out. I was able to earn money and could always have the love of a woman. Unlike courting, where if I couldn't perform sexually I was ridiculed, in this situation they didn't take it personally. What I also realised at this point was that what I wanted and never got was the approval and the love of my hard-working dad. I kept this routine up for about twelve months; it was fairly uneventful apart from the occasional fright at sea and the odd arrest for being drunk and, if not incapable, then it was disorderly conduct. I do recall at some point I actually went home to Sevenoaks in Kent, where I was born. My family still lived there. I can't really tell you much about this except that my father, at some point during my visit, held me against

14

the wall of our living room and said, 'You are not welcome here.' He also said, for some strange reason, 'Leave my wife alone.' I also had a black eye, and I don't know to this day where that came from. It seems odd to me now that at the time these events meant nothing, but here I am some 36 years later realising they are all part and parcel of where I am today.

At this point, I must mention a girl I met; I still think of her now even after all these years. She was just 18 years old. She came from a rich family and was also beautiful. I loved her, as I know she loved me. The attraction I felt for her was that I knew she was loved. Loved by her father and mother, and that to me was worth all the riches this world could possibly offer. She acted as if she were loved. She was my opposite, as I was hers.

I was standing just outside the Mission, with dungarees on and no shoes. It was summer and it was very hot. I didn't have in any way what you would call good looks, but I knew from the comments of the dock girls that I was fanciable. I was lean, hard, and very tanned. I had black hair. In fact, looking back, I was a menace.

This girl, who I will refer to as Mary, stopped dead in front of me and she bloody well unnerved me. She was stunning. She asked if I spoke English. I replied 'No', and she laughed. I knew in an instant that if I were to fish for the rest of my life, with no shore leave in between, I would never own this girl. She was stunning and I was stunned. In the split-second that it took me to say anything sensible, I thought of my father sticking his fingers up my backside and knew instantly that her father had never done that to her.

Someone, somewhere had taken a LIBERTY. I must have said the right thing because I found myself walking with her towards the causeway; this meant one thing. It was Land's End, and she trusted me; I knew we would be physical. There's no need to go into details as to what happened, just let it be enough to know I will never forget that beautiful day. Although I loved her, my alcoholism didn't. We walked back inland hand in hand. As we passed by the Seamen's Mission and the Bank Stores I could see all the deck crew. Chief Engineers, third hands and even some of the ship's cooks that I had sailed with in the past. They were mostly drunk and mostly laughing, but I was by now quite sober and had been since I fell in love three hours ago. I just couldn't see how, in any way, what they were doing could be fun. We got to the bus stop and spent the next hour kissing each other goodbye – we couldn't wait until nine o'clock that night, for that was when we had arranged we would next meet – for dinner at her father's house.

That was my mistake. I managed to find her father's house with the help of a local taxi driver. It was a country house six miles from town. The trouble was, when I left Mary at the bus stop I went straight to *The Bank Stores*. I was now standing outside the massive wrought iron gates, having just paid the driver off. I had managed to have a shower and put clean clothes on, but I had also managed to drink a few bottles of wine with the boys before I got the taxi here.

Again that was my mistake. I tried the gate and, for some reason, was surprised to find it open. It just seemed to me that such a place ought to be locked up. Perhaps it was just me who ought to be locked up. I walked up this long gravel drive; the grounds were immaculate. I remember there were a couple of caravans to my left, and further up to my right was a big beautiful paddock with horses running about. Inside, as I got to this massive great front door, I was surprised to see it was wide open. At this point I hadn't actually seen anybody, although you could feel it was a very lived-in place both inside and out. I looked in through the door and had never seen anything like it, let alone had dinner there.

It was less than an hour ago that I was drinking with the boys, totally confident and full of myself. Now, staring through this doorway, I was suddenly very nervous. I might have been Jack-the-Lad in the pubs, but I certainly wasn't here. I'm no way a country boy but it did occur to me that now might be a good time to brave all those miles of fields and try to get back to town. I didn't have time to think about it any more though; Mary appeared.

My heart stopped; I had never ever seen anybody so devastatingly beautiful. In that instant I was the happiest I ever remember being in my entire life. In the time it took her to introduce me to the rest of her family, I realised I was also the saddest for I knew in my heart, despite her beauty and the acceptance of me by her family, I wanted a drink. I also knew this feeling would be recurrent for the rest of my life.

The few things I do recall from that dinner make me glad that I don't remember the rest. Apart from the few hours I spent making love with Mary that afternoon I had been, which was always the case whilst ashore, drinking all day. We were drinking wine with our dinner. It was at this point that it happened. I was suddenly insane; sane, normal and natural in my drunken world, but insane among this sober, normal family. There was, as I recall, sitting at the table, the mother, the father, a German student, a Nigerian student, an auntie, Mary, and myself.

Now I probably wasn't dressed as well as they would have liked Mary's new boyfriend to be, but they must have been decent people because they didn't try to make me look or feel awkward in any way. I attacked the father. It's as simple as that; it was a totally unprovoked attack. They were going to a concert and would be back later, and were glad I would be with Mary until they returned. The father kissed Mary goodbye, and then came over to me with an outstretched arm to shake my hand. He was about two feet away from me; I punched him full in the face. I have never done anything like this before in my life, but he was senseless. The students saw what happened and, in short, beat me to a pulp. Now I was senseless!

One tried to hold me while the other called the police. Mary, her mother, and the auntie were now screaming hysterically. I don't know how, but I managed to get away. I lost my T-shirt and one shoe. They, in fact, gave me a bloody good hiding. I managed to get back to town. I did try to call a taxi but I couldn't tell the driver where I was because I didn't know myself, so I had to walk.

Darky Dawson, the ship's runner, found me the next morning. I was out cold among the nets under the fo'c'sle of the share boat I was on. He managed to get me over to the Mission where he called an ambulance. I had many injuries, but the most painful was my broken jaw. It was obvious I could no longer stay at the Mission in case the police came looking for me, and Mary's father with his obvious wealth would also be able to wield a lot of power. I had a feeling that things somehow were going to have to change.

Because of my injuries and the fact that the Skipper and First Mate wanted to keep me as a Decky on the *Sutton Queen*, the company agreed to keep me on wages with extended shore leave. The actual wages were very low; we made our money on what they called the poundage. But they did agree to pay my B&B and I knew where I was. It was where I first started my new career as a seaman. That was over a year ago now. The place was exactly the same as when I first booked in, Billy drinking his whisky, and me drinking my vodka.

Although I did a few more trips at sea, my heart was no longer in it. I could no longer hang around the Bank Stores or the Mission. At this point, I was ashore more than I was at sea. I was now drinking continuously: vodka and cider. My routine was to get drunk first thing in the morning and go and sit down by the docks. It also gave me time to reflect on my life so far. I know I was desperately lonely and, although I came off worse, I still couldn't get over how I had so suddenly and inexplicably attacked that man.

3

The End of My Career at Sea

I left Lowestoft in 1970; I was 23 years of age and a chronic alcoholic. As hard as it was, I went back to the town of my birth. I wasn't welcome and I understand why; I was inadequate, and I didn't and couldn't function like other people.

My mum, while worried sick about me, made me as comfortable as she could. She made a bed up for me in the downstairs spare room; I loved that bed and I loved being close to my mum again. Because of my mum, my father tolerated me; we were all in a very tense and awkward situation. Not only did my father never speak to me, but he couldn't even look at me. This rubbed off on my younger brother, and although none of it was their fault, it was a wretched period. I was becoming more and more depressed, and would get drunk at every opportunity; it was breaking my mother's heart.

My most cherished memory of this particular time was when I would come home at night and everyone had gone to bed except my mum. She would be sitting by the fire with her hot water bottle on her lap, and in the kitchen would be a freshly made sandwich covered by a plate. She was and still is always concerned about my eating. I wanted to hug her, but I couldn't and she knew it; we would just sit up and talk.

However, struggling to bring up her family and do all the housework at the same time was beginning to take its toll. By this time of night she would always be tired, so I always looked forward to, and treasured, the few nights she was able to stay up and wait for me to come in.

We talked mainly about my father, and she would tell me little snippets about my father's early life. How, at just fourteen years of age, he, for whatever reasons, was put on a ship bound for America. For some reason that none of us knew, he ended up somewhere in the north of England, and the biggest industry in this particular city was shipbuilding. It's here that he somehow managed to work despite his young age. I was three years younger than that when he put me through the cold bath ordeal.

My mum told me he had a particularly hard time because there were signs put up in a lot of our northern ports which read, *no niggers, no dogs, and no Irish.* I remind you, as I remind myself, he was fourteen years of age and alone. I was always interested in what my mum had to say as I was desperate to know why he hated me so much; I wasn't even aware of my father until I was about four years of age. I guess I was about four because in those days you didn't start primary school until you were five.

I was leaning against the back door frame of our council house, and crying. I remember my mum in the kitchen on her hands and knees, cleaning the floor around the boiler area. There was an argument going on, and they were shouting. I had no idea what they were shouting about, but I do remember even today my mother shouting at my father, 'if you hit him again, I'm leaving'. I don't know what I had done.

As I turned round I saw my reflection in the outhouse window – the outhouse was where the coal was kept – and while my mother always kept the outside of these windows sparkling clean, the insides were black with coal dust which transformed the window into a mirror. I could see my reflection quite clearly and, where I had been crying and had wiped my eyes with the palms of my hands, it had formed black circles around both my eyes. I knew what a clown was because I had seen pictures of them in books, and that's what I looked like – a clown. The only thing missing was a smile; I didn't know how to.

That was my very first awareness of my father, and that's why I was always interested in what my mum had to say. It was important to me to know where I had gone wrong, for if I could work that out I might be able to address my problem and stop drinking myself into a state of foolishness and oblivion. It didn't work then and it certainly wouldn't work now; too many people have already suffered. I don't know how long I stayed at my Mum's house, but it was whilst living there that I met the first girlfriend who I had actually lived with.

We managed to find a flat and moved in just as soon as we could; we had only known each other for about two months. My girlfriend found a job in a hairdressing salon, and I did some private work as a painter and decorator. It wasn't long before I found myself in a situation where I was being paid on an almost daily basis just to enable me to drink every day, and it didn't take me long to reach a point where I was drunk more than I was able to work.

It was about this time, on one of our visits to her parents' house, that her dad, who I liked very much, took me to one side and told me his daughter was getting very concerned about my drinking. I don't know why but it made me angry. He also mentioned he could smell drink on me as I was speaking, and that, where I had parked my car, one of the back wheels was actually on the kerb.

He knew I was drunk and it made me furious; we left shortly afterwards. We drove home in total silence, neither of us daring to speak. I just kept thinking, why the hell couldn't these people leave me alone? That was my mentality at the time, childlike and unreasonable. On the few occasions we had sex, it was basic and almost animalistic; I just couldn't express my feelings. I always knew the right things to say, and I also knew how to conduct myself, but I was empty. This situation carried on for a few more months.

Then one day I came home and saw there were no curtains; I assumed they were being washed, put my key in the door, and walked in. I stood there in total shock; the flat had been emptied completely, and there was just a fine layer of dust covering the hardboard where our carpets had once been. In the centre of the floor was a small pile of my clothes, a plate, a cup, knife and fork, and a letter with Brian written on the top of the page.

It was short and to the point; she wrote: *I cannot tolerate your drunken behaviour anymore, you've abused me.* That relationship lasted exactly twelve months, and that letter was to be the first of many similar letters I was to receive in the coming years. All these years later, I now know that that's what I did; I abused her. How long I stayed in that flat, I've no idea. I only know it was the early to middle '70s.

In 1976, I applied for, and got, a job as dining hall supervisor at a Butlin's holiday camp in South Wales. I worked there the whole summer season, and then went back to my mum's for the winter. Once again I was in the spare room and, I don't know how, I muddled through until the spring of '77 when I returned to Butlin's for the following season. This time it didn't last; I was sacked halfway through the season for being drunk whilst on duty. I was surprised I lasted that long.

1 left Wales and went down to Devon with a new girlfriend and five of my waiters and waitresses. We rented a holiday cottage for £70 a week (£10 each). I was by this time as black as the ace of spades from the sun. Although I was malnourished and had a vitamin deficiency I actually, from the outside, looked quite well.

At this point, I have to mention scrumpy cider – Devon and Cornwall is where it's made. I was alone in the cottage, the only one unable to work, and decided to go down to the store to buy some scrumpy; I'd heard it was strong. I walked the short distance down to the store and bought two quart bottles of what they called Rough Rider. I was already quite drunk before I bought the cider, and I hadn't eaten for some days. I walked back to the cottage and drank the two quarts on my own.

My next recollection was somebody calling my name. Somewhere in the murky distorted depths of my dysfunctional brain, I heard, 'Brian, Brian, Brian, get by here. Get by here now or I will kill you.' It was my girlfriend, who came storming over, pulled me to one side, and started slapping me.

I had gone back to the stores and was standing in a queue. I was going to buy some more Rough Rider. The reason why she was so angry with me was that, whilst I was moving languidly with the queue towards the counter to get yet more cider, I was naked; naked that is except for my girlfriend's pink and very feminine nightie. I was on a different planet.

She dragged me back to the cottage and left me outside in the garden. I came to at dusk. I was cold, and lay there like that for a few minutes so I could re-adjust myself and get my bearings. There were no lights on, and the house was silent. I crept inside and went to sleep downstairs.

I woke up and could sense the place was empty; there was a note on the table. I didn't have to read it; the waiters and waitresses that had so loyally left the safety of their jobs to take a chance with me travelling down to Devon on the day I was sacked, just because they liked me, had all decided to leave me in the still of night. They simply couldn't, and didn't have to, put up with me. I leant forward and picked the note up; it read, *We can't stand your drinking anymore, don't try and contact any of us.*

Déjà vu. I knew I had to leave the cottage, although while I felt alone on my own, I was also lonely in company. I don't know how I did it, but I managed to get back to my home town and the safety of the spare room in my mum's house.

I was thirty years of age, with no possessions, not even a wristwatch. I was a qualified painter and decorator with City and Guilds certificates. I was also an able-bodied seaman and a qualified deckhand, and yet here I was back in my mum's spare room, with my father providing the warmth and shelter. I was in absolute turmoil; I hated, and yet I didn't know who or what that hatred was aimed at. All I knew for certain was that it was ruining my life, and all those lives that came in contact with me.

It was in my spare room, where over the years I had sought refuge, and my mother had given it to me, that I started to have mini breakdowns. I wouldn't and couldn't sit in the front room where it was warm and the rest of the family would gather. Whenever I had to go through there, it would go strangely quiet. While the hatred my father felt towards me was

21

unspoken, it was almost tangible; my brothers and sisters sensed it and, while they never spoke about it, it upset them.

With the exception of my much-loved younger brother David, it scared them. My younger brother David was scared of nothing and nobody, and despite everything he loved me, as he still does today. Anybody who hasn't had to rely on a younger sibling for love and support will never understand the gratitude I felt then, and still do to this day.

My breakdowns always happened in the privacy of the spare room; I would find myself on all fours crying hysterically and uncontrollably. This would last for two or three hours. Occasionally the door would open, and it would be one of my brothers or sisters. They would just look on for a second or two and, unable to help me because they just didn't know how, would close the door quietly and go back to the front room, confused and embarrassed. They couldn't help me because none of us knew, myself included, what was wrong with me.

It was at this point, whilst I was in the depths of despair, that I considered suicide. The only thing that put me off, apart from my cowardice, was an article I'd read a long time ago which had stuck in my mind. A psychiatrist had written an essay about suicide and, apart from miles and miles of polysyllabic words, the bottom line was: suicide is only committed by people who selfishly want to alter events in the lives of their immediate friends, family, loved ones, or people who in their mind have somehow done them wrong. I can only think that this psychiatrist had never suffered depression, or actually known anything about it at all, but at least it made me think, and I'm still here.

While this was going on, I somehow managed to do the odd private job; the situation had to be right as by now I was unable to mix with people unless I had a drink inside me. I used to give my mum a little bit of money towards my keep, but it was never much; I had to be able to buy my drink because nobody would give it to me. For some reason my father never complained about this, or if he did I never knew about it.

Sometimes, when I was able to go out, I would go to the off-licence and buy my drink, which was vodka if I could afford it, or cider if I couldn't. I would then walk down to the big woods where I had played over twenty years ago when I was just a small boy.

It was on one of these trips to the woods that something strange and frightening happened. As I was passing our next door neighbour – she was a lovely woman – she stopped and started telling me that sometime during the night somebody had climbed over their garden fence and had battered to death all her children's pet rabbits that they kept in the garden. She was telling me how the children were beside themselves with grief. I can only assume that somehow my emotions had got completely mixed up, because I suddenly, and quite inexplicably, burst out laughing. I do not understand what was wrong with me; I was actually crying with laughter and I couldn't stop. I must have looked like some sort of demented banshee; I got so hysterical with this insane laughter that I had to sit down on the wall.

My neighbour turned ashen and walked off; I had frightened her as I had myself. Eventually I managed to stop laughing and carried on to the big woods. I walked down to the roots area and sat quietly by myself. I felt calm. I was totally alone and at one with myself, and I thought of my neighbour's ashen face and the contempt for me that I could see in her eyes. It didn't matter; I simply no longer cared or even knew how to. I sat like this, drinking my cider and vodka for about an hour, when suddenly, without reason or warning, I cried; it wasn't loud and it wasn't hysterical. I simply sat there like a ten-year-old child, and cried.

The last thing that went into my system was the alcohol I had drunk the previous day. I hadn't eaten since I don't know when. I weighed about eight stone, and had just drunk a half-bottle of vodka and a litre of cider; I was ill. For the umpteenth time, I not only realised, but also accepted, that there was something seriously wrong with me. I didn't care what the psychiatrist wrote in his essay about suicides only wanting to alter the course of events in other people's lives. I wanted to be dead.

Rationalise that – I walked home; I didn't know what time it was, nor did I care. I was in a timeless wilderness of pain and confusion. I felt guilty, shameful, and fearful. I went in and went straight to my room. As I walked through the front room, nobody looked up except my brother David and my mother; nobody spoke; none of us knew what to say. I lay on my bed fully clothed with my eyes wide open. I was aware someone opened my door, and that two seconds later it closed again. I didn't move; I was catatonic.

I woke up; it was dark and I was cold; the house was quiet. I went through to the front room, and my mum was sitting by the fire. She had her hot water bottle on her lap. She told me to come and sit by the fire; I loved her. She brought my sandwich from the kitchen, and we both sat in silence until she was sure I'd eaten the sandwich.

She didn't ask me where I had been; she didn't have to; she knew. She told me our neighbour's pet rabbits had been killed; I told her I knew. She said goodnight and went to bed. I sat there for about an hour, then went to bed myself As I got into bed, I realised my mum had put her hot water bottle in my bed.

I slept like a baby; I dreamt of clowns with black rings round their eyes, but these clowns weren't smiling. Thanks to my mum, the spare room had been a place of sanctuary for me, but I knew it couldn't last, nor did I want it to. For almost five months I had dwelt in that cold palace of exile and, whatever might happen to me, I had to move and somehow stand on my own two feet.

I don't know why, but I chose Hastings as a place to live. I'm still here now, and have been for the last twenty-five years. It's here that I'm writing my book. I'm married, and have been for ten years; it's my second marriage. My first wife coped with me for eight years until the only thing she could do to save her own sanity was divorce me. This might sound corny and old hat, but after our divorce we really did become good friends.

4

My Abuse

It is imperative that I make clear that the abuse I suffered was not of a sexual nature in any way. I am certain that my father derived no sexual pleasure or gratification from his cruelty and ill treatment towards me. His actions were purely and solely meant to demean, humiliate, and degrade me. My problem now is that I am unable to understand how he managed to build up such hatred for me in such a few short years. Given that during the first few years of a child's life, they are barely able to walk or talk, let alone cause harm to anyone else, and that my most vivid memories are around the age of seven years old, that would have left my father something like four or five years to develop that hatred; to despise me to such an unnatural extent. I really do have a problem with this. The saddest thing is that everybody I come into contact with now, even though they know nothing of my past and what he did to me, become affected by his abuse themselves.

My attitude to life, and how I relate to people now, is a direct result of the emotional cruelty my father meted out to me when I was a kid. To this day I find it difficult to cope with any show of affection, both in receiving it, and giving it. I understand Groucho Marx now, who, when he was granted entry to a certain club, responded by saying, *Please accept my resignation. I don't want to belong to any club that will accept me as a member*. That's how I feel about the human race. Anyone who loves me, or wants to be with me, must have something wrong with them as far as I'm concerned.

Something perverse happens if someone is stand-offish with me and treats me with any lack of respect. It makes me feel as though I need to know them, become connected to them. I feel servile in a way, and am thrown into an attitude of automatic respect. A bit like an animal whose owner constantly whacks it with a newspaper. Eventually, the very sight of the newspaper sends the dog into the corner, tail quivering between its legs in fear of its owner. The owner interprets this as the respect he believes his servile pet owes him.

My sexual relationships with women have been many and varied. With hindsight, I'm pretty sure that for most of the women involved, the relationship was probably unsatisfactory. I could attract women when I was younger, but already the effects of alcohol on my body made sure that I was, physically, pretty inconsistent. Not only was I impotent at an early age, I was also rendered infertile. My GP has told me in no uncertain terms that this is a direct result of drinking from an early age.

I've mentioned in previous pages that, although I'd taken my first drink during the Queen's coronation in 1953, a further six years were to pass before I actually began to use alcohol. I realise, as I write and look back with more clarity on my life, that this was inaccurate. I actually started drinking when I was ten years old. When I had my stomach pumped out for the first time I was twelve and had been drinking steadily for two years. I was an alcoholic then, but didn't know it. A conspiracy was born around me at about that time. A conspiracy between alcohol and me. Between us we would kill me. It was, and remains, just a question of when.

As I sit here now, I'm in pain. My liver is severely cirrhotic. Our livers contain what the medical profession call GGT, an enzyme that goes by the full name of: Gamma Glutamyl Transferase. (Gamma GT/GGT). GGT is very sensitive to recent liver cell damage, and becomes raised by excessive alcohol intake. It becomes permanently elevated in people with chronic liver disease. The normal range for GGT in an adult liver is for males: 8-78 u/l, and for females: 8-47 u/l.

Just prior to a recent admission to Alex One, a detox unit at the Maudsley Hospital in London, the amount of GGT in my body was a staggering 1,800!

No wonder I wasn't feeling too good.

One day, my friend and I were delivering pamphlets, something to do with our local church, I think. As we approached one house, we saw the owner doing his garden. His cigarettes were on the wall just by the front door, and to this day I remember that they were John Player's Navy Cut. My friend and I stole them, but when we got back up onto the road we were disappointed to discover that there were only three left. But never mind, we went straight to the Big Woods and sat down and smoked them. Although I didn't realise it during our nicotine-induced reverie, that theft was about to cause me great pain, suffering and confusion.

Tony and I went to see if we could get hold of some cider, but as we came to the edge of the woods, I froze on the spot. There, right in front of me, was my father. He was white with rage. Somehow, the bloke whose fags we'd stolen knew where I lived and had gone to the house and told the old man what we'd done. Naturally, my father immediately believed him, before he'd even given me a chance to explain myself. Now he was going to kill me. Quite understandably, Tony legged it. My father's hefty hand grabbed my scrawny neck and he dragged me behind him all the way home as though I were a stray dog.

When we got home, he took me upstairs to the bathroom, ran a bathful of cold water and told me to undress. I was scared witless. I'd heard that drowning was a horrible death and I was convinced that was to be my fate. He ordered me into the bath and told me just to sit there. He told me he was going to teach me not to steal. I sat hunched and motionless with my arms clasped around my knees. I was freezing, but afraid to even shiver. I was too young to have heard of hypothermia, but after about half an hour sitting in that bath, that's where I was headed. I heard him coming back up the stairs. He came into the bathroom and went over to the toilet as if to urinate. Then he turned and pointed himself at me, laughed, and said, 'I'm going to piss all over you'. Which he did. He stood there and urinated all over my back.

Now this is the part I'm confused about. The sudden warmth of his urine running down my freezing cold back, in some strange and perverse way, comforted me. He left the bathroom, laughing all the way down the stairs. I'm still confused about why or how I accepted that punishment. I'm confused about the way I could feel comforted by such a cruel thing, how his urine gave me the only good emotion I could feel. But even then, as now, all I knew was that I wanted a drink.

And I wasn't even eleven years old.

There's one more little gem I want to tell you about. He would never use my name. For example, if on a rare occasion he felt like helping my mum lay the table, as he placed the plates in their respective places he would say the name of the person who would sit there: Linda, Barry, John etc, but when it came to my place, he would just say, 'and that bloke over there'. He meant me, sitting by the door out of his vision. I wasn't allowed to sit at the table, but this was never spoken about. He didn't have to say anything. His body language and change of mood told me that there was danger around that table while he was eating and I'd better keep away. Which I did.

If this routine had been a one-off, it perhaps wouldn't have bothered me over much but, coupled with everything else he'd done to hurt, spite and humiliate me, it was beginning to take its toll. I didn't feel normal anymore. The rest of my family, either wittingly or otherwise, were, by their silence and acceptance of his behaviour, a party to it. And the only time I could feel that I didn't care about any of them was when I could hide in the Big Woods and drink my cider.

I remember another incidence of his cruelty clearly to this very day. I was about five years old and was sitting on a chair in the middle of the front room; a white sheet covered me from the neck down. My father was about to cut my hair. Perfectly normal practice in those days because no one could afford barbers. In order for him to trim around my ears he had to rest the back of his hand on the side of my face. It felt beautifully warm and gentle, and I suddenly felt an overwhelming sense of love and affection for him. I didn't want him to take his hand away. I was enjoying the feeling so much, and reached up and put my hand on his to just hold it there. His immediate response was to slap me so hard I almost fell off the chair.

His face contorted into a mask of hate, and I shall never forget the words he said to me. And I quote: 'Get off, you silly looking slop'. I was five years old and I'd never been as unbearably hurt as I was on that day. Even at that early age, I knew that he'd just killed something in me forever. I firmly believe that it was that incident, and that incident alone, that ensured that I would never be able to be intimate with anybody. I can only have sex with strangers. My father's cruelty on that day 50 years ago has affected every woman who has ever loved me. They were never to know him, but he made them suffer too.

This was still going on when I was fifteen and sixteen. I was an apprentice at the time and, although I was still living at home, I was earning much less than my mates, so it wouldn't be unusual for me to run out of money before the end of the week. Sometimes when I was broke I'd pluck up enough courage to approach my father for a tab. He'd be sitting in his usual chair where he couldn't see me and, as casually as I could, considering how much I'd prepared myself, I'd say 'Dad, could you lend me a pound until tomorrow?' I'd then just stand there waiting. He'd be watching telly or reading the paper, but refuse to look up. He just ignored me for minutes at a time. But eventually he would take his glasses off, take a pound note out of his pocket and throw it on the floor. All this without looking up at me, accompanied by the usual insult, 'you silly looking slop, you'. It makes me feel shame to even say that I always bent in front of him and picked up the note, so low was my self-respect, if indeed I'd ever had any.

I remember my mum once asking him why he spoke to me like he did, but he didn't answer her. He didn't even look up. To him the question wasn't even worth a response. To this man, my "father", I was just a piece of shit. I should have had the guts and self-respect to leave his pound note on the floor, but I didn't. I'm certain that's why I'm possessed of such self-loathing. I should have stood up for myself, but never did. I was afraid of him, and still am to this day. I was aware how much he hated me right from when I was a little kid of four. Funnily enough, I don't actually remember him hitting me, but I can still hear my mum saying to him, way back in my memory, 'if you ever hit him again. I'm leaving you'.

That one memory is burned into my brain, and I don't recall what crime I had committed – looking into our coal shed window and imagining seeing that clown's face: my own reflection, with black circles around the eyes, but the smile missing.

5

Buying Cider at Ten Years of Age

We always used to play in the big woods. We called it that because, to us, it was so huge. At the bottom end of the woods was an old fallen down oak tree. It must have been there about a hundred years. This is where we always played. It was called lovers' log. It lay just about fifty yards from the entrance to the woods, so we could see the road with the path just opposite. At the top of this road, on the right hand side, was a pub. I am not going to mention the name of this pub, or the landlords.

In those days, all pubs shut at two thirty. It was about this time that the landlord used to take his dog for a walk. He was a very ugly man, and also very fat. From the path opposite the woods you could see our lovers' log. Now this landlord always used to stop opposite the entrance, and if we children were playing there, he would walk up to the log.

We never minded this because, not only did he allow us to smoke, he would also give us cigarettes. But if you accepted one of his fags, you had to let him put his hand up your trousers – we all had short trousers in those days – or if you were a girl, up your skirt. He was allowed to keep his hand there until you had finished your fag. Now obviously at that age we didn't know exactly what he was doing, but it used to make him go red. He would huff and puff, and sometimes his fag would drop out of his mouth. Then he would go quiet, say absolutely nothing, and leave. But at least some of us got a smoke.

Now none of us had even heard the word paedophile; I doubt even our parents had, but we now know that is what he was. I also knew he sold bottles of cider. Every pub in those days had what was called an "off sales", a tiny little bar where you didn't actually drink but you could, if you were old enough, buy your cigarettes and bottles of drink there.

There's an area to the right of lovers' log called the roots. Now, from sitting by the roots you could see the people on the path opposite, but they couldn't see you. It was here I would sometimes sit if I wanted to be alone. And it was here I was sitting one day when I saw the landlord. He didn't see me.

I saw him stop at the entrance to the woods, but as there were no children playing there, he walked back to his pub. I had four shillings

(20p) that my Aunt Kit had given me, so I waited until he had got back to his pub and then followed him up there. I walked in to the off sales as bold as brass and said to him, 'could I have a bottle of cider please?' He said, 'are you alone?' I said, 'Yes.' He then said, 'Of course you can, but you must hide it, and not tell anyone where you got it.' I said, '1 won't.' He put the cider on the counter and I gave him the money. He went to the till and brought the change back. He lifted the flap of the counter up and walked round to my side. He said, 'You mustn't lose your change; I'll put it in your pocket.' He put the change in my pocket and started to play with me. I grabbed my cider and ran out the door.

1 went back to the woods and sat by the roots area so I could be alone with my cider. I was now in a good position, as that pervert's lust for little boys and girls was so great that he would even risk his licence just for the chance that he might be able to touch us.

The trick now was to let him keep thinking that there was a chance. When he put the change in my pocket and started playing with me, he started his huffing and puffing again. While he had something I wanted, cider, I also knew I had something he wanted even more. I worked out my cider had cost me half a crown (12½p), so my plan was that, whenever I had the money, it had to be exact. That way, as soon as he put the cider on the counter, and before he could lift the flap up, I slammed the exact money down and shot out the door. That's how I was able to buy cider at ten years of age.

6

Personality Disorder

Dear counsellor,

I'm still angry and, forgive me but I think both of us have had enough of the bollocks over the years, don't you? After all the work we've done together, you still haven't a clue where I'm at, any more than I have myself. Please understand that I'm not addressing any individual in particular. There are those of you but for whom I'd have been dead many times over down the years, and you will forever have my gratitude.

But the world sees people like me as a "type", and it must be difficult for you not to do so, after trying so hard for so long to get us to change. We eventually absorb our labels, and our labels absorb us. And unfortunately some of you, in spite of your best intentions, have helped that process along.

I'm also aware that there are those who also see you as a "type"; they demonise incompetent social workers (and why not?), and label you do-gooders and bleeding-heart liberals. But think on. Some of you DO fail us. Clinicians, nurses, social workers, psychiatrists and counsellors, from God knows how many disciplines, have been part of the fabric of my life for more than twenty years now. And each time I see someone new I'm asked the same stock questions time and again. Can you imagine how crushing it is to have to repeat yourself countless times to members of a profession whose *raison d'être* is to listen? Trust dies and you begin to disappear.

Something fundamentally good in you compels you to engage with us and yet the process, over time, separates us, and no matter how hard you try to empathise with us, the divide has become too great.

I moved to Hastings in 1978. By 1979, I was up in court on a charge of Drunk and Disorderly. I was remanded to Lewes prison for 21 days to await psychiatric reports, but I didn't see a psychiatrist during that entire 21 days.

I appeared before the magistrate and, lo and behold, there before the magistrate was a psychiatric report! It was lengthy and detailed, and that day, standing in the dock, I learned from the magistrate that I had a personality disorder. This was news to me.

Again, counsellor, what do you think? Is it just the way the mop flops? I was at pains to point out that I hadn't seen a psychiatrist during my 21 days on remand. So, realising their mistake, a duty psychiatrist was called pretty sharpish, and I was assessed just prior to being called back into court. What meticulous clinical practice! His assessment concurred that indeed I did have a personality disorder.

What really pisses me off is that I have that label, PERSONALITY DISORDER, still hanging over my head. As if I haven't got enough troubles. So every time I meet a new counsellor, as far as they're concerned, the mop has already flopped, but in the wrong direction for me.

This is how the interview with the psychiatrist went.

'Name?'

'Harding.'

'Date of birth?'

'23-10-47.'

'Are you tidy at home?'

'I try to be neat.'

'I mean, are you meticulous?'

'What does that mean?'

'It doesn't matter. Do you wet the bed?'

'I have done on occasion, but then again if you drank like I do, I expect you would too.'

No response.

'Are you aware that walking around the town drunk and disorderly can be offensive to other people?'

'Yes I am.'

'Is there a purpose to it?'

'To what, me walking around town drunk, or this interview?'

Again, no response.

'Thank you, Mr Harding; that will be all.'

I thanked him, and was taken back to my holding cell.

I was called about an hour later. The magistrate informed me that I was a total disgrace and a poor example to other young people of my age, before handing down what he thought to be an appropriate sentence.

I realise that my booze-addled mind may not always be fully accurate in terms of memory but believe me, the impact of that psychiatric report is burned into my brain, and I'm reminded of that interview every time another counsellor starts asking those same old questions.

I don't recall exactly what sentence I was given for this heinous crime, but I do know it was either a bender or a fine. It couldn't have been bird because I would have remembered that! However, little did I know that at a later date this personality disorder would work for me and not against me.

Once again in prison, I was serving 15 months for something that's lost in the depths of my hazy memory. I started off on remand on F wing, and was then weighed off at Lewes crown court where I was granted a 15 month custodial and billeted in A wing with the rest of the convicted "cons". I was then transferred to Wormwood Scrubs, which at that time was an allocation nick. From there I was shipped off to Northeye.

Northeye was a semi-open nick; an ex RAF camp made up of billets housing between 16 and 20 prisoners. It was horrendous. You couldn't even lie on your bed without being looked at by another con. It was far worse than a closed prison, where once you were banged up, providing you had a decent cellmate, you were at least alone with your own thoughts. At the risk of sounding corny, it really did give you a chance to reflect on your life and deeds. Mind you, that could obviously work the other way. If you were in prison for a really grave crime such as rape, murder or child molestation, then I would have thought that reflecting on the past would be the last thing you would want to do.

Anyway, there I was in Northeye. I had just under two months to do and for the past week I'd had a raging toothache. Not only had I heard good things about the prison dentist. I'd seen at first hand examples of his handiwork. Now, to be able to move about the prison in working hours, you needed a pass which had to be signed by a warden detailing where you were going, what time you left your place of work, and what time you were expected to arrive at your destination.

Such a load of red tape just to have your tooth out, but there you go. I got my pass and headed off up to the dentist. I was stopped a few times by marauding screws looking for trouble, but luckily I wasn't out of bounds without permission. The dentist was housed in a brick-built shed. It didn't even look as though it had power on, nor could I see any connecting telephone lines. Well, that's how it looked to me. Within fifteen minutes I was to be proven wrong. I handed in my pass and the dental nurse signed it, writing down the time I'd arrived. There was no waiting room. You just stood there until they were ready. When my name and number were called, I went in.

34

As instructed, I lay down in the chair and the dentist said, 'Open wide'. No introduction or small talk with the cons. He informed me that he had to take a tooth out, and would I mind? I said, 'of course not, if it will stop the pain'. He asked me how I was with injections. 'No problems at all.'

Suddenly he turned around. The syringe was already loaded. He then did something I hadn't been expecting. He injected me in the arm. He clearly hadn't emptied the phial because he then proceeded to inject what was left into my gum. The injection in the arm had been relatively painless but when he put the same stuff into my gum it was excruciating.

Now, at this time, I had been serving Her Majesty for eight months, and had neither taken drugs nor used alcohol for that entire time. I was now suddenly drugged. I was disorientated and scared. As I lay there watching the dentist, a total stranger preparing his tools, having administered a drug I knew nothing about, I thought, something's wrong here. What the hell's going on?

I tried to be rational. Here I was in prison, coming towards the end of my sentence. I was in a dentist's chair about to have a tooth out. The nurse had checked my pass. Everything was in order. *People know I'm here; don't be scared.* Then began a sudden rush of euphoria. I felt really contented. Even the ceiling was fascinating me. The sound of the dentist arranging his tools was gentle and soothing, melodic even.

And then the nurse appeared. She came from nowhere. She wore a white uniform. Her legs were bare and my euphoria was at its height. I couldn't get any higher. She wasn't anything special to look at, but she was a woman and she stood less than two feet away from me. I reached out with my hand and ran it straight up between her thighs, right up to her crotch! I remember it was warm. It was soft and sensual. I could actually smell her.

She let out a shriek and, dropping whatever she was doing, fled the room. The dentist hit the riot button, and suddenly half a dozen screws charged in. That was it. I was straight down the block. I don't know where the euphoria went, but went it did!

If you've ever spent time in solitary, you'll know it brings you up with a start. I'd done it before on the odd occasion. The cardboard chair, cardboard desk, biro to write out your plea of mitigation with no shell on it, just the innards, in case you stab yourself. I lay on my bunk and thought bloody hell, I only wanted a tooth out!

I thought I'd get another six months for this transgression. After all, this was indecent assault. Not only that. I'd committed it whilst doing bird! I was taken before the governor the following day, and present were the assistant governor and his deputy. 'This looks serious,' I thought. 'What the hell's going on?' Now I've never thought of myself as any more unlucky than the next bloke, but at the same time you wouldn't describe me as the luckiest either. But it transpired that they'd got my medical notes mixed up with someone else's, and the dentist had given me the wrong drug – and too much of it to boot. You'll never believe me, but he took full responsibility and I was completely exonerated.

Just goes to show how wrong you can be about people. The dentist hadn't even acknowledged me when I'd walked in. I'd put him down as just another arrogant screw. And when he did deign to look at me, I hated him. But he could quite easily have kept quiet about this, and no-one would have known.

Arrangements were made for me to have my teeth seen to the following day.

7

Exclusion from the Family Holiday

I think I was about eighteen years old, and my mum and dad had decided that the family should all go for a week's holiday. Everyone got together and decided to go to a place called Leysdown, somewhere cheap and nasty on the East Coast. Like the rest of the family, I was getting quite excited; we'd never been on holiday before.

All this was about 35 years ago, perhaps in 1965. I know I'd just started my apprenticeship, and I remember my mum saying to me, 'Have you found a place to stay yet?' I didn't understand, and asked, 'What are you talking about?' She just came out and told me, 'Well you know your father doesn't want you to come with us.' I asked if she was serious. I asked why. She said she didn't know. 'He just doesn't, that's all.' I was flabbergasted. I had four brothers and three sisters. I had long been painfully aware that I was the oddball, but I'd assumed that I would at least be joining them on holiday.

There were still two weeks before the off, so I thought I'd give it a week and try and talk to Mum again. But it wasn't to be. My father, on one of the few occasions that he had ever spoken to me, collared me one day, just as I'd finished work, and told me in no uncertain terms, 'Look you, we are going away for a holiday and you are not coming with us. Do you understand?' What could I say, but, 'Yeah, OK.' I regret not sticking it out, but I just felt knocked back and hurt. Meek is a word I used to describe myself at times when he spoke to me like this. Strange word, but it fits the bill. I had no fight-back in me; not much sense of self at all.

You'd be forgiven for thinking that, at eighteen, being old enough to vote, fight for my country and drink, that I was old enough to be able to find lodgings just for one week, and that this shouldn't be any problem at all. Well it wasn't looking for lodgings that bothered me. It was the fact that my father didn't want me to go on holiday with the family. Mind you, when I thought about it, a "family holiday" didn't really appeal to me either and, although these days an eighteen-year-old wouldn't dream of going on holiday with their parents, that was no consolation to me at the time. It hurt that none of my brothers and sisters questioned this decision. Why had not one of them asked my mum, 'Why can't Brian come?'

There had to be something wrong with me. It was the only conclusion I could come to. Was it my clothes? Was it my attitude? It couldn't be how I ate because Dad had never seen me eat. I'd never been allowed to sit at the table while he had his meals. I wasn't even allowed to be in his line of vision.

I felt unbearably, desperately rejected. I didn't know who to turn to; I was too afraid to tell anyone I was feeling this way in case they said, 'well what do you expect, look at you?' I was totally convinced that my father had to be right. There was something wrong with me.

It wasn't until about seven months ago that I told my mum I intended to put some sort of book together about my life. She was immediately enthused, and instinctively felt it was a good idea. Then she fell silent. I told her I'd be able to tell people about how my Auntie Kit used to sneak me a little bit of pocket money without my brothers knowing. Mum didn't respond. Her mind seemed to be elsewhere. Then I said, 'I can tell people about that horrible bastard who put me up for the week when you all went on holiday; do you remember, Mum?' She had tears in her eyes. 'What's up, Mum?' I said. 'At least I had a roof over my head.' She took my hand and said, 'I'm sorry, duck, I didn't understand.'

She too had suffered all those years for not making my father take me on holiday with them. She'd also suffered the guilt of forcing me out of the family home, and making me stay in some strange lodgings somewhere while they were off enjoying themselves. To say my mum suffered as much as me throughout my life would be an understatement. And do you know, the horrible stark reality is that she still suffers today. I have to accept that I'm part of my mother's suffering. From an early age I'd always felt her love. I knew she loved me but just couldn't show it. If I'd been more of a man, I would and should have accepted that; that, at least, would have been good enough.

When I first moved into those digs all those years ago, I did a strange thing. I can't explain it. I didn't understand it then, and I don't understand it now. I went to Boots the chemist and bought what they called in those days a bottle of QT (Quick Tan). You smeared this lotion on all over yourself and you turned brown almost immediately. Then I went out and bought a sombrero and a pair of sunglasses. I went back to my digs, stripped off and smeared myself from head to toe in this stuff. Within minutes I was almost black. I didn't want to be me; I wanted to disguise myself. The few friends I had at the time were so embarrassed that they didn't even ask what I was doing. When a few bothered to ask why I was living down Cramptons Road, I would just say that my family was away on holiday and there was no way I was going with them! Although none of them said anything, I knew they realised this was all rubbish. They knew my father wouldn't even take me to the graveyard, let alone on holiday.

I'd never felt so alone. I couldn't even bring myself to go to work that week. God knows what I did for money. I was desperate for my family. Why did they leave me on my own? What was wrong with me? I had no idea what mental illness was. I just naturally assumed that if my father didn't want me with the family, then he must be right. There was something wrong with me after all. I'd just have to live with it. All this was going through my head while I was sitting in Knoll Park, entirely alone. I didn't even have a drink with me. I was so angry, frustrated and confused. In fact "angry" didn't cover it. Murderous was the word; bloody murderous.

I was just about to finish my apprenticeship, and was doing really well with my City and Guilds. It's not as though I would have had wild parties in my parents' house while they were away. I don't have that many friends for a start. The truth is, nobody was allowed into the house if they had anything to do with me. My father hated me so much he was of the opinion that if anyone liked me or found me interesting, there must be something wrong with them as well.

I don't remember much about my stay at Cramptons Road except that (although I didn't realise it at the time) I was depressed. But as I write, little things come back to me. I did have a small amount of savings in the Post Office, certainly less than £20, otherwise I would have been considered a wealthy man, and wealthy I was not! I remember taking out £2, more than enough to get me what I wanted – alcohol – and I knew exactly which kind. I went straight to the off-licence and bought what in those days was called "the final selection". It was barley wine. I was booze-wise enough by then to realise that although they were only 250ml bottles, they were 10% by volume. These little beauties would get me drunk. I thought it best to get as near to my digs as possible without being seen. I knew of an old disused gas plant, which, although fenced off, was easy enough to get into if a bloke was determined. It's funny what comes back to you when you begin writing about the past. I recall clearly that the last thing I'd had to eat was a piece of toast on the previous morning and it was by now 4.30 the following afternoon. As I didn't weigh more than nine stone soaking wet, it didn't take much to work out that eight bottles of 10% barley wine would make me drunk, and that was exactly what I wanted.

I'd like to be able to say that I sat there and got pleasantly drunk and reminisced about all the pleasant things that had happened in my life. But not so. I sank into some sort of deep, deep depression. I sat there and sobbed on and off for about four hours. I don't know if I was wallowing in self-pity or if I was clinically depressed. What I was certain of was that I needed the love of my family. I was desperate for it. At some point I fell asleep. It was almost dark when I came to, and I drank the last two bottles of barley wine before sloping off back to my digs.

As per my plan, I was only a couple of minutes away, but when I got to the door, I couldn't find my keys. I'd either lost them, or more than likely just hadn't bothered to take them with me. Either way, I was forced to knock on the door. By God, if anyone was an oddball, then the bloke who answered the door was. He was totally expressionless. As he walked, you couldn't help but think his knuckles are going to scrape on the floor any minute. He called out, and a woman came. He said, 'That bloke's here from the back bedroom.' I heard her say, 'Give him his case.' Without a word, he pulled my case from where it had been placed in the porch, and put it by the front door. It was like a scene from a horror movie.

'Why are you giving me my case?' Still no response from the landlord; he simply stared blankly at me, but she came storming out and yelled, 'I want you out, out of my house!'

'OK,' I answered, confused, 'But I'll want some rent back.' 'Rent back?' she howled. 'You've soiled my sheets with your make-up.' She was talking about my liberal application of QT. With that she slammed the door behind me, and I walked away from Cramptons Road.

There was now only one place left. The big woods. I'd slept there as a kid, but certainly didn't expect to be kipping there at my age and especially not under such circumstances. It was now about nine o'clock. I had my Post Office book, but I didn't actually have any money. I knew a bloke who lived on our council estate, an ex-seaman who used to regale us with stories of when he was at sea. Well, to be honest, he never regaled me. I just thought he was a bit of a bore. But he did let us drink his cider!

I found his house and explained my situation. Would he take my Post Office book as security and lend me a couple of quid until morning? When I told him I was sleeping in the woods that night, he agreed to take my PO book for safekeeping. He gave me a couple of quid and said, 'I ain't working at present, so pop round when you like.' Bear in mind he'd known me ever since I was a little kid. It's funny when I look back, people just assumed I was living in the bloody woods!

I shot down the offy as quick as I could, and got myself a couple of bottles of cider. There was a chip shop next door, so I thought I'd better get myself something to eat. While I was waiting for my chips, I caught sight of myself in a full size mirror on the wall. I had a hell of a shock. What a mess! I was partly black with the QT, partly red from the sun, and the rest was ghostly white, probably because I hadn't had a decent meal for so long. I really was just absolutely wiped out.

Luckily, I knew those woods like the back of my hand, and it didn't take me long to make myself comfortable. Funny. I felt safe. I drank my cider, ate my chips and, believe it or not, slept like a baby.

Morning came and it was freezing. I was desperate to clean my teeth and have a proper bath, but where? I would go up to Toby's. I knew Toby wouldn't be bothered if he smelt booze on my breath, so I polished off the rest of my cider. I made my bivouac look as unlike a bivouac as possible, and made my way to Toby's.

It was only half past six, but he was already up. He welcomed me in and offered me a cup of tea, or "something else". He made polite enquiries as to how I'd slept, and I said, 'I'd love a beer, please mate.' He didn't even answer, just brought me through the beer. 'What on earth are you doing kipping in the woods, for heaven's sake? Why don't you go home?' I told him about the old man. He said, 'Fucking hell, is that still going on?' He asked how much longer I had left on my apprenticeship. I told him there was a year left to serve. He said, 'Right son, as soon as you've finished, you fuck off. Get as far away from that bastard as you can. I don't know what's happened between you, and I know there's always two sides to every story, but I've known you since you were a kid and, apart from being a little bastard yourself at times, as kids are, you ain't never done no wrong.' He then told me they were crying out for blokes like me to join the "Merch" (Merchant Navy). Little did I know then that within two years that's exactly where I'd be.

His wife shouted down that the bathroom was free, and I went up for a good wash and scrub up. When I came down and joined Toby at the table, it seemed that a subtle change had come over him. In fact I probably wouldn't have noticed it had it not been for what Toby was to say next. Quite out of the blue, he said, 'Do you know, it was odd how they never got to the bottom of that Mr M–, and your sister being pregnant when she was eleven or twelve.'

I was dumbstruck. How the hell did Toby know? I had no idea anyone knew anything about it. Don't forget we're going back nearly forty years, and things were different then. What I can't accept till this day

41

was that my father did absolutely nothing. There was only ever one suspect, and when questioned by police he admitted to having sex with his own daughter, and his daughter was my sister's best friend. They lived and played together. Hardly a night went by without my sister visiting their house. The man's dead now, but my problem is, how cowardly does that make me? I realised my father's own cowardice at not confronting the bastard. He was just too scared.

For years I lived in absolute terror of my father. He was so strong and powerful, but now after all these years I realise what a cowardly little man he was. Please God, don't let me be like him. And do you know? Not one single member of my family has ever mentioned it. It takes some believing doesn't it?

It was Thursday and I had two days before my family came home. Toby had given me an old groundsheet and one of his old sleeping bags left over from his younger, less settled years. Although I felt quite safe in my bivouac, my main problem was loneliness. I used to go up to Toby's first thing in the morning and have a wash. Then I'd go and get my drink from the local offy and make my way up to Knoll Park where I'd sit completely on my own until about two in the afternoon. I'd then wander up to the bus terminus where there were loads of people and just sit and watch them go about their business.

I've previously described how people en masse remind me of ants, but now I think I can give a more accurate picture. You see, if you study ants going about their daily business, they all seem to be scurrying about, they walk so fast and purposefully it's as if they're on some kind of mission. That is, until they come to an obstacle. Now, they don't seem to even try to negotiate this obstacle. They don't try to climb it or go round it. They simply change course and carry on walking just as purposefully, but in a completely different direction. This is how I would sit, and this is how I would see people. "People-watching". That was my favourite past time. I do love to people-watch.

For those two days, waiting for the family to come home, I flitted between Toby's, the park and the bus terminus. It was while I was sitting there on the Friday, the day before they were due back, that I realised I had a week's money due to me. Because the holiday was booked weeks before, I'd forgotten that I was entitled to either two or three weeks paid leave from the firm I was apprenticed to. Now, with all the nonsense going on in my head, with the rejection I felt from my father, the isolation from my brothers and sisters, getting banned from my digs and having to sleep in a bloody bivouac in the big woods, none of which I deserved, I had simply forgotten I had money to pick up.

When I spoke to the cashier at the office, it turned out that I was indeed owed one week's holiday money, and she handed it over. As an apprentice, I didn't get as much as my mates, but I knew I'd eventually be able to earn more even than they would. That's what kept me going at the time. Toby offered to put me up that night. It was OK with his wife for me to sleep on the couch. That way I'd be more refreshed for meeting the folks. He appreciated that it would be a difficult time, and after a good kip I'd be more able to cope. We sat up drinking and talking into the small hours, Toby and me. The alcohol loosened the tongue and made it easier for me to ponder the whys and wherefores: why hadn't I had the guts to ask my father why he didn't want me with them on holiday? What was I afraid of? Surely it was a reasonable question?

I still ask myself now, and in some of my more depressed moments, usually in the early hours of the morning, I still believe he must have been right to exclude me. Perhaps I was worthless. Perhaps I was a "silly looking slop". The *Collins English Dictionary* gives the definition of "slop" as *liquid refuse and waste food used to feed animals, especially pigs*.

Shall you and I, reader, suppose that the name my father called me was an offence, for which he had been charged and now appeared in court? Let's suppose it's our job to defend him. How would we go about it? First, let's be philosophical. He wasn't clever enough to actually know what "slop" meant, or to use it in the right context. It was simply bad English. What he actually meant was, "Son, I love you".

Let us also assume, in his defence, that when he poked his fingers up my arse, put them to his nose to smell them, and handed them round for all my friends to smell them too, that that too was an act of love. By the way, this was never in private. It had to be done in public to ensure the maximum amount of degradation, humiliation, pain and hurt.

Shall we then assume he did all this because he loved me? Or should we dare to speculate that there was perhaps something wrong with him? Or perhaps for some reason he just plain didn't like me. What do you think? When he urinated all over me when I was in the bath, allegedly for some offence – grand theft I think, aged ten at the time...

Would the court like to take a rest, or shall I carry on? Do you, the jury, honestly think he loved me then? There was no-one there to impress. He just simply pissed all over me. Perhaps it was an act of love between father and son, something that fathers and sons do. It's just that I didn't

43

know what it was that fathers and sons did back then. If this is all normal behaviour, then I'm making excuses because I just don't feel right. Maybe the next time I see my brother-in-law. I'll ask him if he sticks his fingers up his son's arse. I know now that if I did that, within seconds I would be unconscious. He would just, plain and simple, knock me senseless.

Over the years I've had countless health workers, counsellors and rehab workers become overwhelmed by me as a client. I know they've become impatient and confused. All *their* efforts and *still* Brian can't change. Then it becomes "won't change". Eventually their ineptitude becomes *my* fault. They just don't have the skills in their repertoire to *make me* change my life. *I've* made it too complicated. Then we get to the bit about not being able to change the past. What a cop out that is! So *they*, not I, decide there must be one simple obstacle to stop me resisting their ministrations. *I* have to let go of the past.

Now, I'm totally fed up to the back teeth with hand-wringing (for hand-wringing is the desperate stage *they've* got to by now), telling me that I must forgive and forget. Can't they see I'm totally bollocksed? I'm in and out of nut houses more often than off-licenses. I've got one counsellor who actually gets the point. Without her I would, at the very least, be in a nursing home, but more than likely I'd be dead.

So, all you good upright members of our community, for the benefit of those professionals who are of the opinion that forgiveness is the only way for me to stay alive, shall we all agree that my father didn't really mean me any harm? He was just a bit misguided, that's all. Probably had serious problems of his own that made it more likely that he behaved that way. Probably needed therapy himself. Whilst I, on the other hand, am the nasty little bastard who is just using my upbringing as an excuse for my alcoholism. And while you're making your mind up, based on the evidence so far, could you try and pinpoint the year when I first decided to make alcoholism my career move?

I don't remember much about the day they came home. I think I was sitting on the wall outside number 92, where we lived. I don't know if any one spoke to me. I expect my brother David did, but I don't remember anyone else turning their head. Their return didn't bring about feelings of happiness or sadness. But what sticks in my mind is that my father was laughing and joking with the driver, and I thought, what a bastard. They were all inside and unpacking, and Mum came out and asked if I was all right. I said 'Yeah, I'm fine.' She made some casual enquiry as to how I'd got on with Mr So-and-so – forget his name. I told her he'd thrown me out on Wednesday. She said, 'No, what for?' A bit of feeling was creeping in now, and a bit of sarcasm seemed appropriate. 'I don't know. Mum, why did you throw me out?' 'Oh, don't let's start all this again; you know it's your dad.' 'Oh yes I do, Mum.' Keen to let my tone, and what I meant, pass, she ushered me indoors for a cup of tea.

I mentioned muddling through my apprenticeship. Well, for the next and final year, that's exactly what I did. I simply muddled through. It was when I'd finished that I decided I wanted to go to sea. By this time, alcohol had got its grip and it was impossible for me not to drink. I'm aware that I've just revisited a time that has formed other parts of this story, but when I look back at different stages in my life, I become overwhelmed by how difficult it is to put it all together on the page. The chronology is so hard to remember. The only consistency has been my drinking. The continual contamination by alcohol of my thinking processes has left the recall of my life in such a vague state that it really is hard to keep my thoughts in order. I suppose what I'm trying to emphasise, when I repeat that drink took over my life after my apprenticeship, is that I want you to realise it's not melodrama. It's the literal truth as only I can see it. "Through a glass darkly", I suppose you could say.

8

The Loss of My Virginity

1 was fifteen years of age, and there was a group of us hanging around the bus-stop down by the Bat and Ball area, which was the nearest parade of shops to our council estate. We could have caught a bus up to town, but that cost money and there were policemen up there. It was also a long way from the big woods, where all the mischief used to take place and, if we ever didn't want to be found, for whatever reason, the big woods was the place to be. Parents, the police, nobody could find us if we didn't want to be found.

There was a group of about six of us, all basically using the bus-stop like a monkey swing in a park playground. Of course there was a lot of tutting, and "what do you think you're doing?" coming from the genuine bus-stop users, but as teenagers we didn't take any notice. It was while we were playing on and around the bus-stop that this beautiful woman walked over to us and asked if we had seen Nelson. Now, Nelson was about five years older than us, so to us he was an adult. We all said we hadn't. Nelson was a man to be feared; even our parents feared him, and he was always in trouble with the police. What made us so in awe of him was that the police didn't frighten him either.

Although this woman was beautiful, she was also old – old to us that is, to us fifteen-year-olds. She asked if one or any of us would go over to *The Castle* pub just to see if he was in there. Although fifteen, we were actually quite naive, otherwise we would have said, 'why can't you go and see?' For some reason I volunteered; actually the reason was I wanted to impress her with my bravery, so I went over to *The Castle* and looked in both bars. He wasn't there, and I was so glad he wasn't in there because he also frightened me. I went back over to the shelter and told her. Then she asked if I would go down to *The New Inn* to have a look, which I did; he wasn't there either. Next, she asked if I would go over to *The Railway and Bicycle*, and she would wait outside. She said she would buy me a packet of fags, so in I went – no Nelson.

He was barred from the remaining pubs in the Bat and Ball area, so it would have been no use going in any of them. While I was in *The Railway*, she had been over to the machine and got me ten fags, and as I got up close for her to give them to me, I could smell her. She smelt like some kind of flower. She was beautiful, and had massive big tits. It was summer time so she only had some sort of small crop top on, and her jeans were so tight I could actually see the crack between her legs. Now this to a fifteen-year-old all those years ago was like looking at a porn star; up until this, my 15th year, I'd only ever masturbated, the same as most lads my age. My hormones were more drunk than me. She asked me, if she paid the fare, would I go up town with her to help her find Nelson. Legally, I wasn't even allowed in a pub, so I asked her why she didn't go, and she told me that pubs frightened her – I was later to learn that she was barred from almost every pub in town – so I said yes. I couldn't resist her. My plan was to go in to any pub that she asked me to and, whether he was in there or not, to say he wasn't.

I wanted sex with this grown woman, and I didn't know how to go about it. All I knew was, I wasn't going to let her go. I didn't care about Nelson; my hormones were suddenly stronger than my fear of him. We got the bus up town, but we boarded it down by *The Railway and Bicycle*, so that we didn't have to go back to the bus-stop that we had been using as a monkey climb. However, it did stop there to let some people off, and all the lads saw us. They all grabbed their crotch, stuck one finger up, and jeered and cheered. They knew what I was up to, and looking back I rather fancy she did as well.

We got off at the bus terminus in the town centre. It was her idea to wait at the terminus where there was a shelter with a seat, but she asked if I would get her a bottle of gin before I went to look for Nelson. I had already noticed she had a small bottle of orange in her bag which she hadn't touched yet. I asked if I could have a bottle of cider and she said, 'Here, take this and bring me the change', handing me a five pound note. I remember my wages at that time as an apprentice were three pounds ten shillings (£3.50p).

1 shot over to the offy and got her gin and my cider, took her gin back, and told her I would visit every pub in Sevenoaks, and that I would see her in a while. She told me not to be long, and also not to tell Nelson that she had a bottle of gin. I said I wouldn't, and off I went, straight round the back of the picture house to drink my cider. I had become so sexually aroused by this woman that I really had become like a cat on a hot tin roof. I was trying to be calm and rational. I tried to pace myself with my cider, not because I thought if I drank too much I wouldn't be able to get a hard on, because that was the least of my worries; in fact I had a hard on while I was sitting there.

My worry was how to go about it. I mean, she was a mature woman and I really was just a kid. If I made a move, would she laugh at me? I shot into a pub I knew just round the corner and got a double vodka; that was like an entire day's spending money to me, but it did just give me that little bit of courage. I'd been away from her for about an hour, so I thought it was about time I went back. What did occur to me was, with Sevenoaks not being a particularly big town, what if Nelson had found her? What would she say about me? Women know women, like men know men, and he would know what I was after. I hardly had Samaritan written on my forehead; I never have had, and that's why I'm always getting nicked. And if the police would nick me, I'm damned sure he would, and there wouldn't be a trial. It would simply be a good hiding.

Anyway, my lust, hormones, libido, whatever you like to call it, was stronger than all this. She was still in the shelter, and I could see she was pissed. It was she who spoke first. 'You haven't found him, have you?' I said, 'No. I've been in every pub in the town and he's nowhere to be found.' She said, 'Oh, fuck him.' I said, 'Are you going out with him?' She said, 'Sort of.' I suddenly felt pushy, so I asked, 'What are you going to do now?' 'I don't know,' she replied, 'can I sleep at your place?' I said, 'You're joking, I live with my family.' 'So where am I going to sleep then?' My mind was racing ten to the dozen; she was actually asking me where she could sleep, and I was brain-dead.

Finally, I said, 'Look, it's a nice summer's night, how would you fancy sleeping under the stars in a good quality, waterproof, quilted sleeping bag in the big woods? I will look after you. It's a double, so there will be plenty of room.' I was astonished at her reply. She just said, 'How do we get down there?' I was so stunned that she had agreed to it, I couldn't think straight for a minute. I said, ' It's a beautiful night; we could walk it.' But she said, 'No, let's get a taxi.' I said I hadn't got any money, but she said she had, and sent me off to get one.

We got the taxi down to my house, and I asked her to sit on the wall while I got my things together. I walked in and said to my mum, 'As it's Friday, I'm going to stay at my mate's for the night.' My mum was knitting at the time, so she just looked up and said, 'Let me have a look at you; you'll do.' She always used to say that, and I never knew what she meant. As it happened, I did have a really good quality sleeping bag; I was buying it on my mum's club.

While I was getting my stuff together, I peeped out of the window at the woman sitting on our wall waiting for me. It made me tingle to think I may be able to touch her breasts, or even more. I may have looked calm

48

and cool on the outside, but my innards were in a frenzy. Of course, all of us had messed about with the girls on our estate; some of us had actually felt their pubic hair. Mind you, they were in the minority. I told my mum I would see her in the morning and she said, without looking up, 'Be careful, duck.' I had four brothers, and it was usual for my mum to make a plate of sandwiches and leave them under a plate for us boys to eat as and when we came in. I took half of what was there, and left.

Fay and I left for the big woods, me with my sandwiches in one hand and my sleeping bag under my arm. I remember this night so well for three reasons: one, I had been formally accepted as an apprentice, two, I had bought and paid for my first pair of Levis – I remember this because the jeans had cost the exact amount of my weekly wage, 3 pounds 10 shillings (£3.50p) – and the three, probably the most important reason, I knew Fay would at least let me feel her boobs.

I knew exactly where to head for; it was called "the clearing". Now, although it was called the clearing, it was anything but; in fact it was very dense. It was only called the clearing because the council at some stage were going to clear it and plant some special trees there, until they realised what the natives were like.

Fay and I made our way to the centre of the clearing. It amazed me just how clever she was. When I said I had a good quality sleeping bag, I meant it. It was double-lined, quilted, and waterproof. If you were to hold it up on a hanger, you could unzip it from the top to the bottom; then when you got to the bottom, you could unzip it horizontally to form a groundsheet.

This was a hot summer's night, and all I had on was a pair of jeans – my best Levis – and a tee shirt, and all Fay had on was pretty much the same. I had no drink whatsoever, but Fay had about a quarter bottle of vodka. As we prepared for bed. Fay took off her jeans. I couldn't believe it; I was going to feel her bare legs, but then she took off her top, and I'd never seen anything like it – a fully-grown woman dressed in just her bra and panties. I must admit I didn't quite know what to do; I still had my tee shirt and jeans on.

I whipped my jeans off and used them as a pillow. Fay got her fags, lighter and the rest of the vodka, and snuggled up next to me. I was beside myself, wondering what to do next. I could feel the warmth of her body next to mine so I started to kiss her, and she responded. Whilst just a few minutes earlier I had felt not only awkward but almost a bit of a pervert because I was going to ask her if she would mind taking her bra off, now I was doing it just as natural as you like. At this point I had such an erection, I thought she might think I was vulgar. It just goes to show you how little I knew about women. She let me kiss and suck her nipples and, while I was doing this, she arched the small of her back, raised her bottom off the ground, and took her panties off. I made a headrest out of my elbow and hand, and just lay there looking at her. She was so beautiful. She was body beautiful.

I was a virgin, but now I was in charge, and the reason I was in charge was because what we were doing was natural, and things came easily. I was able to touch her pubic area, and it was the most natural thing in the world. I slid down our homemade groundsheet, parted her legs and started to kiss her most intimate parts. It was so sensual. She smelt womanly, wanton. She was moist. I looked up at her and said, 'I think I'm going to let you down.' She raised the top half of her body off the ground and said, 'What's the matter?' I told her, 'As soon as I get anywhere near you, I will come.' She said, 'I know, but please do it.' The veins in my cock were pulsating so much they were becoming almost varicose. I slid into her and, if I were to say it was over in a minute, I would be exaggerating. It was more like seconds.

I apologised, and she just said, 'I expected it; it's your first time, isn't it?' I nodded. She said, 'Don't worry, you'll be all right in a minute.' We snuggled up together, and sometime during the night one of us had zipped us both up. We really were as snug as bugs in a rug. It being mid-summer, dawn came early, and with it came the dawn chorus. I'd never felt so good in all my life. The zip to the sleeping bag was on my side. Fay reached over and unzipped us right down to the bottom, and then along the bottom to her side, to form a sort of duvet.

Although there was a slight early morning chill, we could feel the sun's rays just beginning to come through. Fay was naked whilst, sometime during the night, I had put my shorts back on. She leant forward and took my shorts off. We both lay there naked, and I surprised myself because I wasn't a bit embarrassed. In fact, I was half-aroused. Fay slid down and took me in her mouth. It was breathtaking; my whole body was charged. It felt as if I was being electrocuted, only in a nice way, a glorious way. She lifted her head gently up and straddled me. I was so rampant, and I could hardly believe this was happening to me. She impaled herself on me, and I suddenly felt like a man. Then she put her fingers in my mouth and gently swayed from side to side so that her boobs brushed gently across my face at the same time. I instinctively raised my hips. I was hers, and I wanted to be, and I had to be, and I would be for all my life if that was what she wanted. She began to ride me, slowly at first,

50

then faster, then even faster, and then she suddenly slowed down; she was now hardly moving at all. She started to gasp, as if she was having trouble breathing, and then tears appeared in her eyes before she fell on me and said, 'I love you.'

I couldn't believe it. I had just made love to a real woman. She was in fact 22. We pulled the makeshift duvet over us and just lay there for a while, neither of us speaking. We didn't have to; we had just said it all.

We roused ourselves about an hour or two later, and now it was time to sort out some practical stuff. I asked her if she had any gin left. She looked at me incredulously and said, 'Are you joking?' I was surprised at her reaction. It didn't even occur to me that she wouldn't want a drink; why, I don't know, but I just took it for granted that she knew I was addicted to drink. To smooth things over, I said, 'Oh, it was just a thought.' She said, 'Gin at this time of day, god, how could you?' She had no idea; she also had no idea that that was all I was thinking about: when and where I could get a drink.

It was Saturday, and pubs in those days opened at ten o clock. It was now nine thirty; 30 minutes to kill. When I'd gone home the previous evening for my sleeping bag, I had also got some money, so I was OK there. I asked her what her plans were for the day, and she said, 'Well, one thing's for sure. I'm not looking for that bastard. Nelson.' She asked me if she could have a wash at my place, but I told her that was out of the question, my old man was a bastard. So I said, 'why don't you go home?' She said, 'Because I've fucking run away, that's why.' I don't know why, but I wasn't surprised. I asked her why, but she said it didn't matter. 'I have to tell you, reader, at this point, that Fay was her real name, but I can't tell you her surname; not only would it be unfair, it would also be very upsetting for the remaining family. Although this all took place some 40 years ago, there are quite a lot of her family still alive.

I said, 'Well, you can't kip here forever; what about this Nelson bloke?' She said, 'It's out of the question; he's at it all the time.' "At it" meant burglary. He'd left school at 14, gone almost straight to borstal, and had only been out a year. Don't forget I was only 15, and apart from drinking anything and everything, I suppose I was well-behaved, by comparison that is. I said, 'Right, you go down to Charlie's cafe; he'll let you have a wash there, and I will go home, have a wash myself, and I will see you here tonight. Is that all right?' She said, 'I've got no option, have I?' I didn't know what to say.

I thought of the previous night, how tender and loving she had been; the look on her face and the way she was trying to tidy herself up was breaking my heart, but what could I do? She looked so pathetic, my heart bled, and while I know my mum would have been sympathetic, she was the exact type of person my father would have had shot. She too would have been called a "silly looking slop".

I'm glad I didn't know it at the time, but the look she had on her face that beautiful summer morning was a look that I would recognise often in the future, and it would become all to familiar over the next 40 years. She made to leave, and I naturally went to kiss her goodbye, for now that is. Anyway, I kissed her on the cheek, but she didn't kiss me back, she just turned and walked away. She had got about ten yards away, and I couldn't stand it any longer, so I went after her. I said, 'Look, my mate's mum and dad are on holiday; I know he'll let you wash and bathe there.'

Jake was one of the lads messing about with us the night before at the bus stop. He lived at the other end of the estate, about 20 minutes walking distance. I was hoping he would be in even more than Fay was, because his dad had a drinks cabinet. I don't why I hadn't thought of it before. I rang his bell, and he opened the door almost as if he was expecting us.

He was expecting someone, but not us. He thought it was his girlfriend, and the look on his face was a picture. He asked what was up. I asked if we could come in, and he said of course we could. I introduced them both to each other, but all he was interested in was what we doing knocking on his door at that time of morning. I just said, 'Oh, it's a long story. Is it all right if Fay has a bath?' He straight away said, 'Of course. I'll show you where it is.' He couldn't wait for her to get in the bath, so he could find out what had happened the night before. He showed her where everything was in the bathroom, closed the door, and shot downstairs.

Talk about prevarication, his first words were, 'Did you get her tits out?' I said, 'I'll tell you all about it on one condition.' He said, 'What's that?' 'Is there any chance of me getting a drink?' You see none of my pals were addicted like I was; some disapproved; some didn't care either way, and just a handful had the same predilection as myself. He said yes straight away, so I told him everything about me pretending to look for her bloke, sleeping in the woods, right up until we rang his bell.

Then I asked for my drink, so he went over to his father's drinks cabinet and took out an unopened bottle of wine. He chose the kind that there were most of, in the hope that his father wouldn't miss it. He then asked me to do him a favour. He said that if his girlfriend rang the bell would we go, and meet him later at Bligh's. I agreed. Bligh's was the only dance hall in the whole of Sevenoaks town; in fact it was the only venue in the town where people could drink and dance and sometimes sing together.

Fay came downstairs. She looked beautiful. I asked her if she would like a glass of wine. She said, 'Oh god, no, how could you?' Jake was just about to tell her how I drank, when he received a subtle kick in the shins. He got the message, and kept quiet. Jake made Fay a cup of coffee, and I asked him what time he was expecting his girlfriend. He said it could be anytime before mid-day. It was now just on ten thirty, so I asked Jake if he would mind if I shot home to have a quick bath, and be back in less than thirty minutes. He said, 'Sure, that's fine, but try not to leave it any longer.'

Luckily my old man was out; my mum was in the kitchen, and she asked, 'Did you sleep all right at John's?' I said, 'Yeah, fine.' 'Well, that's odd,' she said, 'because he was here not 10 minutes ago looking for you... Well?' So I told her I'd slept in the big woods with a girl, and she said that if my father found out he'd swing for me. She told me to be careful, and I went off back to Jake's.

When I got to Jake's, Fay wasn't there. He said she'd just gone over to the phone box to make a call. I asked who she was calling, but he didn't know. He was desperate to know more about oral sex, but I didn't have time to tell him because Fay came back. I said, 'Who have you been calling?' She said, 'Oh, just someone.' She obviously didn't want me to know, so I left it at that.

Fay said she was going to walk down to Bat and Ball and catch a bus up into town, and that whatever happened she would meet me right outside Bligh's at exactly seven o'clock. I said I would be there. She left, and as we were watching her walk down the road, we saw Jake's girlfriend walking up the road, so I nipped out the back, over the wall, and into the back end of the big woods. I still had about half a bottle of wine left, so I went back to the clearing where Fay and I had slept the night before, and finished the wine.

What a contrast between 15-year-olds today and 40 years ago. Nowadays most 15-year-olds were doing what I had done the night before long before their teens. In my naivety and ignorance, I found a secluded spot and examined myself to see if I had contracted any sort of venereal disease. I don't know what I expected to find, I hadn't a clue, but I still had to look at my cock because although I'd had a bath at home, it just didn't seem right to look for something like that in my mother's home.

It was unusual for my old man to be out, so I thought I'd make the most of it, and sauntered off back home. If he was in, then I would come back out; if he was still out, then I could be with my mum for a while. He was out, great. I told her all about the night before. I didn't go into all the details about sleeping arrangements, but she knew anyway. My mum knew everything, and she asked when I was going to see her again. I said I was seeing her again tonight. She asked where we were going to sleep, and I said, 'In the woods, I hope.' 'You've no idea what you're doing, have you?' she said. 'What's up then, mum, so she's 7 years my senior, so what?' 'It's not that,' she said, 'ask yourself why she ran away, why she's got nowhere to stay. You obviously had sex, didn't you?' I said, trying to sound manly, 'Of course we did.' Then my mum asked, 'How long have you known her?' I was now beginning to feel silly, so I said, 'Some time.' 'How long? An hour? Two hours?' She said, 'Put it like this, how would you feel if one of your sisters came home and said she'd just slept with a bloke that she'd never met before, and they'd had full-on sex, no precautions. How would you feel?' I said, 'I'm going up to my room to get ready to go out.' As I went upstairs I heard her say, 'Just think on, that's all.'

All of a sudden I was furious. Wasn't she ever 15? She was married to a bloody sadist, at least she was as far as I was concerned. Before I had left the big woods, I had got myself a bottle of cider, so while I was getting changed I drank it. While last night was all new and exciting to me, this road I was on now was oh so familiar; on the one hand I wanted to go back downstairs and say sorry to my mum, but on the other hand, I wanted her blessing. Blessing for what, I'd no idea, but I wanted her of all people to understand me. Why won't anybody stick up for me, why couldn't I stick up for myself?

While all these thoughts were going through my mind I was standing in front of the mirror, having drunk my two pints of cider and Jake's bottle of wine. I was jack the lad; you wouldn't see me standing with all the other blokes tonight. I had a date, and we had done it properly, all the way and every way, and she was mature.

As I was standing there preening myself like a cockerel, I heard my father's voice. Damn, I'd wanted to say sorry to my mum before I went out, but I thought that's OK, I'll loiter in the kitchen until I can get her attention. This is what drink does to me; my rationale is so totally different to what it is when I'm sober. The trouble with me is, when I'm drunk I think I'm invisible. I had one last preen; I wanted to see my image as others would see me when I went into Bligh's. It was a false image, because I was drunk. I know it now because as I write, I'm sober.

54

I tried to adopt a sober state of mind because, to get to the kitchen, I had to go through the front room, where the old man was. Luckily, my mum was still in the kitchen, so I pulled the kitchen door closed behind me and said, 'Sorry mum.' I had to say it in a sort of whisper, and she said in a sort of whisper, 'You're drunk.' I told her I was OK, but she said, 'You've got nothing on.' I had my best pair – only pair – of Levis on, and a singlet, and boy, did I feel fit. She asked me about my sleeping bag, so I told her it was already in the clearing.

What an odd place Bligh's was, and what odd people we were. This is how it would go: bearing in mind that the only thing on everybody's mind was sex, you would think that we would integrate. After all, Bligh's was the perfect venue: live bands, drink and an equal proportion of women to men, but do you know, the odd thing about this mating game, well especially in our era, was that the blokes would all congregate at one end of the bar and the women at the other end. Some of the braver ones would actually dance round their handbags, but us blokes could only make contact after we had sufficient drink inside us to give us the courage to go over and try to chat them up. I of course was in a different league now; I'd actually gone the whole hog.

The bus dropped me off at the terminus; I could already hear the music coming from Bligh's, but I wanted to go in a pub first, so I went in the nearest one to Bligh's and had a couple of pints. I had told Fay I would meet her at seven; it was now 7.45. I walked into Bligh's after paying my entrance fee and went straight down to the bar. I had a couple of shorts, and suddenly there was some sort of rumpus going on in the main hall. I had to have a look. We didn't have paramedics in those days, we had ambulance men, and when I went into the main hall the music had stopped and there were about half a dozen ambulance men in attendance. And then, just as suddenly, there were policemen – a lot of them. Something was definitely wrong here.

All the lights came on and we were asked to leave as quickly and as quietly as possible. A crowd had formed in the centre of the dance floor. I pushed my way through and my heart sank; there was Fay, lying face down. She was wearing the same jeans that she'd had on that morning when she left Jake's, and there was a small pool of blood round about her midriff.

As I'd had nothing to eat that day and I'd drunk quite a lot, this whole scene was taking on some sort of surreal vibe. I couldn't for some reason help but notice how dirty the floor was; it was littered with dog-ends and spent matches, and the people who were looking on looked like clowns.

55

We all looked ridiculous, myself included, and there was Fay lying face downwards in a pool of blood that was by now spreading wider across the floor. What on earth was happening?

We all sort of dispersed to the surrounding pubs where all sorts of rumours were going around, the favourite being that she had been stabbed and they already had a man in custody. Some said she'd overdosed on hard drugs. What frightened me was that nobody knew her name. I did, I just did not know what to do. It was obvious they would find out who she was, probably within hours.

As it turned out, it was lucky for me that I was late for my date, for when Fay had made that phone call from outside Jake's earlier that day, she had called Nelson and arranged to meet in the town. They had spent all day drinking before going to Bligh's; he obviously had some sort of hold over her.

I would like to think that she did feel something for me; after all I never actually spent a penny on her, so she wasn't after me for my money. I just think she was spellbound by this Nelson bloke, but then again my mum was probably right all along although she didn't even know the girl. She was typecast like me. What had happened that day was that Nelson thought she was two-timing him and, quite simply, he stabbed her. I can't put it any other way. We were all to learn later through the local paper that she spent several weeks in intensive care, critical but stable. He in turn was sent to prison, but I don't know how long he got. Fay pulled through, and the last I heard she was married to a smashing bloke and is now a grandma.

I did say earlier that a tragedy was to hit this family; well it did. It had nothing to do with Fay, although she was affected by it, but I'll finish the chapter on this note: Fay and her family are happy and my mum was, as always, right, but we'll never learn, will we?

9

The Puppet and the Puppeteer

I call this my puppet trick, and this is why. We all of us at some time in our lives have seen a puppet. Now the puppet's operated by the puppeteer, who pulls the strings attached to its limbs. He can make it move any way he wants, and it has no control. This is what I'm like first thing in the morning, but you can't see my puppeteer. My puppeteer is alcohol. There are no strings. I suffered from what I call my puppet trick most mornings throughout the 1990s.

It hasn't happened since I came out of my latest detox. It's an horrendous and frightening thing while it lasts; luckily that's only about 30 minutes, providing I can manage to get some alcohol down me. When it first happened to me, I thought it was just a one-off thing, but it happened the next morning, and then again the following morning. I was having to go through this ritual every single morning. If there are any young people out there who may find themselves in a detox unit for their very first time, then read what I'm about to tell you and pay heed, for after all, I was no different from you when I first started:

I wake up in the morning covered in sweat, new and old; my tee shirt and shorts stick to me like glue. I have a hideous taste in my mouth, and my breath smells. I know what's going to happen as soon as I get out of bed, so I just lay there for a minute. I take stock; I need to know what day it is, how much drink I have left, and how much money. After making a mental note, I get out of bed. I stagger through the lounge, and get myself as comfortable as I can in my chair with my small table in front of me.

I place a bucket in between my legs; the bucket is clean. I washed it the day before. It is lined with two carrier bags for sanitary reasons, so I can easily dispose of the mess that is just about to come out of my mouth. This ritual takes place every morning, and it's not a pretty sight. I always make sure before I go to bed that there is nothing immediately near me; I don't want to damage anything or hurt myself.

I roll a fag as quickly as I can because within just a few minutes I won't be able to do anything for the next half hour. The retching starts; my stomach expands and contracts, and I now look like an old starving yard hound that is just about to die. At this point, because of the spasms, it looks as though I haven't got any stomach at all. I heave, and I heave, and out it comes; it burns my mouth and stings my eyes. The pain is so intense I try to grip the table, but by this time the puppeteer won't allow me control over any part of my body, and sometimes I even miss the bucket when my head swings from side to side. I'm also at this point quite likely to be incontinent.

Whilst all this is going on, and in between gasps of breath, I howl; it helps to relieve the pain. The whole thing takes about 15 to 30 minutes. It is such an ordeal that I then have to sit there for another 30 minutes, sipping my drink very slowly, to make me well enough to be able to perform my ablutions. Then I scrub my mouth and use a strong mouthwash, I put clean clothes on, dispose of the mess and go and sit down. Later I will clean the bucket ready for tomorrow.

That's what I call my puppet trick. I said earlier that alcohol and I conspired between us to kill me, and sadly it looks like I'm keeping my part of the bargain. It was a conspiracy in that I wouldn't admit I was an alcoholic.

I would like to tell you about a drug I took, or possibly didn't take, in about January 2002. I received a call from my local Community Alcohol Team. They wanted to know whether I would be interested in a new drug trial programme that would last 46 weeks. If I was interested, I was to take the drug for 34 weeks, and then for the next 12 weeks they would analyse the effect on me. It's important that you know I have never used drugs. I was told by the CAT that it was possible there could be some pretty nasty side effects but up until then there hadn't been any fatalities.

They gave me time to think about it. The drug they were talking about was called Nalmefeme. Basically it was formulated to stop any cravings for alcohol. The physical symptoms of alcohol abuse can normally be taken away with a 7 to 10 day detox, but the psychological symptoms were a different thing altogether. So this drug appealed to me.

Among the side effects that were listed were incontinence, impotence, dizziness, nausea, numbness of the feet and hands, cramps and sweatiness. All of which I already had anyway, so I thought let's do it! I contacted CAT and made an appointment to talk about it. This is how the trial would go: I would be picked up at my flat once a week and taken to the Bexhill medical centre where the drug would be administered.

Now here was the tricky bit: to determine whether I was both physically and psychologically dependent they included a placebo in the trial. Neither the doctor or I would know what was being administered until the end of the trial. After the administration of the drug, they would also supply a car to take me home. I agreed to the trial and had to go down to CAT and sign a form. The form I agreed to sign explained that I had read and understood all the possible side effects, and the fact that it was a new programme, and that my name was just one of 150 people picked throughout the UK to undertake this programme.

Had I been what we call a binge drinker, one who was able to stop drinking from time to time, then I wouldn't have qualified. It was aimed specifically at people exactly like myself who just couldn't stop drinking. I was to be a guinea pig. The problem now was, whilst I was able and even encouraged to carry on drinking as I normally would, my system had to be alcohol free before I could take the first tablet. How on earth was I going to do that?

CAT and I talked about this and decided that if my blood alcohol level could at least be below a certain limit, then it would be OK to start the programme. This was to prove easier said than done. The date was set for my first appointment. I naively thought that as long as I didn't drink on the morning of my appointment, I would be OK. I had a shock because, although I didn't drink at all that morning, I had so much alcohol in me it would have been illegal for me to drive so I was now in a situation where not only could I not drink in the morning, I also couldn't drink the night before my appointment.

We made another appointment for the following week. I told my wife I wouldn't drink after 5pm, and by 8pm I was climbing the walls. I just had to have a drink. I kept my appointment the following day and of course failed. Two weeks had now passed and I hadn't even taken my first tablet. We made another appointment for the following week. I was desperate to start taking this drug that possibly might stop me craving alcohol.

As the day grew nearer for my third appointment, I was becoming increasingly more drunk each day. On the morning of the day before my appointment I woke up drunk. I was still at this point having to go through my puppet trick every morning. I was in total despair; if only I was able to get started on this programme there could possibly be some hope for me.

I decanted my alcohol into a soft drinks container and walked down to the enclosed part of the shopping precinct. I sat there amongst all the people, watching them being busy; they all seemed to have a purpose. I envied them and, even amongst all these people, I felt totally isolated. I thought about the following day; it would be my third attempt to get on the programme and, so far, it had taken three weeks. Then I had an idea. It was a long shot, and it wouldn't be easy for me, but I was desperate; I would call my mum.

I put my drink in my bag and walked down to CAT. They contacted my mother for me, and I explained everything as best I could over the phone. I told my mum the situation I was in and promised her that if I could stay with her and my dad for the night, I wouldn't drink. Like most men, I had an instinctive inbuilt respect for my mum. Whilst I held the phone, she spoke briefly to my dad and in less than a minute told me to get the first train and come up straight away.

I knew I was going to a place of safety, I knew I wouldn't drink in the presence of my mum. Powerful as alcoholism was, it was no match for the love that my mum had for her number one son. I went home and packed my overnight bag. It contained one bottle of cider. I took no clean clothes and no toiletries; this was business, and my goal was to present myself.

The following morning, I would have an alcohol level that would read what was required to enable me to start this course of treatment. I was lucky I had only eight minutes to wait for my train. The journey would take one hour and ten minutes. I settled down with my one bottle of cider, looked at my watch and gauged the time against the amount of drink I had. I knew I couldn't drink after I got to Sevenoaks station. After all, between now and my appointment at the Bexhill medical centre, it was myself and my mother against the all-powerful alcoholism.

Sometime between Hastings station and Sevenoaks station, I messed myself; I had an involuntary bowel movement. I knew nothing about it until I went to get off the train at Sevenoaks station; I smelt it first, and felt it soon after. I felt like Linda Blair from the film *The Exorcist*.

I went straight to the taxi rank and tapped on the window. He wound the window down and, before I could give him my destination, he wound the window back up; he had obviously smelt me. I went to the second taxi; he didn't wind his window down so I intimated through the window that I wanted a lift. He mouthed the words through the window, 'Get in'. I climbed in the back. He asked where I wanted to go and I told him; neither of us spoke for the whole journey.

As we pulled up outside my mother's bungalow, I saw my mum waiting by the door. I paid the driver and walked up the path. My mum held her arms open, and I fell into them and cried. My mum cried, we both cried; here I stood, a fully-grown 54-year-old child. Whilst my mother loved all her children equally, we both knew we had a special bond; she loved me, and always had. I felt it in my heart.

60

Whilst my father waited in the lounge for me to come in, my mum and I stood on the doorstep and sobbed. Between my father and me we had put my mother through so much; neither my father or I knew why, we just knew we both felt guilt.

I went into the lounge with my mother, and Dad and I said hello. My mum showed me to the bathroom where I was able to wash myself; I also washed my shorts out and hung them over the radiator ready for the morning. I went back into the lounge and sat down. It was bizarre sitting so close to my father, as nearly all my early life I had feared this man and yet strangely enough, sitting so close to him, I felt protected.

My mother, whilst never being a physically demonstrative person, had from day one always loved me. I felt it in my heart, and as I had always had a problem with physical affection, her unspoken love suited me. It was genuine and heartfelt.

As I entered the lounge, my father turned the television off. We were silent; this was going to be more difficult for them than it was for me, because at this point I started to have the shakes, peripheral neuropathy (nerve damage), and I knew that whilst I would suffer, I wouldn't be quite with it. So it was more intense for them than it was for me.

All three of us were only too aware of the delicacy of this meeting. We knew it could be fraught with danger, as the three of us had never before all sat down together. We had one common aim, and whatever we had to go through we would get me to the medical centre tomorrow. That was our aim. We were all careful not to lift the drains covers up on our relationship.

It worked, nobody at this point wanted to get upset. We talked mainly about my brothers and sisters, and about how they were doing. I have three sisters. Each married shortly after leaving school and looking back, I know this was to get away from my father. I am pleased and proud to say they are to this day all still very happily married; they all have children, and some have grandchildren. In this day and age, that's some achievement.

There were times during this surreal evening when my father would just momentarily nod off. On one of these occasions I stole a look at him. He looked vulnerable, and even though I was now a middle-aged man, that night I still wished I could touch him, but I remembered the last time I tried some 50 years ago.

I mentioned earlier that when I went to put my hand on his, at just five years of age, he slapped me so hard he nearly knocked me off my chair, and also abused me verbally. I said, whilst I didn't know what it was, something in me died. I now know what that was; it was my spirit. He also, all those years ago, disarmed me. From that day onwards and up until the present day, he emotionally disarmed me. I have never since that day been able to deal with my emotions. You may think that because he was able to break my spirit just like that, even as a child, I couldn't have had much character; well I didn't.

We struggled through the evening and, at about nine o clock, decided we should all go to bed. My mum nudged my dad who had just nodded off again. He shook himself, stood up, and shook my hand. He wished me all the best for the following day, and went to bed.

My mum wanted to talk to me alone. She asked me to try and understand that, whilst she desperately wanted to comfort me when I was a small boy, and she did in her own way, she couldn't do it in front of my father for fear of incurring his wrath. Funnily enough, I already knew this even when I was young. My mum need never have worried, I knew.

She gave me a pair of my dad's old pyjamas and showed me to the spare room. It was actually my dad's bedroom but, just for that night, he would share my mum's bedroom as there were already two separate beds in there. My mum made sure I got into bed all right and said goodnight. I asked her if she could leave the door wedged open just in case I had a seizure during the night, for now it had been some time since I last had a drink, plus I knew within an hour I would be hallucinating.

I slept badly, sweated profusely, and had horrendous hallucinations. My dad woke me at five in the morning, and then went back to bed. I got up, got dressed – my shorts were by now dry – and found the kitchen. I made myself a cup of tea and somehow managed to drink it, but I neither washed nor cleaned my teeth as my only aim was to get to the medical centre and be breathalysed; nothing else mattered. I walked into my mum's bedroom; it didn't feel proper to go near their beds so I thanked them, told them I would ring just as soon as I had been tested, and left.

Although Sevenoaks station was about two miles away it was all downhill. I managed to get on the main road. At some point, walking down Sevenoaks High Street, I suddenly stopped walking. I knew the puppeteer was about to do his work on me. He had never caught me out in public before. I automatically went down on all fours for safety, and I was in this position just as it started. I retched, I heaved, I gasped and I howled. A postman walking by stopped. He knelt down, put his hand on my shoulder and asked if I was all right. I couldn't speak so I nodded yes, I was OK, and although he turned round several times, he did keep walking, and for that I was grateful. I just didn't want to be seen.

This was Sevenoaks town, the place of my birth. It was something like 6.30 in the morning, and there I was on all fours in the gutter just like a dog. It occurred to me while all this was going on that it was a good job I had clothes on, for had I been naked I'm sure somebody would have called the RSPCA. and they would have shot me stone dead as an act of kindness. This was alcoholism at its best.

Alcoholism and I had never understood each other better than on that day. I got to my feet, rested my head on my arm and leant against a nearby wall. There was still stuff seeping out of my nose. I managed to get to the station and boarded the train, got off at Hastings and went straight home. I walked in, picked the phone up and called the medical centre. I still hadn't had a drink. I explained the situation, and a car arrived within ten minutes.

I pressed the buzzer and was let in straight away; the doctor's door was already open and he beckoned me in. Neither of us spoke as he handed me the breathalyser. I blew into it and the doctor took the reading. It was just below the level required for me to start the new wonder drug. I had finally done it, despite my puppeteer's efforts early that morning to thwart any progress I might make against him. I had done it.

The doctor gave me my first tablet and we talked loosely about the possible side effects. He gave me a couple of phone numbers in case of an emergency and a copy of the agreement I had signed. I noticed at the top of the page there was one sentence in slightly larger print which read, *This programme is not approved by the British Medical Board*. We made an appointment for the following week. The receptionist ordered my car; it would be there in ten minutes. I thanked her, and told her I would wait outside as I needed a smoke.

I knew there was an off licence nearby so I bought a bottle of cider and came back to the centre. I stood in a position where I would be able to see the car but would be out of the vision of the receptionist. I didn't want her to think I was taking a liberty. I drank the cider in one go; at this point I hadn't eaten for 72 hours, and my whole being stank.

The driver recognised me from the previous weeks, and asked me how I got on; I didn't answer. He wouldn't have understood, and I didn't know. He told me his next door neighbour was an alcoholic, and again I didn't answer. I got home, went indoors and drank another bottle of cider, then I went to bed and slept until about midnight.

I got up and went through to the lounge. I checked that my bucket was clean for the morning, and sat down and cried. I was frightened that I might be going mental. In my last detox, at Alex One, we had to attend Health Education classes where we discussed the symptoms of alcoholic dementia, and I was frightened that this is where I might be heading, but I could not stop drinking. I had one more drink and went back to bed.

I dreamt I was alone in a room with my mother and father. I woke up early, went through to the lounge and did my puppet trick. I had one glass of cider, ran a steaming hot bath and performed my ablutions. I then cleaned my bucket ready for the following day. I knew the magic pill – or not – that I had taken the previous day would take several weeks to kick in, so I didn't expect any miracles there.

I kept my appointments for several weeks – it was easy, they would pick me up and drop me off. Whilst I had experienced incontinence in the past, on some sort of irregular basis, I now had to deal with the fact that every time I went out I would probably shit myself. This did actually become a problem. I can only talk about the occasions I remember.

One such occasion found me in some shrubbery just on the outskirts of the town centre and not far from where I lived. I was walking home and knew I was going to shit myself. I hid as best I could in this shrubbery and managed to get my trousers and shorts down to my ankles, but by this time I was covered from my waist down to my ankles in my own faeces, and somehow my mobile phone and my spectacles were also covered. I lay there for some minutes trying to think what to do: I'm drunk, covered in my own shit and I'm on a drug that nobody knows about. What can I do? I decide to call CAT, my local Community Alcohol Team.

Verna answered. I explained the situation I was in, and she said, 'Give me your exact location, and I will try to get an ambulance to you.' Between us we managed to pinpoint my location. The ambulance arrived; the paramedics put on surgical gloves and approached me with caution. They managed to get me to my feet and took me to the ambulance. They laid out a disposable sheet and told me to take a seat. They said all they knew about me was that I was an alcoholic and that I had had an accident.

They then stepped outside the ambulance and, although the conversation was covert, I did manage to understand that the general concern was whether to take me to the hospital or take me home. At this point, I interjected. I said I was fine, and they could just drop me home. They called someone on their radio, then turned to me and said, 'OK Brian, let's go home.' They dropped me right outside my front door.

I am not psychotic; I don't take illegal drugs and, as far as I know, at that point I wasn't mental. I could only think that when I sought oblivion all those years ago through alcohol, it was my first step on my journey towards alcoholism, and that's the only reason I found myself on that fine afternoon in that shrubbery covered in my own faeces.

Nobody was to blame but myself; I can say this with confidence, because nobody knew except me the power alcohol had over me. I'll say again to anyone out there, young or old, if you happen to find yourself in a detox unit for the first time, regardless of the circumstances that brought you there, take a good look around you; and don't ever think that the other patients must have something in their genes or some weakness that you don't, because they are no different from you. They are there because, as with you, alcoholism is beginning to tighten its grip.

Regardless of your status in life, if you invite him in he will destroy you and all those who love you. He is not discriminatory; take heed. As hard as it was for me to get on to the new wonder drug programme, I just couldn't go on living like this. My involuntary bowel movements were now causing me serious problems. I had to assume it was the new wonder drug, so I simply stopped taking it. What puzzles me, even to this day, is that neither the doctors nor my counsellors have ever mentioned this period. As far as I know, there were no observations or reports noted about either my behaviour or response to this drug. The only possible reason for this could be that they had just given me a placebo, but I have to doubt that.

10

In and Out of Detox Units

About 22 years ago, this first started. I had an appointment with a consultant psychiatrist, a Doctor Michael Bott. He was a really nice man, and certainly knew all about drinkers. At the time I met him he had already been dealing with chronic alcoholics, incorrigible alcoholics, reformed alcoholics, recovering alcoholics, dry alcoholics and functional alcoholics. Now he had to deal with me. After speaking for just a couple of minutes, we both knew this wasn't going to be easy.

We arranged that an ambulance would pick me up at my flat, and take me to Hellingly psychiatric hospital. For the first time in my life I was to be detoxified. It was to be the first of something like 16 detoxifications over 22 years.

The ambulance arrived on the date arranged at the exact time. As I had never been detoxed before, the idea frightened me. On the morning I was to be picked up, I had already drunk a full bottle of vodka. Whilst being able to walk and talk, I was very, very drunk. There were already five people in the ambulance, myself making it six. Three of us on the left, and three of us on the right.

There was a partition dividing the driver's cab area from us passengers. I got to my feet, unzipped my fly and urinated, right in front of the other passengers. They put their hands to their mouths and looked on in shock horror; I was insane. As the ambulance turned to the left, it caused my tide of urine to flood to the right, and as it turned to the right, so my urine flooded to the left. Each time this happened they had to pick their feet up. I remember someone banged on the partition to alert the driver. The ambulance stopped, and the back doors were thrown open. The driver and his mate pulled me from the back of the ambulance and threw me in the gutter.

1 just lay there until the police came and arrested me for being drunk and disorderly. They took me to the cells where I spent the night, and I appeared before the magistrate the following morning. I was fined £35. There was no mention of my behaviour in the ambulance.

I went home that day devastated. The next few days were spent in a drunken haze and I was now becoming depressed. I was lost in a

66

wilderness of pain. The girl I was living with at the time, who was later to become my first wife, managed to get me another appointment with my psychiatrist. He had heard through various sources of my escapade in the ambulance. He was furious with me. When I spoke with him for the second time, it was two weeks to the day since I had tried to get in for my detox. Although he was furious with me, he had seen it all before and actually was very kind. We agreed that I wasn't to leave the building. He would organise a welfare car to take me straight to Hellingly.

I came out of his office and went back into the waiting room. My wife- to-be, said, 'How did you get on?' and I said, 'OK, but I must go and get some cigarettes. I ran straight down to our local Co-op and bought a bottle of vodka. So as not to be missed, instead of drinking it there, I ran straight back. My wife-to-be, Pat, knew what I had done; although she hadn't seen the bottle, she just knew.

As I sat down, Ronnie Milligan walked in. He was there for his daily Heminevrin "alcohol substitute". I animated with my hands, *do you want a drink?* He knew what I meant, and nodded. Ronnie and I went into the gents. Again, so as not to be missed, we drank the whole bottle in less than ten minutes. We came out and I sat down; I was again very drunk. In less than ten minutes, my name was called, 'Welfare car for Mr Harding.' Pat and I went out and got in the car. I sat directly behind the driver, and Pat sat behind the driver's mate. Again I was on my way to Hellingly. This time I wouldn't blow it.

To get to Hellingly, you have to go through a small town called Battle. It was while we were driving through Battle that I decided to kill the driver. I took my seat belt off, reached forward and grabbed the driver by the neck. I tried to strangle him. As he had control of the car, he couldn't take his hands off the wheel. Pat sat mortified. The driver's mate tried to break my hold around the driver's neck. His efforts were futile; I was again insane.

The driver managed somehow to steer the car into the police station. The driver's mate jumped out and ran inside. Suddenly there were at least six policemen. I still had my hands round the driver's neck. They managed to release my grip, drag me out of the car and wrestle me to the ground where they manacled me.

I was back in the cells. I was at this point suicidal. Sometime during the night they transferred me to Bexhill Police station. I was still manacled. I fell asleep in my new cell, and when I heard my cell door open, it was morning. Sometime during the night, I had pissed myself.

As expected, the jailer checked my name, read the offence out to me, and asked how I was going to plead. I said, 'Guilty'. He said, 'Right, you'll be the first one up, court one.' He was a policeman of the old school, with plenty of experience. He knew I was just a drunk. He also knew that after my ordeal the previous day, and with no alcohol to steady my nerves, I would be in a "whipped cur" state and therefore wouldn't give him any trouble. I asked him for a cigarette and he obliged. Within minutes of him giving me a cigarette, something strange was to happen – an act of genuine understanding.

The jailer's superior, a sergeant, came to my cell door. He was, he confided in me, a functional alcoholic, that is an alcoholic who can still, although drinking, function. He had done a CRO on me and discovered that two weeks previously I had been arrested for the same offence whilst trying to get to the same detox unit. He understood and empathised with me. Whilst he didn't go into details about his private life, he told me he understood me. He said Pat was waiting in his office for me, and he explained that if I agreed, when they called my name, he could just say the charge has been dropped.

He said he would only do this if I, as one alcoholic to another, gave him my word that I would leave the police station and make my own way directly to Hellingly. He had made inquires, explained the situation to them and told me they had said my bed was still available. There was no mention of the assault on the driver, just as there wasn't two weeks previously about urinating in the back of the ambulance. I think all those who were involved with me at around this time quite simply thought I was insane.

I agreed immediately. I was asked to sign for my personal property. Both the sergeant and I realised that I was, by now, shaking so much with the DTs that I was unable to sign my name. Pat had to do it for me. We went straight over to the railway station where I bought a single ticket for myself, and a return ticket for Pat.

At some point during the previous night in the cells, I had woken up. It was deathly quiet and in the dim light I was able to look round my cell. I was a caged animal and I was frightened. I knew that night, in that cell, that if I kept this up I would die. I realised I didn't want to. It was with this resolve not to die that I bought the tickets. Had I chosen not to buy the tickets, one of two things would have happened: I would eventually become insane with "Korsakoff's Psychosis", "Wet Brain", or I would die. I wanted neither.

I checked the time the train would leave, to make sure I didn't miss it, and went straight to the nearest pub. By now I was shaking uncontrollably. It was almost 24 hours since I'd last had a drink. I could not remember the last time I had eaten food. I ordered a large whisky and a pint of beer. I asked Pat to get a straw from the barmaid. She thought it an odd request but she gave her one. I drank half the pint of beer through the straw, which enabled me to pick the glass up without spilling it. The whisky I had to drink all through the straw; I simply couldn't pick it up without spilling it.

Long gone were the days when, as a little boy in the big woods I used to drink my cider without a care in the world. This was business. I needed alcohol to live, and yet it was killing me. That's how insidious this thing is. I drank as much as I could before my train was due. The nearest place to Hellingly hospital where the train could stop was a small town called Polegate. Pat and I got off, I went to the first pub I came to and asked the barmaid if she would call a taxi for me for one hour's time. She ordered the taxi, and Pat and I took a seat. I had a pint of beer, no straw, and was as steady as a rock.

This is what alcohol does to you; it is the battle that will get you the wounds, but you have to engage it to get well. The taxi arrived; I gave Pat what remaining money I had, kissed her goodbye and left.

Amber ward, where I was to reside for the next 56 consecutive days, was a purpose-built psychiatric unit. They would, and were able to, detox you (a) if you were referred, and (b) if they thought you had either emotional or psychiatric problems. I had both, severely.

I went through induction and reception like I wasn't really there. I had a thorough medical examination. Everybody seemed so kind; that's because they were. Pure and simple, kind. When they had done with me, and given me some medication, they took me through to what they called their community room.

Because of the amount of alcohol I had consumed in the weeks leading up to my admission, I can only think I must have been desensitised, because I was looking at a scene from hell. Although there was very little noise, these people were from a different planet. I didn't in any way feel threatened at all; they didn't even notice me. I could have been a doctor for all they knew, or cared, for they were miles away.

There was one chap who was sitting there knitting. He had two cigarettes in his mouth, and I put him at about 30 years of age. There was an old lady sitting before him, cleaning his shoes. I put her at about 60; she had hot pants on, with a blouse that was undone almost to her waist, and she wasn't wearing a bra. Had I known that this was to be my front room and lounge for the next eight weeks, I would have run away then and there. A girl came up to me and asked for a cigarette. I was just about to give her one of my roll-ups when a nurse appeared from nowhere and told me not to give it to her in case she set the place on fire.

The abuse I felt I had suffered in my childhood paled into insignificance; these people were in pain and they, unlike me, didn't have alcohol to deaden that pain. It was to be another three days before I visited this room again. I had a fit, right there and then. I recall absolutely nothing about having this fit; it was the doctors who told me later when I came round. I stayed in bed for the next three days. I was very ill.

The community room was the only place we were allowed to smoke. It was there I spent all my days and all my nights. I got to love it. I think of my father and the day he sat me in a bath full of cold water and then urinated over me, the day he slapped me and called me a silly looking slop when I was just five years of age, and that punishment was for just one single show of affection towards him. I look at these people around me and think what a cowardly man he was. Please God, don't let me be like that.

It was in the community room that I met a girl called Jane, who was very bright and had a string of 'O' and 'A' levels. She was in her late 20s and a manic depressive. She was also very highly sexed, and we formed a relationship. She, like me, had a problem with being intimate. She loved sex, but could only do it with strangers, which suited me fine. For the eight weeks I was there, we enjoyed a full and satisfying sexual relationship.

The day arrived for the doctors to assess my progress. They were pleased at the way I had responded to my treatment, and felt there was no point in keeping me in any longer. They said it was now up to me. I was given a discharge date of one week's time. I was given an out-patients appointment, a prescription for some vitamins pills and told that this detox was my wake-up call. Jane and I were able to enjoy a few more hours of pleasure in the gazebo before I left. This was my introduction to a life of detox units. I was 32 years of age.

DATE: I4 May 2003. It was only a few years later that Hellingly was to close and was no longer to be used as a psychiatric hospital, due to underfunding and too few resources. We were then having to rely on a more local hospital called Queen Charlotte's. This was a hospital that used to specialise in chest complaints that seemed to be rife at the time, such as emphysema and tuberculosis. Part of this hospital was then used as a

It was while I was here on one of my many detox stints that I was to witness an incident that was to shake my faith in, and understanding of, some of the medical staff. It was to confuse me and leave me more than a little bit frightened. Unlike at Queen Charlotte's, security at Woodlands is of paramount importance. The staff, including the doctors, the nurses, the cleaners and the catering staff, were extremely vigilant. Whilst you were a patient at Woodlands, the concern for your health and safety was as important, you felt, to all the Woodlands personnel as it was to yourself and this is why I was so shocked by this incident. I didn't understand it, which made me wonder whether these people knew something we didn't.

Exactly opposite the entrance door to the day room was a door that allowed you access to an area outside where you could sit and smoke or, if it was a nice day, just enjoy the sun. On this particular day, among the dozen or so patients who were either sitting or just wandering around the day room trying to find something to occupy their wretched minds, there was a girl who I shall call Rose. I had seen her before at various times, either in the dining room, the OT room or in the day room, where she was now sitting. All I knew about Rose – not her real name – was that she was anorexic, and I guessed her weight to be around six stone. She was an extremely timid girl, but also had a kind nature and surprisingly would always be ready with a smile if you ever spoke to her. As I entered the day room, I was aware of Rose sitting, as usual for her, on her own. She would spend hours like this, just looking straight ahead. I always had the impression that, although at first glance she appeared to look vacant, there wasn't much Rose missed.

Among this company was another person who I was very acutely aware of. He was a giant of a man, probably six feet four inches tall, with such a full beard you had the impression that to grow it that long and thick, he must have been born with it. He also had incredibly huge shoulders and yet, despite the incredible size of this man, he not only walked upright, but would also sit upright. As he walked from one side of the day room to the other, he looked almost god-like. Whilst nobody had ever heard this man speak, we were terrified of him. It was an incident between this giant of a man and anorexic Rose that was to shake my confidence in the way that the medical staff viewed us. It wasn't the actions or the words of the giant or Rose, although that was frightening enough in itself, but the reaction of the staff that frightened me.

Rose had decided to go and sit in the courtyard. I noticed this as it was unusual for Rose to go outside at all. I, like everybody else, had my eye on the giant. He too decided to go and sit in the courtyard. At this point I had been in Woodlands about a week and I had never seen the giant smoke before. He positioned himself just a few feet from where Rose was sitting, and even from where I was indoors I could tell it unnerved her. The giant pulled a pouch from his pocket and made some sort of cigarette. My experience amongst the junkies and alkies on the streets of London told me that it was no ordinary cigarette.

This man was already in Woodlands when I arrived, so I had no idea as to how long he had been in there, and I had no idea what he was in for. I'd never heard him speak and I had yet to hear anybody, staff or patient speak to him. While he was smoking his drug – I just knew it wasn't tobacco – he also pulled from his pocket a half bottle of whisky. He drank about half of this and then began to laugh; it started off as a snigger and that turned into a full-blown belly laugh. Meanwhile he had manoeuvred himself so that he was nearer to the doorway to the dayroom than Rose, who was by now looking around frantically. There was, as far as I knew, no other way in. I didn't know what medication the other patients were on, but it was as if none of them knew what was going on.

By now the giant was laughing like a maniac. Although Rose had turned the other way so as not to make eye contact, you could tell by her skinny, bony shoulders that she was sobbing her heart out. In total fear, she suddenly made a dash for the door. The man smashed the neck of the bottle on a dwarf wall surrounding a flower bed and threatened Rose that, should she say anything, he would ram the broken bottle so far up her scrawny arse that even the surgeons wouldn't be able to get it out. He then threw the broken bottle away and passed out on the floor.

I ran to the office to get a nurse; the nurse said she wouldn't be long. I said, 'For goodness sake, get somebody out there now.' She then realised I was serious. Suddenly the day room and the courtyard were mob-handed with ward nurses, staff nurses, charge nurses, even student nurses. Now this is what not only frightened and confused me, but also disgusted me: Rose managed to get back into the day room and was sitting in her usual chair in the far corner with her head cradled in her tiny misshapen hands, sobbing her heart out. She was also bleeding from her foot.

Most of the patients in the day room, who I thought were oblivious to all this, weren't as stupid as I'd thought. At least half of them had seen what went on, but with even more experience than myself of life in psychiatric units, chose not to do anything. But as soon as they saw all the nurses, and realised that they would be safe, they recounted, as I did, everything they had just seen and heard.

By this time, the nurses had roused the big man and managed between them to get him back into the dayroom. I could not believe what I was watching. The nurses were under no illusion as to what had happened, and yet not one single nurse, not one single member of staff, took the trouble just to see if Rose, who was still crying, was all right. The bearded giant on the other hand was receiving immediate on-the-spot counselling, with the nurses putting their arms around his huge shoulders and assuring him everything would be all right. I just couldn't understand it.

A doctor appeared from nowhere and, along with a couple of nurses, walked him back to his room. Rose on the other hand was still crying, and her foot was still bleeding. She had been scared witless, violated, traumatised, and yet was just simply left to sit in the corner to get over it as best she could. It did occur to me at this point that maybe the whole of the medical institution thought of anorexics in the same way as they did alcoholics – that it was all self-inflicted. Alcoholics, anorexics, bulimics, self mutilators; none of us had a disease, none of us were really ill, we were all just doing it for a laugh. None of us really lost our loved ones; none of us really lost our jobs, our houses, our self-respect, our children, our liberty, and even our lives. We were just doing it for a laugh!

Tell me that when I was just ten years of age and my own father pissed down my back, and all I could think of at the time was I needed a drink, that it wasn't oblivion I sought all those years ago, but attention. Tell me I enjoy my fits; tell me I enjoyed the pain when I was hospitalised with pancreatitis; tell me I enjoy being incontinent, impotent. Tell me I enjoy it when some of my old work mates would see me in the street drunk, and shout out, "look at that wanker", tell me it's all just been one big long career move.

I went over to try and comfort Rose. She told me she would rather be left alone. Whilst all the patients talked excitedly about what had just happened, a nurse came in to the day room and told us it was teatime. We all filed through to the dining room, except Rose who stayed in her chair, still sobbing. Rose didn't actually eat anyway; she was on some sort of special liquid diet that just about kept her alive. I finished my tea and went back to the day room. Rose wasn't there. I asked one of the nurses if Rose was all right, and had anybody had a chance yet to speak to her. She told me they hadn't, but that I needn't worry because somebody would speak to her later. I milled about the day room and the courtyard until about midnight, then went to bed. There was no sign of Rose. I slept badly that night. I just couldn't get this picture out of my mind, of this demented, massive, god-like giant of a man threatening this six stone anorexic little girl with a jagged broken bottle in his hand.

I went through for breakfast, and then I went out to the courtyard for a smoke. I could still see a few pieces of broken glass. A nurse came out and I asked her what had happened to the big man. She said he had been transferred during the night to a more suitable place. I was later to read in the daily paper that the "more suitable place" was a secure unit somewhere in Blackheath. I asked her about Rose, and had anybody spoken to her yet as she was obviously very traumatised by what had happened. She said she didn't know. I was later to learn that, as Rose was in the unit voluntarily, it was her choice to discharge herself at any time, and that's what she had done; she no longer felt safe.

I asked this nurse if she could guarantee our safety while we were in her charge. Her reply shocked me. She said there was no way she was going to risk her life for "any of these fucking halfwits", and if I had a problem with this, then I could bring it up at our twice weekly meetings, one of which was tonight. She stamped her fag out and went back into the dayroom. The meetings she referred to were to give not only the patients but also the staff a chance to air any grievances. In theory, this sounds like a good idea. In practice, it nearly always ended one way – everybody just shouting and hollering, and none of us actually got anywhere. Bear in mind a lot of these people were on some very heavy medication and didn't really even know what day it was.

That night's meeting was to be different. As soon as we'd all sat down and laid out the ground rules, which nobody ever took any notice of anyway, I said s that I intended to make an official complaint to the East Sussex County Healthcare Trust. The staff nurse asked me what it was about. I told her I was disgusted with the staff's response to yesterday's incident concerning the big man and the little six stone anorexic girl. I told her I would just like to ask her one simple question. It wouldn't be a trick question. 'Those of us who were aware enough witnessed your total lack of interest, even callous disregard, for little Rose, whilst you at the same time heaped not only tender loving care but almost praise upon her would-be assailant, which in turn made us greatly concerned for our own safety should the same thing happen to us. Please, therefore, could you respect us enough to give us a straightforward answer to this question. Why did you help him and not Rose?'

She told me that was staff business; it had nothing to do with me, and that I had no idea what I was talking about. I told her that as a fully grown man I'd been in these places so many times, I knew when to be frightened, and with her and her staff in charge of my safety and welfare, I was frightened. She said, 'Then make sure you include that in your complaint.' The meeting was brought to a close, and that particular nurse and I never exchanged another word. I was back in this detox unit some two years later, and whenever she was on duty she would avoid me like the plague.

I went to the office to lodge my official complaint, and they told me I would have to come back in the morning before OT, as the chap I would need to see wouldn't be on duty until then. They asked me to tell them briefly what it was about, and I explained as best I could. The woman I spoke to said she would make a note of it and that I would have to make my complaint to the service manager of that particular department. She said that in the meantime, would I like to consider the implications that it might have on little Rosey. Suddenly all the staff were using this term of endearment "little" whenever they spoke of Rose, when I know that, whatever their reasons, they didn't give a damn about her when she was threatened by that hulking great crazed madman. So I said that, whilst I didn't know little Rose personally, it was for her and people like her that I was doing it. She told me that if they considered my complaint to be valid, it would then be passed on to the chief executive, 'whoever he or she was', and that I would be contacted within three weeks. This really inspired confidence in me, and I actually thought, with hindsight rather naively, that I just might be able to do something for this little Rose "whoever she was".

The following morning I went in to the office after breakfast. There was a different lady on duty. She had a lovely big smile and seemed very pleasant. She asked me if I had had my medication, and I told her I had. She asked me if I had a discharge date. I told her I was expecting it some time that week, when I had seen the ward round doctor. She then asked me if I thought I would be able to fill in the necessary forms as part of the complaints procedure. It was then that I realised where she was at. I had been used to dealing with corruption on the street, but to deal with corruption when it's done under the guise of respectability, I was not in their league. I knew there was no way in the world I would be listened to. Whatever should happen, I knew none of these people would be held to account for what took place between the big feller and the little girl. I told the lady that perhaps she was right, and whilst I understood that she and I were strangers to one another, and would quite probably never meet again, we would always have one thing in common and that was we both knew that the people who were on duty that day were guilty of gross negligence. She didn't answer, and I left to carry on with my occupational therapy.

11

Sleeping Rough on the Streets

The clatter of the Borough's council trucks wakes me up; they are the early morning cleaners. They will quite literally hose us down, so we must get up quickly. I guess there are about forty of us here, underneath what they call the arches. I only know it's the bottom of their Villers Street or Villiers Street. I do know we are right next to Charing Cross underground station.

Once again, in my wretched alcoholic life, I was witness to, and part of, a scene from hell. There were something like 20 of us to the left hand side of the arches, and about the same number on the right hand side. If you were to stand at either end of the arches and look at the rows of people, we would look to you to be in various stages of decomposition; to a drug-free, sober person, it was that horrific.

I had arrived in London some weeks previously from a halfway house somewhere on the Isle Of Sheppey in Kent. I was in the halfway house because I had just left a rehabilitation centre in Sittingbourne, Kent. I was in the rehab because during one of my stints in the spare room at my parent's house, I was charged with, and found guilty of, making a threatening telephone call with menace. I had rung my psychiatrist and told him I would kill him and smash his out-patients' clinic up; yet again I was insane with alcohol.

1 was then banned from my mum's house and I had nowhere to go; I was an incorrigible alcoholic. Social Services gave me a cheese sandwich and a travel warrant to the Sittingbourne rehabilitation centre; sounds grand, doesn't it? In fact, it was a doss house where all the inadequate alcoholics were housed in a massive dormitory.

On my first day there, I was told to get in the shower, and I was then deloused. Whilst at reception, waiting for the paperwork to be done, I went to the bed space that had been allocated to me, put my change of underwear on my bed, and went back to reception to complete the paperwork. When that was done, I went back to my allocated bed space and found that someone had stolen my clean underwear. I was furious.

Several of the beds around me already had the occupants laying on top of them. I knew they were all looking at me, waiting to see my reaction. I looked at all of them and said that whoever nicked my underwear was taking a chance as I had full blown AIDS. They all looked away. I was at that point quite emaciated and probably looked the part; nobody came near me after that.

I knew I had to get away from there as soon as I could but, while I didn't have AIDS, I did have gonorrhoea. I don't know where or who I got it from but I did know I needed treatment. I had been there about two weeks when I went to reception and explained my predicament. They gave me a travel warrant to Minster, a town on the Isle of Sheppey, just over the water.

I kept my appointment at the STD clinic and got some medication. I was glad to be away from the rehab, and took the opportunity to look round the town. As I hadn't had a drink for 16 days, when I noticed a job centre I felt confident and capable of doing a job, so I went inside. There was a vacancy for a qualified painter and decorator, so I got the details from one of the centre's personnel and said I would like to take the job.

They told me they would need proof of my apprenticeship, and proof that I had City and Guilds certificates. I lied about everything surrounding the reason why I was on the Isle of Sheppey, and asked if it would be possible for them to contact the company where I had served my apprenticeship. They told me to take a seat. A lady came back ten minutes later and gave me an introduction card to a local well-established family firm.

I went along and got the job just like that. All I needed now was a place to live. I had passed a newsagent earlier with a whole window full of adverts. I found the newsagent, read the ads, and found that what was once a hotel was now what you call a halfway house. A halfway house is where the owner can charge extortionate rent to people like myself who for whatever reasons are inadequate and unable to cope alone in the community. The local council pays the lion's share of the rent so the owners cannot lose. They become very rich and you become very depressed.

I went along to this place, where there were several vacancies. As I walked through to reception, I noticed the bar was still open and it was now about 4pm. Pubs closed in those days at 2.30pm and didn't open until 6pm. I commented on this to the receptionist and she said the bar was open all day up until midnight; I couldn't believe my luck. Although I had never been in this place before, and certainly couldn't have known anybody, I had already picked out the serious drinkers. This was going to be the place for me. I went back to the rehab centre and spoke to the guy in charge. This was the guy who, when I told him my underwear had been stolen, told me if I didn't like it I could fuck off. I told him I not only had a job to go to, but I also had a place to live.

He gave me some forms to fill in to ensure that my first two weeks' rent would be paid in my new place. He also told me he would organise a travel warrant, and that because in my new job I would have to work a week in hand before being paid, they would give me a giro for the amount of my weekly wage; this I would have to pay back at a later date.

I could hardly contain myself. This place was called a rehabilitation centre and yet I had to lie in my bed every night and watch this old man lying on top of his bed stark naked, masturbating while calling out *Mummy, Mummy, Mummy*. Where are the faceless people who think that this type of environment could possibly rehabilitate anyone, even if we were the dregs of society?

The following morning I went, with the person who we used to call the matron, to the stores. She kitted me out with the following: one pair socks, one pair underpants, one tee shirt, one pair trousers, one shirt, one jumper, one pair boots, one pair gloves, one coat. Not one of these items fitted me; I looked like Coco the Clown, but at least they were clean. Again I was on my way, and it was now 18 days since I last had a drink. At this point, I think I was 33 years of age.

I made my way over to the island, found the nearest Post Office and cashed my giro. Whilst I had new clothes on, I didn't actually have any spare ones, but at the moment that didn't matter; what did matter was that I had a proper job to go to. I was sober and I also had a little bit of money. I found the halfway house, went through the bar and into reception. I handed them the forms to sign to get their rent. They showed me to my room, and a couple of the other residents came with me to show me where things were.

One of these blokes was called Lester. He told me that, if at any time the bar was closed, I could just go to the office and, provided I had the money, they would serve me a drink. It was now Thursday, and I had to be at my new job at 7am Monday. Lester, like myself, was an alcoholic; funny how we find each other. He showed me the way down to the dock area, where we spent all day drinking, and then we went back to the halfway house and spent all night drinking.

I woke up the following morning and reached under my bed for my cider. I hadn't eaten for 36 hours. I lay there drinking my cider, and realised I was furious with myself. I had just been 18 consecutive days without a drink, and here I was at something like 7am, drunk again. Lester

82

came into my room. We talked about how I would get to my new job by 7am Monday. I knew I had to get an alarm clock, but didn't want to waste my money – Drinkers' mentality.

Lester and I both wanted a drink, so we decided to buy some vodka and cider and go and sit in the park. I had limited money and this worried me. We sat in the park all day, both feeling hard done by but knowing nobody was to blame but ourselves. We finally wandered back to the house where we continued to drink. At some point during the evening I bought a bottle of cider, took it up to my room and hid it under the bed ready for the morning.

I spent the whole of Saturday down by the docks drinking on my own. I knew in my heart I wouldn't be able to work, but I would go through the motions and see what happened. I made my way back to the house, making sure I bought my cider for the morning. When I woke up Sunday morning and reached under my bed for my cider, I realised it had been stolen sometime during the night. I panicked. I only had £5 left, and still had 24 hours to go before I started work. I was shaking like a leaf, but I knew I had to go to the office and ask them to open the bar for me; it was 7.30am.

The bloke in charge opened the bar, served me my drink, took my money and didn't utter one word, but I could see the contempt in his face. While I was sitting there another bloke came in. The bloke in charge pulled another pint. The bloke paid for it, and neither of them spoke a single word. This again was alcoholism at its best.

He joined me at my table, and he too was shaking. He told me he had received an unexpected giro the previous day and, before he could cash it, was arrested for non-payment of fines, drunk and disorderly. He had only just been bailed, but he didn't mind as it was a Sunday morning and he was rich. He told me the bloke in charge would cash the giro himself for a fee of £10, which is what he did, and that was the reason he was able to buy drink on a Sunday. As he was flush and I was skint, I asked him if he would like to buy my coat from the rehabilitation centre. Although it was of poor quality, it was brand new. He agreed. I gave him my new coat, and he gave me £5.

We sat there for a couple of hours, and then I wandered down to the town. With my newfound wealth, I was able to buy two bottles of cider. I sat on a bench and noticed a woman who had been walking to and fro the last ten minutes. She asked me if I had seen a silver-haired man of about 80 years of age loitering nearby. I said I hadn't. She said she always baked a cake for him for Sunday mornings, and she was worried because she hadn't seen him. She sat down next to me and we talked. She was fairly well spoken, and I put her at about 50 years of age.

I mentioned that I had to start a new job the following morning and was worried I wouldn't be able to get up in time. She told me she had a spare alarm clock and if I would care to walk home with her, she would give it to me. In those days, people tended to trust each other. We walked to her house, talking all the way. I liked her. I asked her, as casually as I could, whether she drank or not, and she said she loved a glass of red wine. She didn't ask me if I drank – something in the back of my mind told me she knew.

She lived in a mid-terrace block. We went in, and she told me to make myself comfortable. She said I could have a cup of tea, or perhaps I would like a glass of wine instead. I think she must have spotted my cider. I plumped for a glass of wine. She went upstairs and came back with the clock; we set it for one hour's time and it worked, so I now had a clock. She cut the old man's cake in two, wrapped half of it up and told me I could eat it at work.

She told me she was divorced, and spent most of her time doing voluntary work looking after the elderly – hence the cake for the old man. Then, quite suddenly, she asked me if I would mind if she took her tights off; I said I didn't. She removed her tights right there in front of me. She said she didn't feel comfortable with anything on her legs; she liked to feel naked. With everything going on in my head, and as steeped as I was in drink, I was aroused. She poured herself another glass of wine. I felt totally at ease with this woman.

1 asked if I could take my shoes off, and she said I could do anything I wanted. she said she felt I was genuine. She poured herself another glass of wine and I laughed, and told her I was the drunk, not her. She told me she had another bottle in the kitchen and I knew then I wasn't going to work. We were silent for something like ten minutes, then I reached over and kissed her on the lips. She responded with a passion that frightened me; we somehow fell to the floor and undressed each other. I've never considered myself to be a good lover, but we made love right there on her sitting room floor.

We got dressed in silence, and both in our own way felt sated. She found a carrier bag and put my piece of cake in it, along with my new alarm clock and a bottle of wine. She gave me directions, and I left.

Lester was in the bar when I got back, so I joined him at his table. We set the clock for 6am, and Lester said he would also give me a call. Next thing, Lester came into my room and asked me what had happened. He

84

said he heard my alarm go off and assumed I had got up and left; it was 6.50am. I told him I couldn't make it, and he said he hadn't thought I would anyway. We sat on my bed and drank the bottle of wine.

I left and went to sit by the train station. I didn't want to go back to that poxy halfway house but I had no money, no clothes and no hope. I heard the guard over the tannoy announcing that the next train on platform two was bound for London Victoria. I decided to cast my fate to the wind. As I sit here now, over 20 years later, I realise just how desperately lonely and depressed I was. My family couldn't cope with me; I couldn't cope with me; I couldn't keep a girlfriend; I had no possessions and couldn't even do a job of work. This was all caused by alcohol.

Out of sheer desperation, I boarded the train bound for London. I don't know how I managed it without any money, but I did. I was accosted a couple of times by one of the guards for my ticket but on both occasions managed to talk my way out of it. I got off at Victoria station, and made my way straight to a group of street drinkers who saw straight away I was one of them. I was beginning to wish I hadn't sold my coat. I drank with them for a few days, sleeping when I could on the station. They told me that if I wanted to survive on the street, and was well enough to be able to beg, then the West End was the place to be. There was a place called the arches there, where it was relatively safe to sleep provided you were able to get up early enough to avoid the early morning street cleaners who, if you weren't quick enough, would hose you down.

I made my way over to the West End. It was now beginning to get very cold, even during the day. I spent my days begging, just for enough money to enable me to buy my cider. I have to mention a bizarre and potentially embarrassing situation that happened whilst I was begging. I was sitting on one of the benches on Charing Cross station, trying to beg from the commuters coming off the trains before they made their way into the city. I saw this bloke approaching the kiosk, presumably to buy his papers. He was immaculately dressed in a pin-striped suit. I approached him from behind and, while he looked vaguely familiar, I couldn't quite place him. He turned slightly to one side and I saw to my horror that it was one of my younger brothers. I was suddenly very aware of how absolutely filthy I was. I froze, then back-tracked to my bench.

I'd known he was an insurance broker and worked in the city, but it just hadn't occurred to me that I might bump into him. Thankfully he didn't see me. A prostitute joined me on my bench and asked me if I was looking for business. As she finished speaking, we both looked at me and burst out laughing. She apologised, told me she wasn't thinking and had just asked out of habit. I was dressed like a tramp, probably smelt to high heaven, and was begging for money to buy alcohol.

She told me a bit about herself, and I did the same. She told me about a place where I could get fresh cardboard every day as my mattress. She also said that, if I was still there that afternoon, she had a coat she would give me. She went off to tout her trade and I carried on begging. I knew a chapel somewhere in or around the West End. It was a tiny chapel with a small grass area and a couple of benches. I collected enough for a bottle of vodka, and made my way to the chapel where I knew serious drinkers would already be congregated. Funnily enough, drinkers were safe there.

I spent the afternoon there, exchanging exaggerated tales of hardship and woe. We were mostly strangers to each other, although some of this company had met before, up and down the country in various rehab centres or halfway houses. Apart from the occasional and predictable snapping and snarling, we had a good afternoon.

I made my way back to Charing Cross station and found the prostitute. She had a coat for me. It was far better than the one the rehab had given me, and fitted me perfectly. I would be the poshest dosser on the streets. I had with me my cache of cider, hidden in a rucksack I had found somewhere. She asked if she could have a sip as she wanted to take a couple of pills. I gave her some of my cider and she swallowed the pills.

She said they kept her just sane enough to live her insane existence without completely losing her sanity. She said she'd had a good day and gave me £5; she wished me luck and said she would see me around. I made my way to the place where she told me I could get some good quality cardboard. I entered the arches, and my heart sank; what a bloody state these people were in.

You now know how I had arrived at the arches homeless, and if you think it was my fault, I would simply ask you to spend, not a year or two years like some people have to, but just one week at that rehabilitation centre in Sittingbourne where the man in the bed next to you lies there masturbating, calling out *Mummy, Mummy, Mummy*, where they would steal the very shoes you walk in, regardless of your age, status or circumstances, where they automatically assume you're lousy and will forcibly delouse you. The shops immediately by the rehab centre refuse to serve you. You may sleep in a bed of sorts, have access to a shower and get fed once a day but people still won't employ you. You are there in that place, you have failed for whatever reasons to fit into society, you are not to be trusted and you have no more status in this society than an asylum seeker.

86

Under the arches, I walk along the rows of bodies, trying to find a bed space. I notice there's possibly a vacancy between two bodies. There's about a two-foot gap between these two people, and the only part of their bodies exposed is the back of their dirty, greasy, uncut hair. I lay my cardboard down and manage to squeeze in. I am so grateful for my new coat but I wake up about midnight and I'm freezing. The girl to my right actually has blankets. I try to lift one of the corners up in order to get that little bit closer to her for that extra bit of warmth, but her hand comes out from nowhere and slaps mine down. I didn't even think she was alive, let alone aware of me.

I somehow nod off, and that's when I'm woken by the clatter of the Borough Council's truck coming to hose us all down. As I get up, I realise the girl next to me has shared her blankets after all. I am one of the first ones to get up and leave. As a new hand at this, I am probably fitter than them.

I didn't see the face of the girl who had shared her blankets with me, and didn't for another ten days, but I was in for a shock. I grabbed my cardboard and my rucksack and made my way up to the hot air vents in the Strand. I drank one of my bottles of cider, then made my way to the public toilets in Leicester Square. I washed as best I could, and went back to Charing Cross station. I was starving, but my stomach had shrunk. I opened another bottle of cider and sat there, just watching all the plankton going by. Some walked purposefully and some just shuffled by aimlessly and once again, I found myself envying people.

I still had a little bit of money left from the £5 the girl had given me the day before, so it was a bit hard for me to get going today. I finished my cider and made my way up the West End. The reason I was in London living rough was that I'd hated the halfway house on the Isle of Sheppey. The reason I'd been in the halfway house was because I hated the rehabilitation centre in Sittingbourne. The reason I was in the rehab was because my mum threw me out of her home because I was charged with, and found guilty of, making a threatening telephone call with menace. The reason I was in my mother's house was because, whilst I was in Hastings, I had a complete nervous breakdown and my mother came down to Hastings and took me back to her house to look after me. Now I knew I couldn't live on the streets forever, and at some point I would have to go back to Hastings, but it was just a question of when.

I wish I knew at what point the sequence of events determines the outcome; that way I would be able to have a little more control. I did reasonably well in the West End, and made my way back via the cardboard place to Charing Cross station. En route I bought myself some sort of burger from a place that looked just like an old shed.

I had already bought my cider, not just for the night but, more importantly, for first thing in the morning. I hadn't been there long when the prostitute came and sat down with me. She told me she had been working all day and was going to take the night off. She didn't have a pimp. She was streetwise and had been doing this ever since her uncle abused her when she was just 11 years old. I didn't dare ask her how old she was now.

She had a quart bottle of brandy and I had my cider; we sat and laughed and watched the people walk by. She got a little bit drunk and asked me if I would like to go with her to her local pub. I pointed out that not only had I had the same clothes on since I left the hallway house, I also hadn't had a bath. Plus I was sleeping under the arches in between two people who stank. She said it didn't matter but I was very self-conscious about this and as much as I liked her company, declined her offer. She said she had to get home, bathe and change, and meet her boyfriend in their local; she told me her name was Lydia and that she hoped to see me again.

I made my way down to the arches with my cardboard under my arm, and found my space in between my fellow dossers. The two people I was sleeping in between never turned round, and as far as I knew would stay in their foetal position all night long. The only time they moved was when I arrived, just enough to enable me to get in between them. As they never actually looked up, I can only assume they either recognised my smell or were used to my routine of taking a mouthful of cider every time I woke up. Either way they obviously thought it was safe enough for me to sleep in between them, and that at least I wouldn't try to rob them.

The cleaners came again and, as usual, I was the first one up – no way did I want to get soaked. I washed and made my way to the station. I had been coming here for some time now, and people were beginning to nod; some would even exchange pleasantries, or drop a few coins in my hat. Lydia came along, which was unusual for that time of day. She told me she had to appear in Horseferry Road Magistrates Court for soliciting, so she thought she would take the whole day off, and asked if I would like to go along with her. I said I couldn't, I needed to earn some money. She said she would see me later, if she got back in time.

I knew my life on the streets of London would have to come to an end soon; not only was I fast becoming malnourished, I also had to appear before Hastings Magistrates Court on a burglary and theft charge. I knew that was sometime in December, and it was now sometime in November.

I walked up the West End and begged a few quid. I realised I rather enjoyed sitting on the station. The arches were only two minutes away, plus I enjoyed talking to Lydia. I didn't realise it at the time, but my stay in London was shortly to be over, but some 18 years later I was to meet Lydia again.

I made my way back to the station, begging on the way. As I approached my bench, I saw there were two women already sitting there. It wasn't until I got closer that I realised one of them was Lydia. I didn't recognise her; she had on a very staid, black two-piece suit. She introduced me to her friend, also smartly dressed, who had accompanied her to court for moral support. She told me she was found guilty and fined. She felt she ought to get off the streets for at least a day or two, and asked if I fancied going with them to her friend's flat where I could have a bath, and perhaps they could sort me out some fresh clothes.

Lydia, me and her friend, who liked to be called Jack, took a taxi to somewhere near St Thomas's Hospital. All I know about this flat is that it was on the first floor, and there was some sort of posh intercom system which Jack didn't need because she had her own keys.

It was immaculately clean and spacious with toilet, bathroom and two bedrooms. I think Lydia might have felt that I would think she was taking the piss by giving me a guided tour of the place, with its luxurious furniture, bedding and carpets, bearing in mind my own living accommodation. So she just said, 'Take your coat off and make yourself comfortable.'

I realised, sitting there in the warmth and luxury of their flat, that since I had been living on the streets of London I had been running on auto-pilot. For several weeks I had been living in horrendous conditions, and yet accepting everything. I can only think that, as a chronic alcoholic, I had decided that I couldn't expect anything else. The die had been cast, and my fate set for life. With hindsight, I think I must have accepted my lot in the same way all those years ago when my father had urinated all over my back.

Lydia said she would phone a friend and see if he could bring some clothes over for me. I was having a job taking all this in; it's funny how some people are just simply kind. Half an hour later, a bloke arrived and he had with him a complete set of clothes, including a hat. It did cross my mind that something untoward might be happening, but nothing did. He simply handed me the clothes and said, 'I hope they fit mate.' Lydia, who had been on the phone for the last half hour, came through and showed me where everything was in the bathroom.

When I came out of the bathroom, although at that time I didn't know anything about drugs, I saw Jack and the bloke that brought me the clothes with some sort of rubber tourniquets round their upper arms. They were both injecting themselves with something; it's obvious to me now that it was heroin. I didn't know what heroin did to you, as I still don't today, but it frightened me.

The bloke left soon after, and I tried my new clothes on. Lydia bagged my old clothes up and put them out with the rubbish. The intercom went and Jack answered it. She spoke briefly then pressed the entry button. A beautiful girl came in – I'd put her at about 20 years of age – and she and Jack disappeared into one of the bedrooms. I realised I had a lot to learn.

Lydia cooked some chicken and rice for us but my stomach was in such a mess I just couldn't eat it. She said she had a regular client coming later but I was welcome to stay if I didn't mind staying in the lounge. Although I was grateful for everything she had done for me, for some reason I didn't want to be involved. These people were living a life I knew nothing about. I told her I ought to get back to the arches, and maybe I would see her tomorrow. She gave me directions on how to get back to Charing Cross station. We gave each other a peck on the cheek, and I left.

I didn't know it at the time, but my residence at the arches was about to end. As I approached the arches, there was quite a heavy police presence and they were questioning the vagrants. When I rounded the corner, I saw an ambulance right by my bedside. I walked up to my lair and had a shock. The person who I had been sleeping with and cuddling for the last few weeks, was a man. He had a full beard. I recognised his hair and, funnily enough, his boots. His whole head and face was streaming with blood.

Apparently some skinhead, high on drugs and drink, had gone down the arches with the sole intention of beating someone up. They know that, while vagrants can stand up to the elements, when it comes to anything requiring strength, we just can't hold up. They had emptied the contents of a metal dustbin over my bedmate's head then smashed the dustbin over his head several times until he passed out. He looked up at me through the blood and, although neither of us had ever seen each other's face before, I felt he recognised me. They took him away in the ambulance.

Both his bed space and mine were covered in blood. The only consolation for that poor man was that where he was going would be warm, clean, dry and he would be able to eat without begging. What a life! What a liberty!

1 knew I couldn't sleep there anymore. I was gutted. I walked up and sat on my bench in the station; I wished Lydia was there. I knew my court case was coming up soon in Hastings, and if I didn't appear there would be a warrant out for my arrest. I was becoming weaker by the day. It was time to go back to Hastings. I knew so many drinkers there, so I knew I wouldn't have to sleep on the streets.

The question was how to get down there without any money. At that point, I think I had about £4. I didn't know how much the fare was, and I didn't want to arrive in Hastings penniless. While these thoughts were going through my mind, a young mum sat down beside me with two small children. Because Lydia's friend had kitted me out in new clothes and I had had a bath, I felt quite respectable.

The woman's shopping bag was open, and I could see her purse. I decided to steal it. My coordination was still quite good. My problem was not that I would have deprived her or her children of anything; that didn't occur to me, but if I managed to snatch the purse, could I make it to the steps, get down them and disappear out on the streets without her catching me? I had no stamina; I hadn't eaten a proper meal since I don't know when. I could have left my cardboard there, but I would still have had to carry my rucksack – it was where I kept my cider – plus, if she did catch me I don't think I would have had the strength to push her off.

There were so many imponderables. It's only now, all these years later, I realise that by living on the streets, you become immoral. If I had thought I could have stolen that woman's purse, and got away with it, then I would have done so. I'm only glad I didn't steal it. I took my hat out of my rucksack and placed it on the ground near my feet. The woman, totally oblivious to what I had just been thinking, gave her children some coins to put in my hat. I thanked them, and all three of them left. When they had gone I cried; I cried for my ex-bedmate, I cried for Lydia, for the man who lay in his bed in the rehab, masturbating. I cried for the woman who gave me the alarm clock, I cried because my father pissed over me, because I stole that man's cigarettes over 20 years ago and because I was me. How's that for self-indulgence?

Tomorrow, by hook or by crook, I would go back to Hastings. I spent the night sleeping fitfully on a bench in the chapel grounds. I dreamt of clowns. Next morning, I went to the nearest police station to report a robbery on Charing Cross station. They took my details, then referred me to the railway's police on the station. Lydia had told me you can get all over the country like this.

They also took my details. They asked me what my destination was and which train I had intended to catch before I was robbed on their station. I told them my destination was Hastings, and that I would now, due to this robbery, have to wait till at least 5 o'clock this afternoon as I had some loose ends that I would have to tie up. They contacted the police station where I had originally logged my complaint, who confirmed that I had reported it to them first. They apologised for any inconvenience that my assailants might have caused me whilst on their station, assured me they would be caught, wrote my false name and address down and issued me with a travel warrant.

I thought it might look like I was taking a liberty if I sat on their station begging, so I went up the West End, in or around somewhere like Piccadilly Circus. There, I saw a school of street drinkers and joined them. I spotted Lydia. She was with a man in a smart suit. I called out to her; she looked round, but ignored me. I couldn't understand it. I stayed there for another couple of hours, then went to St James's Park, wherever that is. I only knew I was there because there was a sign up. I bought some wine and mixed it with my cider.

All of a sudden Lydia appeared. Although the hustle and bustle of the city was only minutes away, sitting in that park we were somehow far removed from it. Taken out of her usual habitat, Lydia suddenly looked so young. She also had what I hadn't noticed before – striking good looks. She apologised for not speaking earlier, and said she'd been with a client. I told her I was going back to Hastings, and that I had used her trick to get a travel warrant. I also told her my ex-bedmate had been bashed up and, as far as I knew, was probably still in hospital. She told me she was sorry, but as in all walks of life, shit happens. She had seen it all before.

She told me that when she was young, and before her uncle started abusing her, her mum used to take her down to Hastings for a day out. She said she adored it, and one of these days she might even go and live down there. She told me where the nearest off-licence was, and asked if I would get her a bottle of brandy. I got Lydia's brandy and bought myself a bottle of chilled wine to mix with my cider, courtesy of the West End punters.

I had grown quite fond of Lydia and was sorry I had to go. We sat there talking and laughing, and got pleasantly drunk. Then she started to cry, which made me cry. There we were, two streetwise people crying our eyes out, and neither of us knew why. We pulled ourselves together and just sat quietly drinking for an hour. As Lydia had been working, she was dressed to attract and so hardly had any clothes on; she was frozen. We made our way back to the station. She gave me her telephone number and made me promise to call, and also gave me the rest of her brandy and a ten pound note.

She said that whatever happened she would come down to Hastings to see me just as soon as she had enough money. For the first time, I kissed Lydia on the lips. She kissed me back, but we both knew that Lydia and I could never be. My father and her uncle made sure of that years ago; Lydia and I would never ever be with anybody, even if we were married.

12

Back to Hastings

I boarded my train for Hastings, and arrived there two hours later. I knew of a café in Hastings that had some sort of living accommodation on the floor above. I went in this café, asked to see the bloke in charge and got a room; it was as simple as that. I was soon to find out why it was so simple. Over the years, due to my low self-esteem and self-loathing, I often found myself living in some appallingly filthy places but this was by far the worst I had ever seen. I daren't mention the names of the establishment or the landlord, because I'm sure he would have me shot.

I had to share a room with two other blokes. One was a massive drunken Irishman who absolutely terrified us, the other was a young skinhead who I think must have had some sort of genetic deficiency. He was an out-and-out bull goose loony psychopath who kept a rat in his top pocket at all times, and if you did something he didn't like he would get the rat out and threaten you with rabies. I'd felt safer under the arches.

I was living here when I had to appear before the magistrates for burglary and theft. I appeared without any legal representation and the magistrate, in his infinite wisdom, remanded me to the medical wing at Lewes prison for 21 days for psychiatric reports. 21 days later, I appeared before that same magistrate but as I hadn't even seen a nurse, let alone a doctor, there were no reports to be made available to him. I had just spent 21 days locked up in a cell and, apart from the jailer, didn't see another soul. The magistrate didn't question this, and neither did I. He sentenced me to three months' imprisonment suspended for two years. I felt I ought to be pleased, but I was already doing my own sentence so I didn't really feel anything.

I walked back down to the town, bought some cider, found a bench, sat down and thought of Lydia. The burglaries I had been found guilty of weren't where I had actually broken in. I would simply walk in to any place where the door was open, whether it was a shop, an office, a house or a flat, take anything that was immediately saleable, and buy drink.

I stayed in and around the café for the next few weeks, managing to avoid the wrath of the drunken Irishman and the contraction of rabies from the skinhead's rat. It wasn't long before I was arrested again. Same charges – burglary, in drink, for drink, with drink to get drink. This time they remanded me to Lewes prison to appear at a later date at Lewes Crown Court. I was now in a different league.

I spent three months on the remand wing and, when I appeared before the judge, received a total of 15 months imprisonment which included my three-month-bender suspended sentence. I was to spend a total of ten months in the prison system and five months on licence outside. I find it impossible to talk about this period; I was a stranger to myself for almost 25 years. I had spent almost every day, one way or another, steeped in drink and now I was sober, I was a complete stranger to myself; it would be like writing about a stranger and I just couldn't do that. While I had the ability to survive in almost any situation, being sober was very hard for me and if I'm to be honest I must say I didn't really like myself, and if that was my perception of myself then I assumed it was that of others. I find this disturbing and therefore won't mention my stint in prison again.

I was discharged on February 3rd 1983 from Northeye semi-open prison which, later that same year, was to be burnt to the ground by the inmates and has never been used as a prison since. I was given a discharge sum of £68, a kit of new clothes and a travel warrant for anywhere I wanted. While I had been in prison, I had kept in contact with my mum by letter. She said that, as I would be sober when I came out of prison, I could spend a week at her house while I decided what to do. A taxi picked me up at the prison gates and I was taken to the nearest town, which was Bexhill-on-Sea – a small town just outside of Hastings.

I went straight into the nearest working man's cafe and had a full English breakfast and, because of my lifestyle over the last several years, and my ill health due to drink, I couldn't remember the last time I'd done this. The halfway house, the rehab centre, my bashed-up ex-bedmate, the begging, Lydia, making love with middle-aged ladies who baked cakes for the elderly, all seemed a million miles from where I was that day. I had an appetite for food. I was sober and I could sit among my fellow men without feeling either conspicuous or paranoid; this was my new start.

However, there are two things that alcoholism doesn't do: take holidays and take prisoners. Whilst neither of us could get to each other while I was in prison, there was nothing stopping us now. I walked to the nearest pub, even though my system had been free of alcohol for 314 consecutive days and nights. I had even spent, for various misdemeanours, a total of three days in solitary confinement. I had been through all this and yet still, I wanted to engage in the battle with the bottle. I don't expect you to understand, and nor should you. I knew the enemy better than anyone, and even I couldn't understand it.

I ordered a large brandy and a pint of beer, and in less than an hour I was drunk. I don't remember much else about that day except that when I tried to board the first train, the guard wouldn't let me on; he said I was too drunk. I went to the local park and slept it off as best I could, then tried again; this time nobody saw me. I arrived at my mum's house in Sevenoaks that evening. I had washed on the station, and straightened myself out, so when my mum opened the door I looked quite reasonable. My dad came out to greet me and we went into their small sitting room.

My mum filled me in on what had been happening to the rest of the family, whilst my dad made us a cup of tea, and I couldn't think of anything to say. She told me that Barry was still living with them, and that he was soon to be married. My other brother Bill was doing the tail-end of a four-year sentence for manslaughter. He had run someone over whilst drunk and killed them. While my mum and I were talking Barry, the one of my younger brothers who I had almost accosted unwittingly on Charing Cross station whilst begging, came in from work and we greeted each other warmly. Then my mum showed me to my room. Bill's old room.

I unpacked my meagre possessions and tried to settle down. This pretence at normality was getting in the way of my drinking. I still, despite everything that had happened to me, sought oblivion. The next couple of days I spent just walking about.

I longed to call Lydia but had lost her number. My brother came into my room Sunday morning and said that if I fancied washing his car, he would give me a tenner and take me to Seal – a small village just outside Sevenoaks – for a drink. He said there was something he wanted to talk to me about. I had been out of prison exactly eight days.

Barry took me to *The Crown* at Seal, and bought me a pint. I realised later that he took me to Seal because it wasn't one of his local pubs, and so when I was drunk I wouldn't embarrass him. As young as he was, he realised that in my battle with booze, I could no longer tell the difference between victory and defeat. He said he thought it was best for all concerned if I went back to Hastings, and he would give me £100 so I could get my own flat. I told him I would go the following day, and could we have one more pint. He said he thought I had had enough, so we left.

When we got back, my mum had our dinner ready. She knew why Barry had taken me to Seal. I ate my dinner and went to bed; I dreamt of clowns with black circles round their eyes. The next day I packed, for what seemed to me to be the thousandth time, and left for Hastings. I

96

rented a tiny room at Undercliff in St Leonards. It was there I was to meet my future wife. My room was no bigger than any prison cell I had been in.

I met Pat on the seafront, just like I had met the cake baker on the Isle of Sheppey. We got on well and I moved in with her. She had been married for 12 years, had one son who was at college, and had been divorced for three years. I managed for the most part to work as a piece-work painter for a local firm. I was also, at the time, receiving a disability allowance for chronic alcoholism, so I was actually quite well off.

Pat and I decided to get married in April 1984. My alcoholism was getting the better of me again, so we decided to sell what few things we had and move to Eastbourne. We lasted there for six months. I drank anything with alcohol in it and we lived in abject poverty. We left Eastbourne without paying our bed and breakfast bill, and moved back to Hastings. I was later to be charged with making off without payment and extracting electricity without intent to pay. A little trick I had learnt in prison – how to doctor a meter.

We found another B&B in Hastings, which was worse than the last one. Alcoholism and I had brought Pat down to my level. When I first met Pat she had a nice two-bedroomed flat, but now she was living in a grotty B&B and whilst she didn't drink, she was a co-conspirator with alcoholism. While we were living in this toilet, I got a tax rebate for £500 – I don't know how they worked that out, but I didn't question it.

We managed to get a one-bedroom flat in St Margaret's Road, St Leonards. It was a basement flat with a garden, and I was to live there for the next 17 years. I was to be divorced there, and remarry there. Exactly one week prior to my unexpected windfall, Pat and I were sitting in our local park waiting for our dinner to be served at the B&B. I remember it was bitterly cold outside, but at least there was a chance I might see someone who would buy me a drink.

I looked in Pat's handbag for my tobacco and realised she had a pound coin. She told me she was having a heavy period and the pound was for her sanitary towels. As I sit here now, filled with shame, I find it hard to believe that I spent the next hour trying to persuade Pat to let me have the pound coin for a bottle of cider, and that I would get her some toilet tissue for her period. As hungry as I was, and despite the bitter cold, I was still desperate for a drink – that's all that mattered to me. I didn't, and couldn't, see how selfish I was. Eventually, Pat just cried and handed me the pound coin. I had hurt her deeply, and yet I couldn't see why, nor did I care. That is why I've said so often that alcoholism not only affects the person caught in the grip of it, but also anyone who has, for whatever reason, any contact with you. They will also suffer; they too are abused which means, because of the way you live, that you become an abuser yourself. This wretched alcoholism is far-reaching, never ending and as I've said before, doesn't take prisoners. It will kill you and inflict misery and hardship on all those around you.

I bought my cider and went back to sit in the park. We sat in silence while I drank it, then walked back to the B&B. There were two other residents in this cold and filthy place. A young lad of about 17, who was later to be sectioned under the 1968 Mental Health Act for indecent exposure, and a Scottish girl who was a hopeless prescription drug addict. These two were sitting in the lounge watching television. The only form of heating in this house was a paraffin heater placed in the middle of the floor. I asked the young lad why it wasn't working, and he said the landlady had drunk all the money the state had paid her to keep us, so there was no money left for paraffin.

Pat and I just sat there and froze. We were almost as cold there as in the park. The landlady came into the lounge to tell us dinner would be late because she was going to church. I asked her about the paraffin heater, and why we had to be so cold. She said if we didn't like the way she ran the place, we could both fuck off. Exactly five days later, I was to receive that cheque for £500 from the Inland Revenue and we moved to St Leonards. I was 35 years old. By now I was a well-known alcoholic and street drinker but was still able, when drink would allow me, to do the odd bit of painting.

Pat and I settled in as best we could, and I continued drinking. Pat took a part-time job that was allowed within the state benefit scheme. We weren't there long before I was called before the Department of Social Security for an independent enquiry by their own medical team as to why I had been signed off work for so long. I arrived there drunk, along with other alcoholics and drug users, and took my place in the waiting room. The doctor examining me reeked of whisky. It's a very recognisable smell. I noticed it straight away because I'm a 24/7, 365-day drinker. I could then, and still can, recognise anybody who comes anywhere near to having an alcohol problem. I've been told that if I were able to be drink-free for just two years, I could counsel people myself. My name was called and I walked drunkenly and robotically to a room where, for the thousandth time, I was to be examined to see if I was fit enough to be of any use in their society.

I received a letter eight days later informing me that I wasn't fit enough to be any use in their community. They didn't use those words but

98

that's what they meant. The actual results of my examination were as follows:

Consultant *Dr C Sobhraj*

Final Report

Sodium	139mmol/1	135.145
Potassium	4.2 mmol/1	3.5-5.0
Chloride	102 mmol/1	95-108
Urea*	1.1 mmol/1	Low 1.0.65 'low'
Cretinine	60 umol/1	
Glucose	5.1 mmol/1	3.5-5.9 (if fasting)
Bilirubin 'total'	7 umol/1	2-20
Alk Phosphatase	122 iu/l	high 20-110
Ast*	47 iu/l	high 7-40
AIT	32 iu/l	4-45
GGT*	832 iu/l	High 50
Total Protein	55g/l	60-80
Albumin	40g/l	60-80
Calcium	2.37 mmol/1	
Phosphate*	2.17 mmol/1	High C.80-1.40

Comment *Dr C Sobhraj –*
This man needs to stop drinking.

End of results and comments.

The above results frightened me. While I had no clue as to what my Bilirubins or my Aik Phosphatase were, I knew I was in trouble. Pat and I muddled through with me drinking almost anything I was able to earn. She had long since accepted that sexually I was a failure. To me at that time, having sex with someone you love was a form of abuse. I don't know why I felt like that. On the few occasions I felt I needed to gratify myself, I would visit one of my alcoholic female friends who like me had the same problem with intimacy.

Strangely enough, while an alcoholic would do almost anything for a drink, they also have a deep sense of morality. I've witnessed this, and have been party to this ethic most of my life. I will excuse myself for the liaison I had with the lady that baked cakes for elderly men!

It was whilst in the early years of my stay in St Margaret's Road, that my doorbell rang at five o'clock in the morning. It was Tony Costeller. He said Ronnie was outside. He had just discharged himself from hospital after being stabbed by his live-in alcoholic lover. He was bleeding badly from the stomach and didn't want to make a mess in my flat, but was desperate for a drink. He knew I would be up at that time of morning, and would have a drink. I told Ronnie to come in.

He told me that they had been drinking in the park. It was mid-winter, and it was Ron's turn to go to the off-licence. He had enough money for a bottle of sherry and four cans of Special Brew. On the way back to the park, Ronnie had bumped into another drinker who had no money and was rattling for a drink. Ronnie sat down with him and between them they drank the bottle of sherry. Ron's lover, who by now was also rattling for a drink, had found Ron and seen he had drunk their sherry. She took a pair of scissors out of her bag and stabbed Ron twice in the stomach. This was all witnessed by someone in the flats opposite, who called the police and an ambulance. The police recognised Ron as a street drinker and so just put it down to a domestic problem. The ambulance took Ron to the hospital where he was to wake up at three o'clock in the morning, himself rattling for a drink.

Pat knew that someone ringing my bell at that time of morning would have to be one of my drinking friends, so she stayed in bed. Ron, Tony and I sat there drinking. Tony himself was a hopeless alcoholic, and yet I've never met anybody, even to this day, who didn't like him. He was an affable, amiable man with an endearing nature. I was sad when I was told that he had died from hypothermia, alone in his lair, drunk and cold. None of us will ever know Tony's story; he simply didn't want to tell it.

13

Tony's Death

Tony's death. Where do I start?

It was about 1979. I'd been in Hastings a couple of months and I was already a street drinker or "bench drinker". The label differed, depending on which part of town we came from. There was a row of about six benches at the lower end of Warrior Square Gardens, which were taken up every day by a regular bunch of my drinking colleagues. When I got there on this particular morning at about 5.30, only one of the benches was occupied. I recognised Ron Milligan, a friend I still drink with to this day, and Tony who I only knew by sight. I'd drunk with him a few times and had always found him good company.

If all I had wanted to do was drink I'd have headed for any of the other five benches, but I cautiously wandered over to sit with them. 'You all right, mate?' said Ron. 'Yeah, I'm fine.' Tony looked up at me. He was very drunk. 'I know you, don't I? We had a drink together on the station the other night, didn't we? Do you remember that bastard who wouldn't give us the price of a drink?' I remembered. We were both drunk, and Tony was begging, and this bloke just wouldn't come across. Mind you, when I look back, I don't blame him.

So I said hello and he shook my hand as if we'd known each other all our lives. And for some reason I felt as though we had. Tony was a very gregarious character, full of fun and always up for a laugh. He lived in one room at the top of a house. The house is still there, and so is the room, which is still let out to people like Tony; people who have no-one to stick up for them and say, 'Look, this isn't good enough.' And it was in this horrible attic that Tony died. From what? Hypothermia. He literally froze to death.

The landlord was yet another one of the sharks that own property and let their stinking rooms out for the maximum rent possible and don't give a damn about the consequences. And do you know, the man who let Tony live there for all those years actually went to the funeral and cried. I want people to know how and why Tony died. He didn't die laughing. He wasn't stabbed in a fight; he didn't fall from a window and break his neck. Something like that would have been mercifully sudden. No. Tony died slowly, painfully. He died freezing, day by day. I knew it, Ron knew it and the landlord knew it. He was a familiar face, and even people who were only on nodding terms with him knew it. This landlord, if he has any conscience, should be beside himself with shame.

Tony and I became good friends. We'd meet up most days with Ron. Ron was the more level-headed of the three of us, but Tony and me were always at it like cat and dog. Neither of us had had much of an education. We'd made it to secondary modern, but didn't get anywhere near taking exams. But when we were pissed, we were not only Einstein, we were Socrates, Byron, and that bloke Wilde who got banged up in Reading Gaol for being a poof. We were everything. We laughed and joked, but what we didn't realise was how empty the day really was. We were just bullshitting our way through each day. Getting through the endless hours.

We were all on limited funds. I got my giro on a Monday, and Tony got his on a Thursday. He had a regular punter, Twilight, who would give him a fiver on a Sunday night and Tony would pay it back when he got his money, so whatever happened he was always assured of a drink on the Monday morning. One Monday, Tony came along to my bus shelter and said he hadn't been able to get hold of Twilight the night before, so couldn't get his fiver. I said, 'So what. What do you expect me to do?' 'Well, could you lend me a bluey?' Naturally I told him to go away. I'd never see it again. But he wouldn't leave off, and pleaded, 'look Brian, I swear I've only had one can of Special Brew. No, Tits brought it for me.' 'Look Tony,' I attempted to reason. 'Say I lend you a bluey and you get pissed and disappear till Thursday, what am I supposed to do?' He just said, 'I don't know, just shoot me.'

I knew what he meant. Anyone dependent on alcohol to the extent we were, would. So I lent him the fiver with the proviso that if I didn't get it back on Thursday, I'd kill him. He assured me he'd do the job himself. How could you not love a bloke like that?

I don't know what happened between then and Thursday, but when I went to my shelter as usual that morning, Tony was nowhere to be seen. Where the hell was he? Ron wandered over and said he'd seen him about six that morning. 'In fact, he was coming to see you. He said something about owing you some money.' He'd been no more drunk than he usually was at that time of the day. But the good news was Ron had come by a bottle of brandy. 'I ain't got a clue where it came from,' he said, 'but let's drink the bloody thing anyway.'

Just then, a woman we knew turned up. No-one liked her. In fact I couldn't stand her, but I asked if she'd seen Tony anyway. She had, and asked if my name was Brian. 'Why do you ask?' 'Tony's in the next shelter. He's shitting himself because he was supposed to meet this Brian Harding at six this morning, and he wasn't there. Are you the bloke?' What could I do but deny it? I liked the bloke and he was honest.

Ron refused her request for a slug of brandy. I'll try and explain why I so strongly disliked this woman. It's a job to put an age on her. Ron and I guessed about 35. We knew her youngest daughter was 11, and two older ones were about 13 and 14. This was the set up. You went into the pub and ordered your drink. You then looked round for this woman and if she were there you'd ask which of her daughters was available. They weren't even out of their teens. Despicable.

Ron and I carried on with the brandy... the vodka and the cider. We could see Tony sitting about 40 feet away on a bench with other drinkers. He couldn't see us, he was blind as a bat, so Ron and I just bided our time. We even went back to the offy and bought another couple of bottles of cider. Having eventually drunk our fill we walked over to Tony's bench. There was a lot of "Nudge, nudge. Look out, here comes Brian", and when he spotted us he jumped to his feet. 'Brian,' he said. 'Look mate, that fiver – I swear to God I put it between the slats of your bench first thing this morning.'...

Tony could always get his money early because his landlord had possession of his benefit book. He'd give him the money out of his own funds, then cash Tony's giro later. They home in on a drinker. An alcoholic needs a drink. He needs to be allowed to drink in his own room. So the landlords buy up any decrepit five-story house that's all but falling down. They then inform the borough council that they have rooms or flats to let, habitable, but in need of a "bit of work". A grant is issued which the landlord either pockets, buys a flash car with, or uses to buy up yet another mildewed hovel. But as far as the council is concerned, there is property available. And that's the sort of place that Tony had the misfortune to live in. But I digress.

...We all walked back to my shelter and there, sure enough, under the first slat, was a neatly folded bluey. I nearly fell apart. He'd taken the trouble to get there first thing because he knew I was an early bird. I apologised. 'Oh, fuck off,' he said, but in the next breath asked, 'can you do the same next week?' 'WHAT?' Then we laughed!

But the mood suddenly emptied. In truth we were weighed down by how utterly pitiful our existence was. Was that all we could find to laugh about? We were a fraternity. We were all as close as brothers grieving together. He asked me where I thought this was all going to end. I said, 'I haven't a bloody clue; are you scared?' 'Yes,' he said, 'Are you?' 'No, it's loneliness that frightens me more than anything.'

We walked back and gave Ron the nod that we wanted to move on. He copped our meaning straight away, and so did a couple of the girls who moved with us to the next bench. They didn't want to be around that woman who hired her kids out either. At some point, someone suggested we all toddle off to one of our hovels and have a party. I knew these girls were alkies too, but they sure as hell hadn't been drinking since five that morning. None of us had anything better to do, there was nowhere else to go, so why not? I also rather fancied one of them. Mind you, if she fancied me, the only thing I WAS confident about was that I wouldn't be able to do the business.

Back at Ron's we drank, we laughed and we cried. There were arguments; there were fights, but nothing serious. I did go to bed with this girl. Just to be naked and lay with someone who, just for that time, you could be close to and trust. I'm pleased to report, however, that I DID rise to the occasion and it was beautiful. She's happily married now with a couple of kids. I see her now and then, but we only nod and smile.

Tony, Ronnie and I roused ourselves at about eight o'clock, and the girls left. I don't know who shagged who, but it didn't matter. They had things to do and we wanted a drink. They had children to tend to and husbands to look after. We didn't. The usual pretence of promising our undying love for each other accompanied their leaving. Of course, we all knew this was bollocks. We were living in an alcoholics' world, and these gigs would only happen when "the outrageous misfortunes of slings and arrows" (to misquote) brought us stumbling into each other's company again. Our stock-take showed that between us we had two unopened cans and two half full – or half empty, depending on your take on the situation – so a return trip to the offy ensued.

Tony and I became good friends over the years. And not just as drinkers. It was odd how I learned that he'd died. Sometimes I would sit right at the back of the park just to be on my own. A woman regularly walked her dog there, and when she passed by my bench she'd often nod or smile. Small gestures like that made you feel a part of the human race for a bit. She never usually spoke to me, but one morning she stopped and said to me, 'I'm ever so sorry to hear about your friend, Tony.'

'What about him?'

'Oh, I'm ever so sorry. I just assumed you would have known.'

'Known what?'

'Apparently his landlord found him in his room, dead.'

I was stunned. She just walked off with her dog. She was normal. Decent. She wouldn't make up something like that. I sat for a minute trying to take it in. Tony, dead? I put my bottle in my bag and went straight to Bottle Alley. Was it true about Tony, I asked. One look at their faces told me it was. Apparently Ron had been looking for me for a couple of days with the news. I turned away and headed back to the park. I couldn't even cry. All I could feel was anger. Why? I didn't have a clue.

The next few days passed in a haze. Everything was just a vague mess. But somehow, Ron and I managed to organise ourselves and a few others to sort out the cremation service. Once the date was fixed, we set about organising lifts to the crematorium for everyone.

I've never seen anything like it. When we arrived, I had never seen so many alcoholics gathered in one place at one time. There must have been about 40 of us, each and every one with a can or bottle in our pockets.

We filed in and quietly took our places. We weren't the smartest congregation that the vicar had ever seen, but you could see he appreciated that we'd made an effort. Most of us had needed him at some stage, and he'd looked out for us over the years in his own small way.

The sermon was beautiful. The vicar recounted some funny stories of Tony's exploits down the years. There was no falseness; he'd taken trouble over this. He made us laugh. We all knew that he'd given Tony the odd pound or two, here and there, just to help him out, provided he wasn't too drunk. When it was over, about a dozen of us all piled into Ron's, and that's where we stayed for two days. All I can say is that life went on.

Bless you, Tony.

14

Memory Loss

My first serious memory loss happened in 1970 when I was 23. I'd left Lowestoft and gone back to live with my mum. She had made the spare bed up in the back room, but made it abundantly clear that if my father was to accept this arrangement it was imperative that I was in work as soon as possible.

I managed to get a job as a theatre assistant at the local hospital. Now this suited me fine. There was a lot of shift work which meant that once I was familiar with the rota, I worked out that I could drink until I was drunk for a certain number of hours, and calculate how long it would take me to sober up ready for work. It helped having the rota worked out a week in advance so I could plan my drinking to my best advantage. There are times when I need a drink at three or four in the morning, and the shift system seemed ideally suited to allow me to manage my cravings and withdrawals, and keep straight enough to work.

I also doubled as a porter, which meant that I would sometimes be called upon to collect patients from the wards and take them down to theatre for surgery. Sometimes there had been an amputation, and my job included disposing of the dead limb. I was supposed to electronically ignite the incinerator, throw the dead weight of flesh and bone on the fire, and stay to make sure absolutely nothing remained.

I loved the work and the theatre environment. I still had a tan from being weathered by my years at sea and the whole hospital, especially theatre, seemed to be teeming with women. I was in my element.

But like everything else in my wretched life, I had to spoil it. I'd been there several weeks, and been extremely careful not to let anybody know that I had a severe drink problem. But as usual, I became complacent and started bringing alcohol into work. You name a place in that hospital, I hid bottles there. It got to the point that I could do any shift they asked me to. And why? Because I was now coming to work, night or day, drunk. Obviously not staggering drunk, but drunk none the less. There were a couple of occasions when the theatre sister asked me if I was OK, and I'd take a couple of steps back to avoid her smelling my breath and reassure her that I was fine, just a bit tired. She knew how many hours I was putting in so that seemed to satisfy her.

My love life was great, too. The student nurses would do something like a three-month stint in one department and then move to a different ward or hospital, so neither variety nor commitment were a problem. But not becoming involved wasn't just an avoidance tactic. Because of the emotional deprivation I'd suffered when I was a kid, I had a hell of a job differentiating between love, affection, sex, loyalty, friendship and abuse; in fact, any show of affection or act of kindness threw me into a quandary. I really didn't know how to deal with it. I feel the same even now.

But I did make one good friend of a chap who was just about to go off to university to study chemical engineering. One night he invited me to a party. He said there would be loads of booze and nurses. I couldn't believe my luck. I couldn't remember the last time that I'd been invited to a party!

Because it promised to go on until the early hours, I arranged to meet him at about ten o'clock. I still ask myself why I wanted to go to this party. I was in a relationship, albeit very casual, and had a good sex life. I wasn't involved, but it was as much as I could handle. But to me being invited out to a party felt like an honour. I was being treated like a normal person, not the outsider I knew myself to be. But...

This is how an alcoholic thinks; how we approach a social occasion: I would pace myself. I wouldn't drink when I got home. I was determined. I planned not to go out until eight o'clock, but I was very excited. For someone to invite me to a party meant that they must like me. Also, they couldn't possibly have known about my drinking. I walked home feeling really happy and went straight through the front room to my bedroom. Mum came in to see if I was all right, and sat on the edge of the bed. I told her I'd been invited to a party, and she was pleased as punch; 'oh, that's smashing duck,' she said. She always called me that. But although she tried to smile, and I knew she desperately wanted me to have a good time, I could see the trepidation clouding her eyes. After a few moments holding my gaze, she softly, but quite firmly, without scorn or malice, asked me if I intended to drink the four cans of Special Brew hidden in the fireplace.

It agonises me to think that mother even knew what Special Brew was. Here, looking into my eyes was genuine unconditional love and affection, and it was impossible for me to reciprocate. I was incapable of showing this wonderful woman how much I loved her. But I did show her. In the only way my impulses could interpret my regret and sorrow, I jumped off the bed, put my hand up the fireplace and pulled the cans out. Giving them to Mum, I asked her to keep them for another day and promised her I had no intention of drinking them that evening.

I went upstairs and had a bath, came back down, opened my bedroom window, reached down amongst the weeds, pulled out half a bottle of vodka, closed the window and secreted the bottle in my working boots. I stuffed a pair of socks on top. This was business. I'd arranged to be at Christopher's by ten. I desperately wanted some sort of social life. I wanted to integrate. I wanted to be a part of something. I wanted to be accepted, but in order for that all to happen, I needed to be drunk. Why, I don't know. Perhaps I was dropped on my head as a baby, but that's to make light of something that was too heavy to face. It would be equally easy to blame my genes. But either way I needed to be drunk. I didn't start at home. I took a slow walk down to the woods, and sat by the roots of a big tree. I knew I'd be alone here. At least until I'd drunk my vodka.

I pondered on my life so far. Why on earth should I feel so bloody alone? I wasn't bad looking. Or so I thought. People generally seemed to like me but I couldn't shake off this enormous, overwhelming feeling of detachment. Everyone except me seemed to be genuine. Perhaps it was down to mixing with "normal" people for the past couple of months. Their normality brought into sharp focus how separate I was from the existence they seemed to enjoy; the reality they seemed to inhabit. I know that "normality" is a weird concept and impossible to gauge, but I knew that I lived on the edge of whatever it was.

It was about 7.30 when I finished my vodka. (I knew because I had enough spare cash to have actually bought a watch at last). I headed off to *The Chequers*, which was only a few minutes from Christopher's place. No sooner had I walked through the door than I bumped into a mate who was in the same year as me at school. I hadn't seen him during the seven or eight years since we'd left, but by God I could see he was bad. As bad as me.

Because we hadn't seen each other for so many years, I assumed he would know nothing of my drinking habits. How wrong I was. He'd heard all about my exploits. It seemed there were loads of stories circulating about me, half of which never happened of course, but from what he was telling me it, I'd gained legendary status! So he naturally assumed I was up for a bloody good drink, and of course he was right.

I remember we played pool (after a fashion) I also remember trying to chat these two birds up, and they told us in words of one syllable, the second being "off", that they weren't remotely interested. My next recollection is standing outside Christopher's house with a bottle of something. When he opened the door, I saw the shock on his face. 'Brian, I've never seen you like this, mate. I can't let you in in that state. How the hell did you get so drunk, man?' He always called me "man", probably because he was going to university. University types always seem to call people "man", don't they?

'Let me in, you prick,' was my less that polite response. Whereupon a couple of his mates came to the door to see what the trouble was. He told them I was just someone from work who'd had a couple too many, and with that someone's fist connected with my chin and down I went. As drunk as I was, I was on my feet and wanting a fight. Fists flying, I was ready to fight anyone or anything, if only I could focus on a target.

The door slammed. No party. I went in search of a cab, but none of them would stop, I was staggering so badly – as if there's any other way to stagger – all over the road with a bottle in my hand. Now this is the part that gives me the creeps. I'll just explain simply what I remember, what I saw and heard.

I'm lying in bed. It's a single bed and it's clean, almost too clean, clinical, even. I'm naked and I'm warm and comfortable. I can hear a voice somewhere in the distance. I open my eyes and find myself looking at a picture. It's a beautiful picture hung on a spotlessly clean magnolia wall. It's a picture of a nun holding a single candle. I look at it for some time, spellbound. But then I realise that I don't recognise the image at all. It doesn't resemble anything I've seen in the homes of anyone I know.

Then the voice I'd first heard on regaining consciousness became a little clearer. I sat up with a start and, looking around me, saw a single wardrobe with both doors wide open and a chest of drawers with all the drawers pulled open wide. I was frightened and couldn't understand what I was seeing. Scattered all over the floor was every single item of women's clothing imaginable. There were knickers, bras, stockings, suspender belts, slips... You name it, it was there. And the voice was coming closer. Next I heard a light tapping on what I took to be a door, and the voice was calling, 'Come along Mary, come along Jane, time to get up Jill, come on Sally.' The voice was coming nearer with each name she called out.

It seemed that my room was one of many in some sort of hallway or corridor. I jumped out of the bed and managed to get dressed in a nanosecond before there came a knock on the door. 'Come along, Wendy,' the voice said. I froze. Then the click of heels, and the voice became fainter as whoever she was walked away down the hall.

Tentatively I opened the door a crack, in time to see what appeared to be a matron or nursing sister disappearing down the hall knocking on doors and calling out names as she went. I left the room exactly as it was and fled in the opposite direction.

Then I came to a big wide staircase and followed it down, trying to look as if I belonged wherever it was. When I got to the bottom, I saw a sort of lodge or reception desk to my right, behind which was a man in uniform. He called me over and asked what my business was. I answered him in French. I knew one phrase in French. It was long but I knew it by heart and I kept reciting it in a very loud, clear voice and kept on walking. He gave me a great big smile and said, 'Enjoy your stay in England, sir'!

I walked through the big double doors and down some steps, still completely bewildered and with absolutely no idea of where I was. I crossed a car park and came out onto a main road. There, I suddenly recognised my surroundings. It was the area known as the Bat and Ball, at the bottom of St John's Road, just near the hospital, and just opposite was the nurses' home. I'd just walked out of it! God knows how or why, but the dream I thought I'd been having suddenly turned into the nightmare of me having actually spent the night there, under what circumstances I've never been able to recall.

By now it was just past eight in the morning, and nowhere in Sevenoaks would serve a drink until nine. I was rattling. Seriously rattling. I hadn't been in Sevenoaks long enough to know where the drinkers would be. There were obviously plenty of social drinkers, but they were still tucked up in bed and would have been no use to me anyway. I needed a drink. I was shaking. Little did I realise at this point that I was in more trouble than I thought.

I saw a newsagent's open and decided to buy a paper. As casually as I could, I asked the vendor if there might be anywhere I could get a drink at that time in the morning.

I was in for one big shock. I'd managed to figure out, because of where I'd woken up, that I'd been in the company of a nurse and that I'd been alone because she'd left early for work assuming that I could find my way out without detection, and she wouldn't get into trouble. In front of me though were the Sunday papers. I was more than a little confused; I was stupefied.

IT WAS SUNDAY. Where in God's name had I been? I remembered arriving at Christopher's drunk, and his mate punching me. But that had been Friday night. It was now Sunday morning. What had I been up to? Why was I naked in a nurse's bed with all her underwear scattered across the floor? Was I a pervert? Had I gone back there with someone, or did I break in? How the hell had I lost 36 hours?

In a daze, I bought a paper and, explaining that I was a merchant seaman just home on leave and didn't know the area, I asked the guy if he knew where I could get a drink. He was a surly old bastard and told me that Sevenoaks had about 36 pubs, all of which would be open at 12 noon, at which time I'd be welcome in any one of them. Galvanised by his razor sharp wit, I paid for the paper and sloped off to the big woods and the roots of the tree where I knew I'd be alone for a while. I was only 23, and already suffered from the DTs (delirium tremens). I did a quick stock-take. I had £17 left. I couldn't go home until I'd had a drink, and I had about three hours to kill. So I just sat there like I used to when I was a kid. The only difference was that this time I was clucking. It had been 15 years since I'd last taken sanctuary there with a bottle of cider.

Suddenly I heard a voice behind me, and there was Mrs Hillary, a lady I'd known when I was a kid. She was out for a walk with her dog. She'd known my family well – or rather she knew that my mum had had an oddball kid. She managed to sidle down to sit beside me in the roots of the tree and told me that she remembered me from those days coming here to the same spot. She wondered why I was in such a reflective mood. Was I thinking about the past? She was being so kind to me that I was caught a bit off guard and started to tell her what had happened. She wondered if the police might be able to help. Now if someone else had made such a ludicrous suggestion, I'd have thought they were taking the proverbial. But I knew this was genuine concern.

However, I could sense that she wasn't feeling too comfortable. I was making her a bit nervous, but took a chance anyway and asked if by any chance she had any alcohol in her house that I could buy from her. She thought for a minute and replied, 'I can't help thinking that if I did, I wouldn't be doing you a favour,' but added that if I liked wine she had a spare bottle. I hated asking her, but by God I craved a drink.

My instincts were right. I'd made her nervous. She got up to take the dog home, but then she paused and offered to fetch the bottle back for me. I honestly didn't expect her to come back but she did, and brought a corkscrew and a plastic beaker. Refusing payment, she then asked me if I would mind if she prayed for me. Well, to my mind that was a bit weird but, holding her bottle of wine, how could I refuse? After asking me not to open it until she'd gone, she placed her hands on my head and spoke a few words. I hadn't a clue who she was talking to, but I assumed it was God. I hoped she was having better luck than I'd ever had, because whenever I'd prayed – only of course, in times of great need, in other words, in trouble – he was never in.

When she'd gone, I set to medicating my DTs, and got to thinking. It was 13 or 14 years previously that that dirty old bastard used to touch us up here, masturbating himself at the same time. He'd give us a couple of fags, and threaten that if we went home and told our parents we'd probably get a clip round the ear for lying. I started to feel particularly maudlin and lost. From an early age, I'd always managed to find comfort crouched down in the protection of those tree roots but now I'd never felt less reassured that things were going to be OK.

I went home, and straight to my room. Where had Mum put my cans of Special Brew? But before long I was asleep. My brother David woke me at about half past seven, and called for Mum. I was in a hell of a mess, and asked her where my cans were. She went and fetched just one and said, 'Brian, in your state I can't let you have more than one.' Where had I been since Friday night? I explained that I didn't know, and Friday was the last thing I remembered until I woke at 3.30 on Monday morning with my body screaming for a drink.

The frantic search began for those cans. Then in a flash of desperate inspiration, I remembered Mum always used to hide things from us in the shed. Sure enough, there they were, snug as three lovely bugs, under a sack of coal. Indoors, I settled in front of the gas fire and polished them off. I was bolloxed. At sometime around 5.30, I heard my father stir. It was time I was in bed. I slept most of the following day until a neighbour brought round a message from the hospital. Now, I knew my supervisor wasn't just ringing for a chat. This could only mean one thing – the sack. I managed to haul my bones into work, but the supervisor was indisposed. A Mr Stoke was able to see me.

He informed me that I'd been seen in the grounds of the nurses' home in the early hours of Sunday morning, and offered me the chance to pass comment. What could I say in my defence? I explained that when you drink as much as me, it's not that easy finding a willing girl and I'd had to do a little hunting. My sarcasm wasn't lost on him and he sacked me on the spot.

When you start drinking in your teens, you expect some silliness; the odd hour or two lost in the haze of youthful exuberance. But when it gets to the point where you lose a couple of days, you know you're in trouble. I was only 23, and the last thing I remember was that I'd had my last drink on Friday night, followed by a smack in the mouth. I'd lost 48 hours of my life, and I was terrified.

15

Going Down to the Bottom With a Bad Man

I can't believe that in this enlightened time, I have to sit here and dispel the myth that alcoholics sit on park benches and drink methylated or surgical spirits, so I won't. I have been an alcoholic for over 40 years, and in all that time have only ever had one pint of it. This is how it came about:

I woke up, and it was 12.45am. I had the DTs and was hallucinating. I was in the spare room of a flat I was living at with a woman who was 17 years my senior. I was in the spare room because a couple of days previously I had embarrassed her in the night club where she worked part-time, so she wouldn't let me sleep in her bed. Plus she said I needed to have a bath.

I was desperate; she had long since made sure there was no alcohol in the flat. I knew I had £60 on my bedside table, but it was no good to me at that time of night. I wanted a drink. There was only one place where I could get alcohol and that was at the club where this woman worked, but I was barred. I had no chance.

I panicked. If I didn't get a drink I would die. My only hope was a mate of mine who was also an alcoholic, but it was nearly one o'clock in the morning, plus his girlfriend hated me. Out of sheer desperation, I walked down to where my mate lived. I knocked on his door several times. Finally his girlfriend opened the door. She saw it was me and went to slam it. I heard Gordon say, 'who is it?' and I managed to shout out, 'It's me Gordon, Brian Harding.' He told her to get out of the way and let me in.

He knew that for me to be knocking on his door at that time of night, something must be wrong. He could see I was rattling and needed a drink. He had no drink in the house and in fact, this was his fourth day without one – he was trying to come off it. I asked if he could go to the club for me and buy me a couple of bottles of wine but he was also barred. He said the only thing he could do was sit with me until the morning. He knew from first hand what I was going through. I was unable to roll cigarettes, so he did it for me.

We sat like this for about an hour. It was obvious I was getting worse, not better. Neither of us were gay, but he cuddled me. He understood. He asked me if I had ever drank meths, I said no. He said he had some in his garden shed, and that if I could just get it down me it would at least stop the DTs. Anything was better than this.

He went out the back door and came back with this bottle of meths. It was an old fashioned pint bottle, full. He then went into the kitchen and came back with two milk bottles; one was full of water, and the other was empty. He poured half the pint bottle of meths into the empty bottle, then topped it up with water from the second bottle. I now had half a bottle of meths and half a bottle of water. He put his hand over the top and shook it up. Then he got a bucket, as he thought the first mouthful might make me sick.

He was right. I took my first mouthful and was almost immediately sick. I waited a few minutes, and then drank some more, and some more. I couldn't believe it. I was beginning to feel centred, and was no longer shaking. Gordon made me up another mixture, half meths and half water. I drank the lot. This filthy shit I was drinking was actually making me feel better. I still had the £60 in my pocket. This is alcoholism. It was then 4am.

Gordon woke me at 8.15am. He had taken a £10 note, gone down the off-licence and bought me some vodka. So the next time someone tells you they see a tramp on a park bench every single day drinking methylated spirits, don't believe them. To drink meths on any sort of daily basis on an empty stomach will kill you in just a matter of weeks.

16

The Urine Taste

Back in late 1977 or '78, I was staying in a squat in Sevenoaks, punctuated by attempts at living in my mum's back room once more. The squat was situated across three floors above the ground floor where the landlord lived. Now the landlord was eccentric; eccentric in fact, to the point of madness. I now realise that he suffered from OCD – obsessive compulsive disorder. But what were we to know back then? To us he was just weird.

His behaviour consisted of continuous scrubbing. He'd scrub anything and everything, from the toilet bowl to the glass lampshades. In fact the toilet bowl was his greatest obsession. All his cleaning had to be done with carbolic soap; nothing else would do, and it made the whole squat reek. We were on the top floor, and even we stank of the stuff.

The landlord never ventured upstairs, but as far as any of us could make out he never seemed to sleep. His behaviour seemed so bizarre to us that I imagine if he'd been living in the community these days, he would have been under close supervision, or more than likely institutionalised. There were often reports of him having a crap in his own front garden. Such was his determination to keep his own toilet unsullied. He always cleaned up after himself, but God knows what he did with the evidence, because it sure didn't go down the bog.

It was quite easy to get into the building without detection. As you came in through the front door, the toilet was situated on the right hand side of the small hallway. To sneak past, all you had to do was wait just by the front door until you heard the scrubbing. As soon as you heard that sound you knew that his head would be quite literally down the toilet bowl. You'd scuttle past the door, up the stairs, and you were in.

Our drinking den was on the top floor, and by God it was a hovel. There were generally between two and six people there at any given time, all in various stages of drunkenness, disarray and incoherence. Unfortunately there was only one toilet in the building as far as we knew, and because of the landlord's weird behaviour, none of us dared blunder downstairs to use it. We just holed ourselves up in our den and didn't venture anywhere else.

Of course, this posed a bit of a problem as far as our own sanitation facilities went. But necessity is the mother of invention and all that. We were forced to engage our addled brains in devising a system to suit Mother Nature's needs and our own. Once a two-litre cider bottle became empty we could use that to piss in and when that was full, which wouldn't take too long, we'd empty it out of the window. Unfortunately, this arrangement was scuppered within a few days because the landlord thought he had a leak somewhere at the top of the building and called in the plumbers. So, forced to moderate our scheme, we stored up the bottles. Those full of piss were kept to one side of the room, whilst those yet to be drunk were on the other.

We had a friend called Sandy. She was 17 and had a Saturday job in Sevenoaks market. Her father was a paedophile and was, I believe, doing an eight-year stretch at the time. Her mother was a part-time cleaner and full-time drinker, known to most of us. So Sandy ended up associating with the sort of people she'd grown up with and came to the squat as often as she could, just to be with us and drink. She neither liked sex nor disliked it but, if one of us fancied having sex with her she'd oblige, often drinking and having a conversation with one of the other lads at the same time. It simply meant nothing to her. It was neither right nor wrong. That sort of ambivalence is something I've grown so familiar with down the years. I've lived so close to the sort of people that have to detach themselves from the reality and horror of their own lives, and of the circumstances they find themselves in, just to survive. To face that reality would do their heads in. You let the body that only ever expects to be used take the flack, and bugger off somewhere else in your head until it's over.

As soon as she had a break, she'd rush down to the squat as quickly as she could. But on one fateful day she was in such a tearing hurry for a drink that she charged straight in and over to where we kept our urine bottles. Before anyone could stop her, she'd unscrewed a two-litre bottle and started necking it like she'd just come out of the Gobi desert. Two of us shouted for her to stop. 'Don't drink that, it's piss.' 'I know,' she said. '1 hate the fucking stuff.' 'No, really,' we said. 'It's one of our piss storage bottles.' But by then she'd already downed almost half of it. Mind you, I realise how hard it is for a woman to piss into a bottle, otherwise half of it might have been her own anyway.

Well, she turned ashen. She was furious and started laying into us for not telling her. We explained that we'd tried, but she was leaping about clawing her tongue out. She was begging for some vodka, but all we had was some "real" cider which she gratefully glugged back to get rid of the

116

taste. She said, 'Look, you bunch of bastards, I wasn't going to tell you this but I managed to nick a tenner this morning. Will somebody go down and get me a bottle of vodka? I think you owe me, don't you?' When the volunteer returned, she downed the lot in what seemed like two minutes flat.

Sandy was suddenly very drunk. We tried to coax her to go back to work because she earned about thirty quid for a Saturday, and she could ill-afford to lose it. But she wasn't having any of it. She was going absolutely nowhere. We didn't know how much money she had before she nicked the tenner, but she'd assured us she had on her enough for "a fucking good drink" as she put it. Well, that was good enough for us. She was wary of the weirdo downstairs, so asked if one of use would go with her while she called a couple of friends from a nearby phone box. BRILLIANT.

We sorted out the money for the drink and change for the phone – no mobiles in those days – and off they went. They were gone more than an hour, and we were beginning to think they'd left us. Sandy was 17 going on 42, but the two mates she brought back with her were 16, and looked like it. They were lovely looking girls, and as drunk as I was. I had to wonder why on earth they wanted to come to a squat. They weren't even alkies, and they certainly weren't druggies – you could tell by the clarity of their eyes and skin. And we must have stunk. We certainly didn't look that clever lying around on the floor with empty cider and vodka bottles, and full bottles of piss everywhere. I wondered then, and still do now, about my own attraction to living in that kind of environment with my fellow alkies. I was completely apolitical back then; not anti-anything or pro-anything. I felt normal when I was with them in that squalor, but removed from it I felt that I didn't fit in.

I can only think in retrospect that these girls were a bit anti-establishment, a couple of Bob Dylans. Knowing, through Sandy, the way we lived, they saw us as having "opted out". We were going to change the world. The truth was that we couldn't even change our clothes.

Sandy introduced us, and we all sat on the floor. There were actually some chairs dotted around, but I think these two thought it was the right etiquette in such revolutionary circles to sit on the floor.

From my experience, I knew this was going to be on. I'd already picked the girl I was most attracted to, and I knew she felt the same. Now, when you're living in a squat with a load of other blokes, you tend not to care too much about your hygiene. In fact, for the most part you rot. I

117

pondered on the state of my shorts, and knew that my breath was rancid from the dog ends I'd been smoking for the past couple of weeks.

I also became aware of a change coming over Sandy. She'd always been at ease around us: not necessarily quiet, but she counted as one of the crowd. Now she was becoming more extrovert, drawing attention to herself a bit. I suppose you could say we'd started to pair off, and Sandy was being a bit too easy, louder than she normally would be. Don't forget that she'd been abused throughout her young life and this sudden intimacy had thrown her off course. She didn't really know where she fitted in. This was her territory.

The girl I was with had made it very clear what she wanted, and it was to be with me. She wanted to have sex here in this filthy room with these filthy people. I looked over at Sandy and thought of all the times I'd been glad of her company, all the times she'd gone down the offy for me when I was unable to move, and I knew she was hurting. She was hurting badly. She was hurting like she used to do when she was a child. I knew it because I'd been through it myself a hundred times. The girl I was with had painted toenails and perfectly manicured fingernails. She was clean and her hair smelt fresh. She had everything Sandy would never have if a million years passed.

I stopped, excused myself and went over to Sandy. 'Can I share my bottle with you, San?' I said, and she put her arms around me saying, 'I'm a shit, aren't I?' I was suddenly overcome with grief. She started to cry, and something made me tell her I loved her. Then I realised that in a strange way I really did. Sandy and I got down to laughing and drinking. Nothing feels worse than hurt on hurt. We both knew that there was little likelihood of either of us ever finding a partner, no matter who fancied us, because before long it would all fall apart. Those sorts of things just didn't happen to people like us.

The girl I'd been with, Jan, sidled over and wanted to join the party, which was OK by us. She seemed to be much more interested in Sandy now. Not sexually. She was just fascinated by her, in how at just 17 she could be so worldly wise. The fact is, she wasn't worldly wise at all. She was just too old for herself, and too much a part of a harsh life that brought with it too much knowledge of the wrong sort, and very little of the sort of wisdom that could have got her away from it.

Sandy didn't know what love was, and had never experienced loving sex. And she certainly didn't know what it was to love and be loved by either a mother or a father.

118

As we were talking, we became aware that the other girl was crying, and then she started screaming and yelling, 'Get off, you bastard.' She was becoming hysterical. Jan just froze. She didn't know what to do. She was way out of her depth. Sandy got to her feet and ran over to where the couple were thrashing about. 'What the fuck's going on? You'll get us all thrown out.'

Apparently this bloke had tried to push a bottle up inside the girl and had bitten her neck. Sandy stuck her foot in the small of his back and, with both hands, pulled at his long filthy hair. She managed to prise him off, and then she kicked him full in the face.

Sandy had told the girls what we were like, how we lived, and what we would probably expect of them, so they knew full well what to expect. But this was depraved and beyond even our hazy boundaries.

When they went to leave, Jan asked Sandy about our relationship; how long we'd known each other, and when told it had only been four weeks she found it hard to believe and asked how come we were so close.

Sandy replied, 'We were just brought up the same way.'

17

The Urine Test

What happened next occurred during a time when I realised that I could no longer earn a living at sea, and once more found myself staying in the back bedroom of my mum's council house. I always felt it in my bones that my mum's brother-in-law, Uncle Bob, disliked me – despised me even. He was a proud, working class staunch union man; a heavy goods vehicle driver with maintenance qualifications, and was very proud. I think this intense dislike came about because I'd had the privilege to have served an apprenticeship. I'd also just spent two years at sea with nothing to show for it. I didn't even have a place to live.

Unlike me, my brother John, who was two years younger than me, was a great mate with uncle Bob. In fact he had a lot of respect and affection for him, and it was lovingly reciprocated. John was courting, and saving money towards getting married and buying a house. And he didn't drink himself into oblivion on a regular basis.

However, on this particular night, I actually had a date. I've no idea how it happened; all I know is, I met this girl in a little country pub just outside Sevenoaks. Now, Uncle Bob's only passion, and I mean passion, outside his work and the union, was buying up old cars cheap, doing them up and selling them. And this was a passion he and my brother shared. On that day, they'd just finished a big job on a beautiful vintage car and I happened to overhear them planning a test drive for that evening. Whenever they did a test drive, they tended to use the same route. And guess what? This route would take them right by the pub where I was to meet this girl!

Of course, my only problem now was the antipathy between my uncle and me, so I tried to wheedle round John and asked him ever so nicely if he wouldn't mind me cadging a lift and them dropping me off. Not to worry, I'd make my own way home. He said, if I was ready on time and I wasn't pissed, they'd oblige. I was also to try and be quiet.

Unbeknown to them, I had half a bottle of vodka in my room, keeping company with a bottle of wine. Now I don't expect you to believe or understand me, but I swear by everything that is right and proper that I had no intention whatsoever of getting drunk. This is alcoholism. I sipped

the nick, and ten minutes later they opened the door. 'Had a change of heart then, Brian?'

'No,' I said, 'but listen to this. You reckon I nicked that bag, hid it in my coat, and that's how I got out of the building without it being seen, right?'

'That's pretty much it, why?'

I said, 'Find out who was on duty between two and six pm because I tell you this Nigerian nurse carried my coat for me right up until we got to the exit. Not only that, she helped me to put it on. She was in her early 20s, as black as your hat, and I know she was Nigerian because she told me. Find that nurse for me officer, and see if she confirms what I'm telling you.'

They didn't even answer, just slammed the door shut on me. I lay on the bunk trying to sleep. I hadn't been given any medication, and hadn't had a drink for about 30 hours. I was in withdrawal and beginning to dread the fitting that would come. Fortunately, my GP later informed me, my fears were groundless as I had been given 40 ml of Heminevarine during my time in hospital, and that had staved off the worst of the withdrawal symptoms. This also explained why I was being so quiet. Normally, when you're banged up for something you haven't done, one does tend to rear up and make a bit of a racket.

I lay there for hours, and I was frozen. But they'd been such contemptuous bastards that I'd freeze to death before I'd ask them for a blanket. I tried to work out what time it was. It must be about six pm by now. In my delirium, I was thinking that if they're not going to mess about, and they do cop hold of this nurse and she does confirm my story, then I could be out of here pretty soon. I knew I had a bottle of cider under my mattress, and I knew a girl who might put me up for the night. That was the fantasy.

The reality would more than likely be that they would find the nurse, she would confirm my story, but the bastards would keep me in overnight anyway because they hadn't been able to intimidate me. Was I going mad? I was in the cells for something I hadn't done, and God knows I put my hands up to plenty I have been guilty of. They had no reason to hate me in particular. Surely they'd let me know once they knew the truth. Being locked up plays funny tricks on your mind; nothing but cell walls and graffiti for inspiration. Enforced confinement isn't natural. Necessary at times, but still not natural.

I drifted off into a restless sleep, half-delirious because I hadn't eaten for about a week. I heard the door go and I was awake in a flash –

immediately, acutely aware. 'Come on, Harding, you're going home. Get your shoes and baccy.' I said, 'what's happened?' The jailer replied, 'The detectives found your Nigerian nurse, and she remembered you well all right because you stank to high heaven of booze. She remembers putting your coat on for you, and I must say she was adamant that as far as she was concerned there was no handbag hidden in it.'

I said, 'Where are those bloody detectives that called me all the names under the sun?'

The jailer didn't even look at me. He didn't answer me. He just told me to sign for my personal. One set of keys, one comb, two false teeth, £1 in cash, and showed me the door.

'Cheers mate,' I said. He didn't answer. He'd seen it all before

I walked off, totally dejected. I was freezing cold. My flat was cold. I was hungry, but couldn't eat. I wanted someone, someone to love. The room I was going back to was smaller than the cell I'd just left. All I had was one poxy bottle of cider and one pound coin. And all this, dear readers, was solely because of drink.

But as down as I was at that moment, I wasn't to know that it would only be about two weeks until I met my wife.

19

Discrepancies

If you find discrepancies in the chronological sequence of events in this book, it is because of the very nature of the beast that I've been fighting all my life. It's played games and addled the thought processes of my mind, and it's just another insidious little thing that alcohol does for you; charming little disease, isn't it?

The times I've pleaded guilty just to get it over with, simply because I do not remember anything; It's likely that I have been guilty of most charges that have been levelled at me, but I'm equally certain that there are charges that I haven't been guilty of. There's one incident that sticks in my mind, and I remember it quite clearly. I woke up in the cells, and I only woke up because I heard the door open, to find the jailer and another bloke who I'd never seen before, and the jailer saying, 'Is this the bloke?' to which the other bloke replied, 'Yes, that's him.' I was banged up again. that was my ID parade.

I was then charged with stealing a crate of spirits from a van delivering to a local wine store. Now at this particular time, as drunk as I was, I do recall quite well that it was all I could do to carry a bottle, let alone a full box of spirits. I just lay there and thought, 'Oh, let them get on with it.'

This all took place sometime around midday. I remember a sergeant who I knew quite well through my past misdemeanours. He came to my cell door, pulled the flap over and said, 'What are you playing at, Brian? What did you think you were going to do with a box of whisky?'

I told him I didn't do it, and with that he opened my door. He asked me what happened. I told him I left my house that morning with a ten pound note in my pocket, went down the offy, bought my quota for the morning, and went off down Bottle Alley. There I met Tony and Ronnie; we had a bloody good drink together, then they went down town and I bought myself a half bottle of vodka and went to sit in the lower gardens. That's when these coppers and this other bloke came along; they said to him, 'Is this him?' He said, 'Yes, that's him'. And here I am.

The sergent asked if anybody saw me in the gardens. I told him the bag lady came and sat with me for an hour or two. She was well known.

She used to feed the pigeons even when there were none around. He said, 'I'm going to close your door and make a few enquiries.' About an hour later, he came back and asked me if I knew what time it was when I spoke with the bag lady. I said I hadn't a clue, so he asked if I knew X. I said I'd heard of him, but didn't have anything to do with him as he was trouble. (I have to refer to him as X for fear of death.) He banged me up again.

A few hours later, I was un-banged again. It was the same sergeant. He said, 'I've got some good news for you Brian. We've just arrested and charged Mr X with the theft of not one but four boxes of whisky. What the constables didn't know at the time of your arrest was that we were investigating the sale of cheap liquor to *The Greys* [*] in London Road, and it was just your bad luck that you do happen to resemble our Mr X. The driver is positive that it was Mr X carrying the box of whisky, and not you. He's actually waiting outside to offer his apologies. I said, 'It doesn't matter, officer, I don't want to see him.'

I asked the sergeant why they arrested me in the first place, and he said that a shopper had seen what they thought was me walking off down London Road with this box of whisky. He said, 'You're not stupid, Brian, everybody knows you, and if I'd seen the back of you, I'd have thought the same. And by the way, the bag lady's not as stupid as some people might think; she told us she was with you about an hour and there was no sign of any boxes of any sort. She even told us that if there had been, she would have nicked a bottle herself.' He asked me if I wanted a lift home. I asked him if they had confiscated my personal drink. He said they hadn't, so I said that I'd walk home and finish my drink.

I cut across the oval, went down to the putting green, and sat on one of the benches. I could see my house from where I was sitting, about a hundred yards away. I'd just had a couple of swigs of vodka when Shakey appeared and plonked himself down, asking if he could have a swig of my drink. I said NO, absolutely not. He said, 'Well, I'm barred from the offy. I've got some money; can you get me some drink?' I told him I'd only just got out of the cells, and he said, 'Please mate. I'm dying.'

I asked him where Selina, his girlfriend, was; she usually looked after him, that is if she wasn't kicking the shit out of him. He said she'd been off the drink for six days, and he was trying to avoid her, because if she wasn't drinking, then he wasn't allowed to. Well, I knew I had to get my drink for the morning, so I said, 'Let me finish this and I'll nip down there.'

---

[*] *The Yorkshire Grey*

I don't know what time of year this was, but I do know it was in the 80s. I finished my vodka, and it was painful. I could feel every inch of it going down into my stomach. It burned. I don't know what it is that takes it down to your stomach, whether it's your gullet or what, but it was painful, so painful in fact that whatever it was travelling down to get to my stomach must have at the least been ulcerated, if not lacerated.

Shakey gave me enough for two litres of cider and I bought three, two for tonight and one for the morning. When I got back to the putting green, my heart sank; there was Selina sitting next to Shakey. I approached them very tentatively, not knowing what mood she would be in, but my fears were unfounded. She still wasn't drinking; she was OK. Selina told us about her day; Shakey told us about his, and I told them about mine. Selina told me she knew X had nicked that booze because he was in *The Greys* bragging about it. As Selina wasn't drinking, she was the first to go. Shakey and I sat there drinking our cider and chatting about old times.

It's funny how your mood will alter depending on the environment at the time. It was nearly midnight; both Shakey and I had drink and yet we both became morose, maudlin even. I think it's because we both realised there really weren't many good times, if any. We were sitting on the edge of the putting green with a drink, and yet neither of us was laughing. We both knew we had just got through another day, and that drink was our boss, and that as long as we had a drink, we really didn't give a toss about each other or anyone else for that matter. It was unspoken, but ever present.

We made arrangements to meet the next day in Bottle Alley, both knowing that if neither of us had a drink then neither of us would be there because we would both be out looking for a drink. Shakey had finished his two litres and said he was going to make his way home. I still had about half a litre left so I thought it was a good idea to just sit there and enjoy the night sky; after all, I could have been sitting in a cell right at this minute.

It was so still and quiet. I looked skywards and wondered why the hell I was an alcoholic. This sounds as though I was angry, but I wasn't. I don't know if it was the peacefulness of the night or the fact that I was free, but I felt OK. I walked the few yards to my flat, went in, undressed and got into bed. Just another day in an alcoholic's wretched life.

20

The Theft of My Solicitor's Wallet

Until this point in my life, every single time I had appeared before a magistrate or a judge, they had recognised and accepted that all my crimes – petty and otherwise — were committed while I was either in drink, looking for drink or looking for something to sell in order to buy drink.

So... I was on police bail, waiting to appear at Lewes Crown Court. Not only was my brief, David Harding, a real gentleman, he was a very hard working, diligent, up and coming defence solicitor. I'd been on bail for some time, so we were familiar with one another's ways and I was quite aware of what I had to do; plead guilty to all charges, providing I could enter a plea of mitigation. Our only problem now was to get me to Lewes Crown Court, sober. This needed a plan.

Like me, my barrister lived in Hastings, so my solicitor was going to try to persuade him to give me a lift on the day. Now, with my reputation as a street drinking alcoholic, we both knew this wasn't going to be easy but Mr Harding was a very persuasive man, and had four clear days to persuade the barrister that I could be responsible, and would turn up sober and looking respectable. The day came around. A Wednesday, as I recall. It was five in the morning, and I was retching like a hound dog in the bathroom. I had until 11.45 to get straight enough for my appointment with David Harding. At this point, my entire stock of alcohol consisted of one can of Special Brew, and boy was I rattling. My actual court appearance wasn't until the Friday but today was the day I'd find out if David had persuaded the barrister to take the chance of giving me a lift to court.

My tolerance level at this particular time was extremely high. I needed at least three cans just to get me out of my front door, to look and act normal. I wandered down to where I knew I'd find one of my drinking buddies, and explained the situation to him. I found Ron Milligan, who'd been a drinking friend for more than 25 years, so he understood my plight immediately and donated enough cash for four cans. I went back home and cleaned myself up as best I could.

It was only about a five-minute walk to the solicitor's office, but I planned on doing a bit of begging on the way. I managed to get a pound, but one pound just wasn't enough for what I needed. Anyway, I somehow made it to the office ten minutes early. When he answered the door, David invited me in and straightaway remarked on how well I looked. He asked me to wait in his office while he finished up somewhere else. I'd been there so many times he didn't need to show me the way. Making myself comfortable, the first thing I noticed was a jacket hanging on the back of the door. Now this jacket could only have been David's. A bit of a farewell party was going on out in the reception area, and from my comfy vantage point I could hear the laughter of the few revellers. I knew that somewhere in that jacket there just had to be some money. Now at this point, a simple ten-pound note would have done me fine. I walked over to the jacket and looked in the inside pocket. Sure enough, there was a wallet. I didn't want to take the whole thing, so I just wriggled my fingers in and prised it open just enough to see inside. All I could see was £5 notes. BRILLIANT.

I tried to take just the one, or maybe two, but it wasn't to be. As the wallet and all its contents fell to the floor, I heard footsteps. Now, this just happened to be the last office along this particular corridor and, as the footsteps sounded purposeful and unfaltering, passing all the other doors, I just knew it had to be him. What a quandary. All the evidence scattered across the floor. Anyway, in those days I'd taken to always carrying a shoulder bag. Very useful to hide my drink from the police and, let's face it, from certain fellow alkies. Still do. It was now time to put my booze bag to another use; gathering everything up smartish, I shoved it in just in the nick of time.

David was a nice-looking man in that he had regular features and always a massive big smile. He opened the door with that big damn smile and walked towards me arm outstretched, ready to shake me by the hand. He asked me to pull my chair up closer to the desk, sat opposite me and said, 'I've got some good news'. He'd been in touch with the barrister and, providing I'd had no more than a quarter of a bottle of vodka, he was prepared to give me a lift to court for my appointment with destiny.

It's hard for me to explain exactly how I felt at that particular moment. There was I, sitting opposite the guy who was actively defending me on the burglary charge of which I was clearly guilty, having arranged completely off his own back my transportation to Lewes Crown Court, solely in order for me to arrive sober and thereby increase my chances of a more favourable result in front of the beak. Little did he know that in my shoulder bag was, not only his wallet and its entire contents – cash to the value of £35 – but also something like 20 personalised Eurocheques.

Now, I didn't know what a personalised Eurocheque was, but what I did know was that on those cheques was the name HARDING, and that was my surname!

We shook hands warmly and he wished me well. He reassured me that my barrister could not only think on his feet, but that he could also, while dealing with the most complex of issues, think ten steps ahead. This should have brought me comfort, but all I felt was shame and sadness. I was about 39 and pretty articulate, but right then I felt about ten years old. I wanted to give Mr Harding his wallet back. I wanted him to comfort me and tell me he forgave me. I wanted him to tell me he understood. I wanted him to go to the police. I wanted him to speak to the judge. I wanted him to speak to my family. I wanted him to speak to my brothers and sisters. And more than anything in the world, I wanted him to speak to my father. I wanted forgiveness. I didn't want to be sitting here with this man – so different from my father – who was trying to help me, with his wallet in my bag, knowing that within five minutes of leaving his office, I would be in the off-license buying alcohol to deaden the pain at the heart of my very being.

We stood up at the same time. I left feeling wretched and went straight to the off-license and bought four Special Brews and half a bottle of vodka. I sat on a bench opposite Lloyds Bank, the bank that issued the cheques, and gave one of my "Brews" to a fellow alkie. He was made up with it. By the time I'd polished off one of the Brews and the vodka, I was drunk enough to go into the bank. On one of the cheques I wrote, *please pay cash to Mr Harding, the sum of £100*. The teller did it automatically, asking only if I would like either ten or 20 pound notes! 'Tens will be fine, thank you.'

I felt neither proud nor clever. I wanted my solicitor's attention. I wanted my father's attention. I wanted the teller's attention. I wanted the attention of the small crowd of no-hopers who could see that not only was I drunk, but that I had some money.

I really didn't know what I felt. I had just over £100 in my pocket, and I suppose, as an alkie, I should have been happy. But I wasn't. Even some of the people I'd drunk with in the past were giving me a wide berth. While I make no excuses for myself please accept, not by way of an excuse but more by way of explanation, that I was in total conflict with myself. I wanted anonymity and yet I was screaming out for recognition. I didn't want to be an alcoholic but I would have used my grandmother's ribs to prise her tea caddy open to get enough money for a drink. I was in total conflict with myself.

I know. That's the second time I've said it, but it's simply how I felt. People walked past, some passing the time of day or even exchanging pleasantries. Some just pointed at me and laughed. They'd obviously seen me in the past. They had no idea I'd just stolen £135, and nor did they care. I was just a drunk. There were still a few hardened drinkers who sat with me though. How many times I shelled out, or how much money I'd given them, I had no idea. I just knew they kept going in and out of off-licenses. By now I was very, very drunk and decided in my infinite drunken wisdom to go home via the next Lloyds Bank to cash yet another cheque, this time for the princely sum of £1000.

It was about ¾ of a mile from Hastings town centre to where I lived in St Leonards-on-Sea, and I knew there was a branch of Lloyds not 50 yards from my digs. I walked in, wrote the cheque out and handed it to the cashier. She took one look at me and asked if I had any ID. What I had with me, for some odd reason, were my indentures. These were my City and Guilds certificates from when I'd served my apprenticeships some 30 years before – nicely aged, so all you could make out was the name Harding. But I could tell she wasn't satisfied with this and she asked me to take a seat. Although I was really drunk, I was with it enough to realise something was wrong.

She disappeared out the back and I disappeared out the front. I knew I'd been nobbled and I didn't care. I actually staggered out the door swigging from my vodka bottle.

I got half way up the road when a squad car suddenly appeared over the brow of the hill and screeched to a halt as I was mid-way through another swig. They jumped out, all four of them. Two were familiar faces, and simply said, 'We hope you've had a nice day, mate, because you won't be seeing the streets for some time. Let's have a look in your pockets, Brian.' Of course they found the wallet and what money remained after treating everybody and anybody to anything they wanted to drink. They handcuffed me, put me in the back of the car and off we went to the police station. It was to be ten months to the day before I was once more released from the prison system.

1 will now tell you exactly how my stay at Her Majesty's pleasure went. Being as the defence solicitor was named Harding and so was the defendant, things were bound to get a bit complicated in court. But add to that the fact that he was actually defending me on a burglary charge and, while he was doing this, I was busy stealing his wallet, how on earth could he defend me? Brian Harding and David Harding couldn't possibly appear in the same court together.

They kept me in the cells until about midnight then, as far as I could tell in my groggy state, took me to Bexhill police station. I appeared before Hastings magistrates the following morning and naturally I was remanded in custody, having been stupid enough to commit a further offence while on police bail. I was sent to F Wing, for remand prisoners, and was to languish there for no less than three months. I was locked up in a cell with a 50-year-old bloke who was on remand for no less than 23 counts of fraudulently claiming £27,000 worth of goods from Marks and Spencer.

His gig was to steal credit cards, go to Marks, buy goods to the value of anything less than £50, take them to the till and simply ask for a refund. You see, at that time Marks and Spencer's biggest selling point was that they would refund anything – absolutely anything. All you had to do, even without a receipt, was to produce the goods and the assistant would simply give you the value of the article in cash. This man and his pretty wife – who was later to divorce him on the grounds that he got nicked – had played this con all over the country for something like four years. Anyway, to cut a long story short, I spent three months with this guy. Unfortunately, he went on to get five years. But as a first offence, he only served 20 months and was given parole… I digress.

I spent three months in that stinking hole. Apart from the odd scam here and there, we were banged up for 23 hours a day. Now, there was a Mr Baker on the wing and although he was a screw, he was a kind old bloke. He opened my cell door one fine Monday morning and said, 'Harding, I've got something to show you.' He walked me along the wing to where the notice board sported the list of those due to appear in court the following week. Yours truly was top of the pile. Two things hit my irony button. The date would be Friday 13th, and the judge presiding would be none other than the notorious Pat Coles. He led me back to my cell and wished me luck. Do you know something, reader? I know that bloke liked me.

It was Mr Baker's duty to sit at the end of the landing to keep an eye on us cons while we were on association. I always felt he kept a special eye on me, not because he was a poof or anything like that, but I just got the feeling that for some reason he felt a bit sorry for me. When association was finished, he would often call me over with some task or other to do. Everyone else would get banged up again except me. The wing would be quiet and he'd ask me to go and make two cups of tea. We'd then just sit at his desk for a couple of hours talking. He was probably about 60, and at the time I was nearing my 40s. He reckoned he had a son about my age who, no matter what, just would not stop drinking. Now, although I liked Mr Baker, and I'm sure he felt some sort of affinity with me, I was probably facing anything up to four years, and what he seemed not to understand was that while his son might be an alkie, he at least owned his own house. I on the other hand had nothing except up to four charges of burglary, at least two of theft, plus I was on a three-month bender! So while I liked this screw very much, he failed to see that we were on different planets. I also realised he was a bit on the naive side after he tried to tell me that Judge Coles was really a pussy cat and that I had nothing to worry about. Didn't he read the local papers? They were full of the type of sentences she was dishing out. He actually said to me, 'I know you know the score, but I somehow think you'll be all right.'

His next day off was the very day I was to appear in front of Judge Pat Coles. I was gutted that he wouldn't be there on my production day, as I knew I was going to get bird. I don't know why, but I wanted him there. I never saw him again.

I'll just drop in a few explanatory details about the intricacies of the sentencing practices in our fair country. A concurrent sentence simply means two terms of bird run at the same time. In easy terms, if I were to be given two two-year sentences, made to run concurrently, I wouldn't serve four. I'd only serve two. But, Judge Coles was in a generous mood and granted me the full compliment; two two-years to run consecutively. A nice four-year lump.

My own personal private thoughts on sentencing on the charges against me were that, at the very worst I might just cop a "four" on all charges lumped together to run consecutively. If so, and I got a knock-back on my parole, then with full remission I'd still have to serve 32 months. But with parole I could be walking out the gates in just 16. The thought horrified me.

Thursday 12th arrived. I had the right to a shower the day before appearing before the judge, but it was gone eight o'clock before the screw let me out. Everyone was banged up, and the only other person on the wing was one of the cleaners, and he was only there because he was shagging one of the screws. The screw that took me to the shower was a bastard. There's no other way to dress it up. He was an out and out bastard. He said, 'Harding, you have three minutes; any longer and you know how Angus likes young skins.' Angus was the aforementioned cleaner who was on remand for the brutal rape of a 14-year-old boy in his care at some hostel somewhere. I went in, got wet, came straight back out again and walked back to my cell. It was locked. Well, there are a lot of thieves in prison.

Neither Angus the rapist nor the screw were anywhere to be seen. I just stood there looking at row upon row of cell doors and suddenly, out from one of the recesses came Angus... followed by the screw. I was in no doubt then, that me and the blokes I drank with weren't in the same league as this pair.

These two pieces of shit, one in prison garb, and the other in the guise of respectability – a uniform that gave him the automatic authority to dictate to people who found themselves at Her Majesty's pleasure, made my blood run cold. As I stood for the four or five minutes it took them to get to my cell door, I thought of all the people that I'd ever drunk with. Most were already dead. I could name them but that wouldn't mean anything to you. But Lydia, for example, was a prostitute simply because her uncle raped her when she was just 11 years old. It would be easy for you to say she didn't need to prostitute herself, but she had compassion. She was honest, and mortified when I told her I was tempted to steal a young mum's purse. She didn't want to sell her body.

Thinking of those old friends brought me up sharp. I wanted to know where I fitted into this great scheme of life. I wanted to know why I was standing outside a cell door waiting for the filthiest, most vile pervert who has the gall to command respect from his peers, the police, the courts and even the government and assumes the right to unlock my cell door and lock me up until morning. I wanted someone to tell me how this was proper, just and morally right.

I'm an alcoholic. I've stolen things I shouldn't have. I became the person I am because I couldn't stand the pain that my father subjected me to when I was a kid. I want to apologise for not being enough of a man when I was between five and 15 years old. I don't want to be standing outside this cell door knowing that tomorrow I will be sentenced to at least a couple of years in a system where the vilest pervert will automatically command my subservience.

I'm an alcoholic, totally dependent on the stuff. I'm both committed and addicted. That's my crime, and everything else is just by the way. Consolidate every crime, every nasty petty little thing I've done and any misdemeanour that you, as upright, sober citizens think I might be guilty of in the past. Lump them all together and charge me with being a chronic alcoholic, and I'll give you my word that I will plead guilty. No plea of mitigation. At least then I could just get on and do my bird. At least I could hold my head up against this filthy piece of shit that gave me the choice of just three minutes to get showered or get fucked by the rapist of a 14-year-old boy. I've since learned that this screw had been at this prison for quite a while. In God's name, didn't at least one of his colleagues think something wasn't right? Surely someone must have known what a sadistic bastard he was.

Friday came and I was nervous. I'd just spent three months on remand, and the thought of spending another couple of years behind bars made my blood run cold. After breakfast I was taken out to the yard, handcuffed, and put in the sweatbox. This is the van that transports prisoners from one place to another. It's usually divided into four cages which measure about four feet by four. You sit handcuffed to a small bench. Luckily, Lewes Crown Court is only minutes from the prison. God knows what it would be like to do a long journey in one of those things. Toilet facilities haven't been given much consideration and there's not much of a view. My fellow inmates and me were settled into the cells in the bowels of the court building. Luckily I was the first up, un-cuffed, and led straight into the dock from below.

There she was! It was the first time I'd seen Judge Coles. I was a bit knocked back by how attractive she was. Apparently she'd even appeared on TV several times for documentaries and the like. I remember very little about what she actually said but, after reading the social enquiry reports I knew clemency wasn't on the cards for the crimes I'd committed. As it happened, I struck lucky. I pleaded guilty to all the charges, which went in my favour and although I got several years, most of them were to run concurrently. So, the bottom line was, I got my two years. Back in the cells, I worked out that with full remission I would have to do 16 months, but if I got my parole I'd be out in eight.

I was right. My parole application was a success, and I was granted pre-parole leave (PPL). When you've been granted parole you automatically get four days home leave three weeks prior to your EDR (estimated date of release). Naturally my entire written application for parole was based around the fact that as all my crimes were committed because of drink. I had, from day one, whatever prison I was in, attended AA meetings. I'd remained in contact with my alcohol counsellor on the outside, and this was a practice I fully intended to keep up on my release. From here on in, drink was history. No more drink, no more crimes.

I'd actually served the full eight months when I was told my PPL was now due. I can't describe how excited I was. I'd been in this poxy system for eight months, and now I was going home for four whole days. It was an absolute disaster. I got drunk on the train going home; I was drunk when I arrived home, and I stayed drunk all the time I was there. It broke my wife's heart. I did actually manage to get on the train back, and got as far as Hove where I was arrested for, you've guessed it, drunk and disorderly. The police did a quick check and soon realised I was a home-leave failer, and marched me straight back to Lewes nick where I was put on the block for the night. From there, back to friendly old A wing.

I was devastated. Up until my arrest, I had just three weeks left to serve and now it looked like I would have to serve the other eight months. I couldn't stand the pain of it. I'd been trusted with four days PPL, and then I'm found drunk on Hove station. Any right-thinking person would understand my thinking that was my parole gone. I was put on Governor's orders to appear before him the next morning. All the cons on the wing commiserated, and knew what I knew; I had another eight months ahead of me.

Two screws were outside my cell door the next morning ready to take me to the Governor. He read out the charge. 'Home-leave failer, what have you got to say for yourself?' Here we go. I explained that I'd had a 30-minute wait for my connection at Hove, and was totally sober. 'I honestly didn't touch a drop all the time I was on home leave, sir. Anyway, I was befriended by a group of language students who insisted, because I was English, that I have a drink with them. I said that was very kind of them and I would like a glass of lemonade, as I didn't drink alcohol. They bought me the lemonade, and all the blokes were patting me on the back and the girls were even kissing me simply because I was English. I don't know how many glasses of lemonade they bought me, but they were obviously spiked, sir. It did seem odd that each drink was in a pint glass though. I just assumed it was railway policy to only use pint glasses.'

The Governor listened intently. His only comment was, 'Thank you, Harding. While your story sounds plausible, it's also possible it's not true. You will know within two days whether or not you keep your parole or lose your remission. Thank you. That will be all.' I went back to my cell and only left it for meals. I didn't want to see or speak to anyone. Two excruciating and depressing days later, my cell door was opened by the Deputy Governor.

'Harding! Ten days.' I sat bolt upright, and said, 'Ten days? What do you mean?' The screw explained, 'You're a lucky man, Harding. The Governor believed you.' All I'd lost was ten days remission! I'd be out on the 15th instead of the fifth. I was pole-axed, and hardly heard him spit, as he slammed the door, that if it had been left up to him. I'd have lost my parole.

I walked away from that sentence on 15th October 1987, the year and the day of the Great Hurricane. While most of Britain was up all night scared stiff, I slept through the whole thing... drunk.

21

Easy Come, Hard Go – The Stabbing

This incident happened while I was living above the corner cafe where, if you recall, I shared a room with a violent drunken Irishman and a psychotic skinhead who always kept a pet rat in one of his pockets. I'd put the year at about 1980-81. As was usual on a Saturday night, the Irishman came in drunk and started to terrorise us all. I couldn't help but notice, however, that he had on him two "Blockbusters" (treble bottles of cider) and a big bottle of sherry. I stole the sherry and took it up to my room. He was so drunk he wouldn't have a clue where it had gone, even if he remembered buying it. Anyway, he'd still be terrorising us whether I nicked it or not.

I was up first thing the following morning, had a quick sluice in cold water and was straight out of that door. It was a bitterly cold January or February morning. I knew a derelict building opposite Marks and Spencer where I could go and drink my newly acquired bottle of sherry. The only problem was that there was only one room with any floorboards left. It was here that all the misfits, the druggies, the winos, the alkies, all those who didn't want to be seen pursuing their habits, would come. They'd do their business and leave. For some reason they always seemed to need a shit, so dotted all around the room were heaps of human crap. You had to be extremely careful where you trod, and I wasn't that keen to hang around for long. I was looking at the fire escape that ran diagonally along the entire length of the Marks and Spencer wall opposite, and noticed that two of the supports were missing from the fence at the bottom which was meant to keep the public out. I was going up that fire escape.

I'd drunk the whole bottle of sherry so by now I was quite drunk. I crossed the road, sneaked through the fence and up the fire escape. It being a bitterly cold Sunday, there wasn't a soul about. I turned left at the top of the fire escape where there was a semi-glazed Georgian style door. I elbowed the pane nearest to the lock, reached through, unlocked it and I was in. And by god, didn't it feel warm. I'd fantasised that I'd be able to wander around all over the shop floor but all the other doors were locked. Never mind. There were two bottles of wine and £15 in cash lying around in this room, so I was quite happy none the less.

Then, stupefied by drunkenness and good fortune, I suddenly decided to take a train to Sevenoaks to see my brother David. It didn't register how filthy I must have been. I went to the offy and bought some cans, and treated myself to some tobacco – I was fed up with dog-ending. I bought my ticket and I was off. I woke up at Sevenoaks Station, mealy-mouthed and hung-over. I don't know how it happened, but when I checked my pockets I only seemed to have one pound coin left. But still, I asked a taxi driver to take me into town. The trouble was, it was in the opposite direction to where my family lived.

Now, some 12 months previously, during one of my temporary stints at my mother's house, I was doing a painting job in an accountant's office in the middle of Sevenoaks High Street. This is where, a year later, the taxi dropped me off. Anyway, there I stood with a completely different attitude to life. I was familiar with the offices, and knew there was a drinks cabinet in the boardroom. There was also easy access to the fire escape. I want to impress upon my readers right now that, when I woke up that morning and when I was downing that sherry in the derelict building, none of this had been on my mind. At no point had I planned to be in Sevenoaks later that day, planning a break-in.

Within half an hour of the taxi dropping me off, I'd been caught breaking into the office. I knew exactly what to do. At the end of the alleyway, separating the adjoining shop from the accountants' offices, was a dustbin. It was there just waiting for me to turn it upside down and use it to hoist myself up and scale the wall, thus gaining access to the fire escape. I headed for the door at the top of the stairs. It was about four o'clock and already getting quite dark. Now the strangest thing was about to happen. As I elbowed the window, I saw a movement out of the corner of my eye. It was a woman who obviously lived above the shop next door, bringing in her washing. The sound of breaking glass on that quiet Sunday afternoon had made her look up, and from the state I was in I clearly wasn't a security guard or emergency repairman.

But I didn't duck down or leg it, I just carried on. I put my hand through the broken window, undid the lock, and opened the door. All the while, the woman in the garden didn't take her eyes off me and carried on unpegging her clothes. I closed the door behind me and leant against it, convinced that within a few minutes I'd hear police sirens and be captured. I weighed up my options. I was hungry, filthy, unemployed, unemployable and with no proper place to live. I already had a court case pending. Nobody wanted to have anything to do with me, and quite honestly I didn't belong anywhere. So what did I have to lose?

While all this was passing through my mind, it occurred to me that the police seemed to be taking their time. Ten minutes must have passed. Well, they hadn't turned up so I decided to head for the boardroom, which I knew to be unlocked, and straight to the drinks cabinet. I selected two or three fine wines, and followed through to an office facing the High Street. Small wall lights had been left on so I wasn't wandering around in the dark. I sat in the comfort of the large office chair and drank the wine. Eventually I started to feel hungry and went to rifle through the staff fridge. Nothing except low fat yoghurt and an energy drink! Oh well. I put a cushion from one of the chairs onto the floor and went fast asleep.

I woke with a start, and remembered in a cold sweat that I'd stolen the mad Irishman's sherry. I don't know how much time had passed but, taking in my surroundings, there seemed to be a lot of drink around. And then it dawned on me. I'd drunk some crap sherry in a shit-infested derelict building, broken into Marks, nicked their wine and some petty cash, and woken up snug and warm in an accountant's office that I'd given a makeover a year ago. OK. Think. This wasn't the problem it could have been. It was Sunday night. Staff wouldn't arrive until about 8.30 in the morning so, if I could find some sort of respectable looking bag, I could take most of the drink home on the train and at least get back into the Irishman's good books.

But plans change. Things were just about to take a turn for the better. As I sat in the chair enjoying what I'd decided would be my last bottle before I jumped the train, I found myself looking at the safe. What a thing of beauty. Such a lovely, shiny, big brass handle. My curiosity got the better of me. I had to see if it would open, but of course it didn't. I sat back down and had another drink. There were three drawers in the desk in front of me. I pulled the handle of the largest in the centre and was surprised to find it opened. And there, bang in the middle of the otherwise empty drawer was a key. And wouldn't you know it, the tag on it read *SAFE KEY*. This had to be a joke – a decoy. Safe keys wouldn't be so easily found. And so, sitting there looking at a key clearly marked *SAFE KEY*, I thought this could mean one of two things. I'm not a rocket scientist, but concluded that this could either be the genuine article, or the decoy I suspected it to be, and there was nothing in the safe to steal.

This was ridiculous. I'd been seen breaking and entering by a neighbour; my fingerprints were daubed everywhere; my DNA was on nearly every bottle and cigarette end in the room, and there was the safe key in front of me on the desk. I'd have to be superhuman to leave there without taking a look. I picked up the key, put it in the lock and turned it

144

to the right. *Click*. It was open. I pulled the brass handle down and the door opened just as easily as that.

Most of what was inside was paperwork, covered in rows and rows of figures. But in the top left hand side of the biggest shelf was one of those old-fashioned cash boxes. I took it out and looked inside, and what do you know? There sat £300 in £10 notes. 30 £10 notes which I felt compelled to liberate. I replaced the box, closed the safe, and put the key back in the drawer. I then picked up the bag I'd filled with spirits and left exactly the way I'd come in.

Now what I should have done was head straight for the station and jump the train. I could now afford a deposit on a nice flat, some new clothes, decent footwear, a proper winter coat and maybe a nice wrist-watch. But oh no, not me. What did I do instead? I got a taxi straight down to my brother's. David worked six days a week delivering meat and poultry round the West End of London, so the last thing he wanted was me turning up on a Sunday night, drunk.

But I knew he wouldn't turn me away, and sure enough he greeted me with, 'Hello mate, come in'. His wife came to the door to see who it was and when she saw it was me, and the state I was in, I felt I heard her heart hit the floor. I'd put them on the spot, I know. I knew they loved me because they knew about my past. But Sunday night with a full week's hard work ahead just wasn't the right time for me to pay a visit, and I knew it. But David took me through to the lounge and I began telling him of this most recent set of idiotic capers, from waking to the delights of the Irishman's sherry to the escapade at Marks, although I thought it best not to mention the accountants in Sevenoaks – bit too close to home.

David and Christine sat quietly and soberly, and I realised as I was relating events to them that they just didn't seem to find funny. David asked me what I intended to do now. Suddenly I felt very stupid. I looked around their house. It had all fitted carpets and it was warm, with comfortable furniture. It was a home. I don't think my brother was ever aware of it, but I envied him so much. Christine came in wearing her nightie and slippers, and offered me something to eat. It dawned on me then why I'd been in so much pain. It was now Sunday night, and the last time I'd eaten was on Thursday when I shared a bag of the mutant deficient's chips. That was three days ago. No wonder I always felt so ill. But I thanked her and declined her offer, telling her I was just a bad eater. I was in no fit state to keep food down just then. She went up and ran me a bath and told me to 'get upstairs and give yourself a bloody good scrub, and I'll sort out some of David's clothes for you.'

When I came back downstairs, the mood had distinctly changed. There was a heavy silence in the room. I'd asked if David could drop me off up west in the morning, but it was Christine's intuition that told her I just wasn't stable enough. She'd kitted me out in some of David's better working clothes, and she wanted me back in Hastings first thing in the morning to look for a flat. David was going to have a beer right now, but I was adamant that I wanted to go to London.

I spent the night on the couch, but not until my little brother had had a chat with me. Now I say this kindly but, although David's not the most articulate of blokes, he did have this ability to make you see, regardless of anything else, the simple truth. And to David, the simple truth as he saw it was that I needed in-patient psychiatric help. He agreed to taking me to London, but with huge reservations. He was clear that he wanted me to accept that it could end only one way, and that would be in disaster. He wanted to know how much I'd drunk that day on an empty stomach. He asked me if drinking a bottle of sherry on a freezing cold Sunday morning in a derelict building where human excrement was liberally strewn across the floor was the action of a rational human being. I knew exactly what he was saying. I knew my behaviour was bizarre. I knew I had no direction in life. David saw I was getting upset. He knew me well enough to know that inside I was hurting. But you see, although I didn't know the answers, I did know he was right.

We were in the West End by 6.30, and by eight o'clock I was sitting in the grounds of a small chapel in or near Soho. I didn't realise it then, but within a couple of years I was to spend at least six months living on these very streets, begging money, mainly for cider and vodka. How pleased I am that I wasn't blessed with such a gift of premonition. If I'd known, the weight of my despair would have been unbearable.

There were already about half a dozen drinkers there, some in pairs, some on their own, some just walking around in circles humming to themselves. I remember one bloke in particular. He was sitting on his haunches on the grass with his head in his hands sobbing his heart out. I went over to see if I could help. One of the blokes wandering about humming tuneless dirges jumped in and said, 'Leave the man alone. It's his pain and he'll deal with it.' I found out later that he'd recently discovered he'd lost his only daughter and, although he hadn't seen her for over eight years, was beside himself with grief Those lost years handed over to living the wretched life of an alcoholic; all that regret for failing the child he still loved dearly, and who he spoke of often, must have intensified his grief to unimaginable depths.

146

I chose to sit on my own. I'd bought a bottle of Scots Mac, fairly strong and easy to drink. I thought about David for a while, and our journey together this morning. His parting shot had been, 'Sort yourself out, Brian, or you'll end up in the Big House' (Wandsworth Prison). God, I was depressed. I thought about the hovel I had to go back to in Hastings, with not even a wardrobe in it. Not that I had anything to put in a wardrobe, mind you. I thought of the loutish Irishman, the genetically challenged skinhead, the rat he carried on him all the time, the burglary I'd just committed and almost certainly would be caught for...

It was while I was in this awful, depressing secular mood that I heard the creak of the rusty wrought-iron gate. Four blokes strode into the chapel grounds, Scousers, all in their mid-20s. Little did I know that I was to rue the day that I'd ever clapped eyes on them. All four came and sat to one side of me. 'Hello, mate,' one said, and asked if he could have a mouthful from my bottle. Well I only had about a quarter of it left and so I said, 'It's OK, I can get you a bottle each.' As I've said before, and no doubt will say again, *When the wet's in, the wit's out.* And never was an expression so apt! I pulled out my wad, gave them 20 quid, and told them to toddle off and satisfy their thirst but bring me back a bottle too.

Then it kicked off. I'd hardly put my wad back in my pocket when one of the bastards punched me full in the face, knocking out a tooth. One tried to grab me around the head, one was just kicking me anywhere he could, and one was trying to get his hand in my pocket. We were no more than 20 feet from the chapel gate, so a sizeable crowd of passers-by had gathered to watch the fracas. The people I'd been drinking with weren't in the least interested. They'd seen it all a hundred times before. All they were concerned about was their drink and, to be fair, that would have been exactly my attitude.

They managed to pull the money from my pocket and made a run for the gate. The crowd let them through. You see, we street or bench drinkers couldn't possibly expect the same civic-minded response to being mugged as an "innocent, ordinary" citizen. But despite my injuries, I did manage to catch the last bloke going through the gate. Another mistake. I grabbed him by the collar and pulled him to the ground, but he struggled to his feet. And then I saw it. He had a blade. Before I could take any evasive action, he'd stabbed me. I don't know where he was aiming, but he stabbed me full in the biceps and, instead of pulling the knife straight out again, he drew it out with a slicing action. Not one of what must have been 30 bystanders did a thing. I was bleeding heavily and going into shock.

There had been about £240 taken from my pocket, but luckily some change remained in the other. It amounted to about £17 when I counted it later. I staggered back to where the other alkies were still sitting. Those left by this time were the more experienced. One of the blokes handed me his whisky bottle to take a slug and, God bless him, handed me a £20 note. He'd spotted one of the Scousers dropping it as they made off. Now that's what I call fellowship and honesty.

I was losing so much blood that I was beginning to go dizzy. In my disorientation, I heard an ambulance arrive and, having done what was needed on the spot, the paramedics took me to the nearest hospital. When I'd been patched up, I was discharged on the Monday night, still not having eaten since the previous Thursday.

I arrived back in Hastings just after midnight. But before I'd boarded the train. I'd called into a deli and furnished myself with a four-pack of Special Brew. Being a delicatessen, they charged about one and a half times the price a normal offy would, but when needs must... These people know when you're rattling, and they know you'll pay the price. So my entire fortune was now £9.

There was no point in going to the corner café at this hour. I only had to wait for opening at eight the following morning so I decided, rather than settle down in a doorway, I'd be better off back in the derelict house I'd started off from on the Sunday morning. The room I used to sit (or stand) in was on the first floor but the stairs had been ripped out and the only means of access was up a small rotting ladder. I managed, with my bad arm, to hoist myself up and, having salvaged a load of discarded newspapers from the train coming down, made myself as comfortable as possible. After the trauma of the past 48 hours, and the lack of any nourishment for God knows how long, I was feeling pretty weak and light-headed. I feared I was also a bit delirious. When you reach this point in an alcoholic's career, with a body pretty much shot to bits, two cans of Special Brew hits the spot damn quick and lasts you quite a few hours. You can be as drunk as you want to be and not even worry where your next drink's coming from.

The room was fairly well lit from the streetlights just outside the window. It must have been the culmination of recent events and my delirium that made me focus on all the piles of crap, large and small, dotted about the room. They all seemed to be in varying stages of decomposition. I found it fascinating the different types of material the depositors of these little heaps had used to clean themselves up with afterwards. Old chip bags, newspapers, a piece of old curtain that used to hang at the window. Another had simply used his own underpants. Someone had used an empty milk carton, and then of course there were heaps where there was no evidence that the depositor had tried to clean himself up at all.

Once more I fell into an uneasy stupor, and dreamt of clowns with black circles around their eyes, and no smiles.

22

The Tyrannical Major and the Lie

It was in 1983 that I first met my girlfriend. I had just completed a 15-month sentence at Her Majesty's pleasure. We dated for about 5 weeks and, as I was living in a squalid bedsit and she was living in a two-bedroom flat, it just seemed to make sense that we should move in together. She was aware that I'd just come out of prison, but had no idea that I was a chronic alcoholic. Neither did she have experience of what an alcoholic was like.

At this particular period in my life I was actually able to work more often than not, so for a couple of months things weren't too bad. But it's the same old story. After a while I was drinking more than working.

As I said, she had two bedrooms and she suggested – due to my drinking – that I move into the other bedroom. We were hardly making love at all. I was nearly always drunk, or if I wasn't drunk I was just plain shaking too much to do anything. This arrangement lasted for a couple of months before she finally threw me out. She'd come to realise that drink was my life.

Now, this is where the Tyrannical Major came into play. The only accommodation I could find at the time, with my limited resources, was a huge B&B place in London Road. It was a massive detached house with something like 15 rooms. It was immaculate. If it had been a hotel, it would surely have had four stars. On the front of the building, the sign read, *Vacancies: DSS Considered*. Now, I was on benefits at the time, but was quite reasonably dressed. I walked along the short gravel drive and rang the bell. It was such a long time before anyone answered the door that I was just about to leave when suddenly it opened. There in front of me was a huge great man. I put him at about six foot four inches tall and bolt upright. Even when he bent down to pick up some mail from the floor, he was still bolt upright.

He said his name was Mr Jacks (not his real name) and how could he help me? I said I'd noticed that there were vacancies, and that I would like a room. He asked me in and invited me into his office. I followed him obediently. The office was massive and overlooked a beautiful rockery. His office was immaculate with not a paper out of place. He told me to

150

take a seat, and gestured with his outstretched hand to a small chair opposite his own throne-like chair.

I'll guess that I was about 35 years old at this point, and yet I sat there like a little schoolboy. First he asked whether I was working or not. I said I wasn't, but that I was in receipt of sickness benefit which meant that the DSS would pay any accommodation or rent. He asked how long it had been since I'd worked and I told him three months; he then asked me what my illness was, and how it rendered me incapable of work. I didn't expect any of this, and so wasn't prepared with an answer. But for some strange reason – and this was entirely off the top of my head – I said I had a ruptured disc in my spine.

All the time I was talking, he was writing and didn't once look up at me. He asked what sort of education I had. I told him secondary modern, plus two stints at college, one to learn all about ceiling and wall coverings, the other to learn how to become an able-seaman, and that I'd spent two years as a trawler-man.

That was the only time he stopped writing and looked up at me. I thought his next question was rather strange. He asked me if I ever drank when I was at sea. I was suspicious. Had he ever been to sea? No, he was "a military man", had been all his life, but there had been occasions when he had put to sea for reasons which I wouldn't understand.

I'm going to contradict myself now, and tell you that I was fast becoming pissed off with this bloke, but I have to say there was something about him that I liked. There was something bothering me, but I couldn't quite make out what it was. Then it dawned on me. It was the silence; not the silence in the office, but the silence of the building. I asked Mr Jacks how many residents he had. 'Five at the moment.' 'How many rooms?' '15.'

He then asked me point blank if I drank. I must admit that by now I was fed up with him, and asked him why on earth he was asking. He answered, 'The reason that there are only five guests is that I will not tolerate anyone who drinks, period! 'That's why I asked if you drank when you were at sea, because in my experience, seamen, ex or otherwise, are notorious for their drunken behaviour. It's the curse of all mankind!'

Do you know something strange? I actually believed him! But whether I believed him or not, I knew that all I wanted to do at that particular moment was to get outside and have a drink, room or no bloody room. But I managed to stick it out and let him prattle on about his rules and regulations. He asked if I had any ID. 'Yes I do, but wouldn't now be a good time to look at one of the rooms and perhaps discuss the rent, considering that if you accept me as a guest, the DSS would be paying the rent as I am, for the time being, incapacitated?' He agreed, but before we left the office he said, 'I've just bought a new special horsehair outdoor mat. Did you use it?' I genuinely thought he was joking until he checked his own shoes, then I realised he was serious. That clinched it. I hoped I did get one of his rooms because I wanted to play this man!

I knew there was more to this bloke than met the eye. We walked up three flights of stairs, each as immaculate as the other: not only the carpet and balustrade, but everything was in pristine condition. He took me into the room facing London Road. As far as I was concerned, it was perfect. There were three rooms on this particular floor, and I was the only occupant. The other inmates were all situated on the other floors.

It was about 20 years ago, so it's difficult to remember the rent, but I did know it was within what the DSS would pay. He opened every drawer and every cupboard just to show me how clean everything was, and made a special point of not only showing me how clean the basin was, but asked me to run my finger across the base to check there was no lime-scale! I told him I liked the room, and asked if he would accept me as a guest. He agreed to accept me provided I went back to his office, filled in the necessary forms to get my rent paid, and take them up to social security straight away.

When we were back in his office, for some weird reason he showed me a list of people who had stayed there in the past. In fact, not only did he have their names, but their current addresses. He told me that these were people he had to ask to leave because he had found out they had been drinking. I asked if they'd been drunk. He said, 'I don't know, but they absolutely stank of alcohol.'

Now, I don't particularly like to use clichés, but this reminded me of a particular saying I once heard, and it went something like: "Nobody is more obsessed with sex than a fanatical puritan." Well, the way Mr Jacks kept on about alcohol, and the fact that he even had the names and addresses of blokes that had long since been thrown out because of drinking – not because they were drunk, but simply because they had been drinking – made me think. A lifetime of mixing with drinkers gives you a certain kind of radar. This bloke was obsessed, for whatever reason, with drink and drinkers. Maybe he was an alcoholic? No, couldn't be. As I walked behind him on the way to the office, he was so upright, his co-ordination so perfect, he couldn't possibly be... could he?

Forms filled in, I dutifully took them up to the social, which just happened to be about five minutes away. The following day I moved in.

The Major – by now, what else could I call him? – made it quite clear that at 11pm on the dot, even though I had my own key, the bolts would be thrown across from the inside and it would be no good knocking because he simply wouldn't let anyone in, and if that was good enough for the other guests, then he was sure that it would be good enough for me.

I nodded in agreement, and wondered how the hell I was going to be able to drink in a place like this, and get away with it. It seemed to me that even if he saw me on a park bench drinking, he'd throw me out.

Now, I've never liked being out at night, except during those heady teenage years. So, what I knew I had to do was get back at a reasonable time, say eight o'clock, sneak round the back with my drink and sit on the rockery. This was a superb vantage point because I was dead opposite his office. I had a watch, so I knew what time it was – when he told me he would throw those bolts over, I knew he meant it.

I managed to keep this routine up for about four or five days. Then one day I got absolutely drunk. It happens with alkies. I remember staggering round the back to my place on the rockery at just past 11 o'clock. I knew that, as drunk as I was, if I'd tried to get in he would have thrown me out. I still had the best part of a bottle of vodka left, so I thought I'd just have to sleep there that night. Oddly enough, as I sat there in the rockery – and I really had made myself quite comfortable – I saw The Major's office lights come on. I checked my watch. It was 11.15. Although he had net curtains up, the lights were quite bright so I had a clear view of exactly what he was up to. He sat down at his desk and opened one of the drawers. I couldn't believe what I was seeing! He pulled out a glass and a bottle. Now, from where I was sitting I would guess the distance between his office and me was no more than 20 feet, but I still couldn't believe what I was seeing – I just had to get closer.

As it was pitch black, I could get right close up to the window and he wouldn't be able to see me. I was incredulous. He had a bottle of whisky. I could actually read the label. It was Bell's. I couldn't believe it but, for some reason, I wasn't shocked. I went back to my little lair in his rockery and the cliché kept coming back to me: "nobody is more obsessed with sex than a fanatical puritan". This tyrant of a man who had made some people homeless simply because they might have had a pint of beer was sitting there drinking whisky.

As I sat on his rockery drinking my vodka, I wondered whether perhaps tomorrow he might like to discuss hypocrisy. How dare he ask if I ever drank at sea? His words "drinking is forbidden, period" – His words!

153

At that moment, steeped in drink, I couldn't be sure what I was going to do but I did rather think that this could work for me instead of against me.

The morning finally arrived. Now, I knew that dead on six o'clock, a bloke would come down and unbolt the doors. It wasn't necessarily his job or his duty, he was only one of the inmates, but I think it just made him feel important. It was some sort of ritual with him. In fact, I don't ever remember him leaving the premises. He was a bit of an odd-ball. I think I only went into the dining room once, and that was simply to avoid The Major, but I passed there often and, each time, this bloke would be sitting there with his back to the rest of the residents, not necessarily eating – just sitting there.

I got up from the rockery, walked round to the front of the building and positioned myself where I couldn't be seen, but would be able to hear when the bolts were thrown back. Sure enough, at six on the dot, BANG BANG went the bolts. Now all I had to do was give Silly Bollocks a couple of minutes to go and plant himself up in the dining room then I'd slip upstairs unnoticed, get myself washed, change, finish my vodka then use my super strength mouthwash just in case Lurcio The Bolt Attendant got anywhere near me. Mind you, that was highly unlikely as I'd been there about three weeks and he hadn't as much as looked in my direction.

Normally at this time of day, The Major would be busy organising things in the kitchen, so I had no fear of bumping into him. It was just bad luck that, as I approached the big main door, there he was sifting through the mail. As I passed him to go out, I just couldn't believe what he said to me! He said, 'I would prefer it if in future you would let me know if you decide to stay out at night.' How on earth had he known I hadn't slept in my room?

He said it so flatly, so matter of factly. He didn't even look at me as he said it. He really did give me the creeps, this bloke. In fact to be honest, I was now beginning to be a bit scared of him. How could this man be so cold, so immaculate, so meticulous, so regimental? So pathologically strict? Bearing in mind what I had witnessed the night before, I really was beginning to think he was some sort of psycho.

I apologised, and told him I hadn't known myself until the last minute. He accepted my apology and, apart from still not looking at me, that did seem to be the end of it. I went straight down to the off-licence to buy a bottle of cider and then walked down to my girlfriend's. Even though she'd thrown me out, she let me in! When I told her I'd got so drunk yesterday, I'd had to sleep in the rockery, it will not surprise you to learn, dear reader, that she wasn't particularly interested. 'Well, what did you expect?' came the comforting reply. For some reason I didn't let on about The Major at that point.

Apart from my drinking, Pat wouldn't let me sleep at her flat because she had a son. However, he was in Eastbourne with his girlfriend until 10.30 that night, so I could stay till then providing I didn't get too drunk. I then had to return to the B&B. I must add that before I left The Major's that morning, even though eye contact hadn't been made, I did tell him I had an elderly aunt who liked me to check in on her between ten and 11 at night, to see the place was secure, and asked if Mr Pangboume (Lurcio) would mind awfully if I actually came in just slightly after 11 rather than just before. The Major said he would have a word with him, but under the circumstances he was sure it would be all right.

I wouldn't expect a non-drinker to understand this – I don't understand it myself – but an alcoholic needs a certain quota of alcohol to keep straight. They call it "tolerance". So I could stay at Pat's until say 10.30 or 11, and she would allow me to drink a small amount, so I always kept back at least a quarter of a bottle of mostly vodka, or sometimes whisky, and I took to drinking this on The Major's rockery. It's an amazing, funny world.

I would arrive on the rockery about two minutes after 11, and the office light would go on at about five past. He would secretly drink his Bell's and I'd secretly drink my vodka. I remember all those years ago when I first started going to sea and had to share a room with a bloke called Billy. We were total strangers. We'd say hello to each other, and Billy drank his whisky and I drank my vodka. Neither of us spoke; we didn't have to. We both knew we were alkies and we both accepted it. And here I was all these years later, still drinking vodka with a man not 20 feet away drinking whisky. The only difference was, he wouldn't accept it and was therefore in torment. He had no friends, he couldn't communicate, he constantly lived a lie, and despite his upright posture and his perfect gait as he walked giving the impression of his being in total control, this man was more lost and lonely than I was. He would probably have liked to mix or socialise with some of his guests. In fact if he were to come out into the open and say without shame – *I rather fancy a tipple myself* – I'm sure people would have warmed to him. I'm not a poof or anything, but he was also what the ladies would have called a fine figure of a man.

My routine of having the last drink of the day on The Major's rockery lasted about a week. I know I said I was a bit scared of this man, but you know, funnily enough I now felt some sort of affinity with him. A bit

155

sorry for him. He owned this massive house, and obviously had a few quid tucked away, but his life between six in the morning and midnight was a sham. Not only a sham, but a lonely sham. I suppose that the only time he could indulge himself was at 11 o'clock when he could have his drink, but even then he was probably scared witless of detection from the Missus. Even his guests probably frightened him to death.

It was now 11.30, and so as not to upset Lurcio I thought I'd better go in. At least that way I would have a drop of vodka left for tomorrow.

I was able to get in, but Lurcio was sitting right by the entrance of the dining hall. I said goodnight and went to my room, but couldn't sleep. In the morning, I thought I could manage a cup of tea so, as a one-off, I went down to the dining room. The Major managed to say, 'This is an unexpected pleasure', and even volunteered that he was off to the cash and carry and that should I need anything, Lurcio would be in charge. I said I was fine thanks, and would be out most of the day anyway. I had my cup of tea then went and sat in the park with a bottle of cider.

I was on my way to Pat's, but spotted a couple of alkies I hadn't seen for some time so I thought I'd join them just for a change. As I sat there chatting to my mates, along came Pat. This was most unusual for her, so I naturally thought something was wrong. But nothing was wrong. She'd seen me walk down to the park and, while she didn't like the people I drank with, she needed a favour. She walked straight over to me, and all my mates said hello. She totally ignored them, and that really pissed me off.

Anyway, apparently a friend of hers worked at a local shop and had asked her if she would take the van up to the cash and carry and bring a load of stuff back for her. Well, she'd only been there a couple of weeks so Pat didn't like to say no, but she didn't think she could manage it all and, in short, would Brian give her a hand to load the van up? Her mate said that as long as Pat could get it back to the shop, there'd be someone there to help her unload. She didn't want anyone in the shop to see me. Charming! To add to this generosity of spirit, Pat said she'd give me a couple of quid. I said I'd be with her in a tick if she could just hang on while I finished my bottle.

I'd heard this place was massive, and it was. Pat went to one of the staff with some sort of docket and we were taken to where the order was stacked. No wonder she wanted a hand, there was loads of it. As we started to load up the van, who should I spot but the bloody Major! I couldn't believe my eyes. Thankfully he didn't see me. Anyway, he was loading up the back of his estate, and I couldn't help but notice a box of

156

Bell's whisky. As he went over to one of the assistants I had to have a peep in this box. There were 12 bottles of scotch! And there was me worried about him catching me with one poxy bottle of cider. He had no idea I was watching him but, even then, from a distance, his very stature commanded my respect.

I made up my mind there and then that I had no reason to reproach myself. He was no better than me or anyone else I drank with.

23

The Tyrannical Major and My Wife

Pat's friend dropped me off at the corner, a respectable distance from the shop, gave me £3 and thanked me very much. I went into the offy, bought a quarter bottle of vodka and a bottle of cider, and walked down to resume my position in the park. Where there had only been two or three that morning, there were now about a dozen.

I plonked myself back down next to Ron and asked him if he'd ever stayed at Mr Jacks' B&B up the road. No, he hadn't, but Tony had. (Tony later died of hypothermia). 'What was it like at Mr Jacks', Tony?' His reply was, 'Don't ever go there, man. He's an out and out bastard.' He added, 'I was staying there when I had that fucking Hep B or A or whatever it is.' 'Hepatitis?' 'Yeah.' Tony had actually become seriously jaundiced and should have been hospitalised. Even his eyes turned yellow. Then he said something very interesting. He'd actually been there for seven weeks, and during that period he obviously couldn't drink. The doctor simply told him that if he did, he'd die. Now, when you drink to the extent that people like I do, it's almost impossible to detect alcohol on each other's breath. But during Tony's alcohol-free stay at The Major's, there were a few occasions when Mr Jacks himself served breakfast, and Tony swore blind he smelt whisky on Jacks' breath. Now, every one of the alkies sitting there drinking knew of this bastard Jacks, and nobody could believe it.

But I knew different. You see this Mr Jacks' attitude towards drink and drinkers was widely known among us "inadequate" street or bench drinkers. While all of us sitting there knew each other by sight, we didn't necessarily know each other's names. What we did know was that each of us had been drinking since we opened our eyes first thing in the morning. It was now something like two in the afternoon and as you can imagine, we were all fairly pissed. Which is probably the reason I took it upon myself to tell anyone who was listening that I had seen Mr Jacks that very morning buying a dozen bottles of whisky. Not only that, I had also seen him, with my very own eyes drinking the best part of a bottle of the stuff every single night for the past two weeks.

There were shouts of "Bollox" and "Don't talk like a cunt". I didn't get the chance to convince them. Although in those days they hadn't set up the non-drinking zones, the police arrived anyway. Someone in the nearby flats had decided we were becoming a bit too rowdy. None of us was arrested, but we were asked to move on. Not wanting to spend the night in the cells we wandered off, mumbling and a little unsteady. I decided to go up to Pat's for the rest of the day. She was just about to go out, but had seen the whole thing from her flat window. Having seen the police arrive, she knew it would only be a matter of minutes before I was knocking on her door. She'd be gone for a couple of hours and, surely at this time of day I'd had enough to drink so, providing I didn't have any drink on me I could come in. I assured her I had none on me at all, but had something really important to tell her, something she wouldn't believe in a million years. 'Oh yeah! I've heard all your drunken stories before.'

So she left, and I went straight in and crashed out in the spare room. She wouldn't have appreciated it if I'd passed out in her room. I knew she loved me but it was this insidious drink business and there was nothing I could do about it. But just before I went to sleep, I decided I was going to do something about this Mr Jacks and his hypocritical stance on drinkers. After all, the DSS were paying him an astronomical sum to put us up there, and half these people were so ill they couldn't even eat.

Pat came back about nine. I'd just woken up. Her son was due back about 10.30, so she told me that if I wanted a drink I would have to look sharp as she didn't want me to be there when he arrived. Well, I shot down the offy as quick as I could and got a bottle of cider. I didn't bother with the vodka because I didn't want to waste it. I'd save that for settling down in my lair, waiting for The Major to hole himself up in his office and do what my drinking friends and I had been doing that very morning, and had been doing ever since we didn't know when.

I was going to ask him why. I was going to ask him why he drank in his office late at night, in secret. I was going to ask him what the difference was between him and me.

Although earlier, when I spotted him at the cash and carry, I said I had nothing to reproach myself with, actually I did. There was a difference between him and me. There was a difference between him and most of the people I drank with, and I wanted to know what it was. I could have understood a lot better if he had just said to me, "Look Mr Harding, I understand that you drink heavily and it's caused you a lot of problems. I understand, but please, I would prefer it if you didn't do it in my company." That way, I might have been better able to understand why he drank alone in his office late at night. If I could get over the hypocrisy of the man, I would have to admit that he wasn't actually doing anybody any harm. This bit of philosophy was short-lived because by the time his lights came on I'd drunk just over half of my new bottle and was very drunk.

The ritual began. He opened the drawer and pulled out a clean glass. I suppose, because I'd drunk so much that day, I had a bit of a "don't give a damn" attitude. I left the safety of my lair and stumbled down to the bottom of the rockery. I pulled up an old box and made myself comfortable no less than two feet away from the window. I studied him for a while as best I could, bearing in mind I hadn't eaten for a couple of days, so was really drunk. He was browsing through some papers, sometimes smiling to himself, sometimes just staring into space. I couldn't resist it any longer. I got up and tapped on the window quite loudly several times. He shot out of his chair, and I suddenly realised that there were three spotlights which, when switched on, lit up the whole of the rockery. All these lights were suddenly activated, and his office lights went out. He could now see out, but I couldn't see in, so I just stood there like a rabbit caught in the headlights. This wasn't bravery. I was desensitised. I had no fear. At that precise moment I had not a care in the world. If he'd thrown me out there and then, it wouldn't have mattered one iota.

I'd always known that there was a back door right next to his office but in all the time I'd been there I'd never seen it open. Suddenly I heard the bolts go back and there was The Major in all his glory. His frame took up the whole space where the door had been. I was illuminated beautifully by the spotlights and he was clearly shocked. He asked what on earth I'd been doing. I don't think he saw my vodka because I'd left it by the box I'd been sitting on. I said, 'I'm ever so sorry to trouble you at this time of night Mr Jacks, but I have a friend who would like to buy some whisky at cash and carry prices. Would you happen to know where I could get some?'

Unfazed, he claimed not to know what I was talking about and demanded to know how I'd got round the back. I explained how easy it had been. I'd just climbed over the back gate, undid the bolt and here I was. Claiming not to know anything about cash and carry whisky he said, 'Whatever happens, you will not be sleeping here tonight or any other night.'

'But, Mr Jacks,' I persisted, 'I was in the cash and carry today, helping a friend, and while I was there I couldn't help but notice you and the 12 bottles of Bell's you were loading into your car. I pointed to the

160

rockery and told him I'd been staked out there for the last two weeks watching him. 'Call it my lair, because you, Mr Jacks, have made me feel like some sort of leper and that's the place where I drink my vodka and cider mix while you've been sitting in your office drinking your scotch.'

Unhappy to have such a conversation out on his patio at that time of night, he invited me into the office. I said, 'I've left my drink over there behind that box; would you mind if I brought it in with me?' He said he didn't mind, but needed to know if anyone else knew I'd been sitting in his rockery all this time. I told him they didn't, and he said to come in, and that we'd better have a talk.

He turned the spotlights off and the rockery was suddenly dead. We sat down, and I must have had the devil in me because I went straight over and sat in his own throne-like chair. He went to comment, but thought better of it. I poured the rest of the cider into the remaining vodka, and that's how I sat there drinking it, straight out of the bottle. He asked me not to, and pulled a second glass from his desk drawer. We just sat there for a minute or two looking at each other. What right did I think I had to sit on his rockery at that time of night staring into his window, he asked.

I told him that I didn't want to be sitting on his rockery at that time of night, or at any other time come to that, but because of his hypocrisy and his downright disregard for anyone other than himself, I felt compelled to. 'Although I'm a street drinker and obviously street-wise,' I went on to explain, '1 couldn't drink in my room because you would have thrown me out. And all the time, you were sitting in the comfort of your office drinking your whisky.'

Since I'd been talking. The Major hadn't interrupted me once. In fact, for most of the time he'd sat with his head bowed. Even though he wasn't looking at me, I knew he was taking it all in. Sometime during the past ten or 15 minutes, our roles had subtly changed and this wasn't just because I was sitting on the "throne". It had nothing to do with that. It was because I was speaking the truth; because I had suddenly realised that I held no animosity towards this man at all. His regimented and disciplined manner was all a façade. He wanted to be friendly, but because he'd spent all his life, man and boy, in the military, retiring at the rank of Sergeant Major, he just couldn't make friends. If he'd tried to make friends with his subordinates in the army, he was just blanked. He felt he could never "let his hair down" and, because he was an officer, his men didn't feel they could trust him, and this just rubbed off in Civvy Street.

Ten minutes of heavy silence passed, then he spoke. During that time, we'd both just sat staring at our glasses, not able to look up at each other.

Strange how I had gleaned all this information from him without actually asking any specific questions. It's as though he wanted to talk but didn't know how to. Now, I could have taken this as either an honour or an insult. Should I be honoured because he trusted me to understand, or should I be insulted because I wouldn't have a clue what he was talking about?

He went on to tell me that he and his wife hadn't had a conversation for seven years. Although they rubbed along just enough so that the B&B ran properly, they not only had separate beds, but separate rooms. I hadn't prompted this outpouring. He just seemed to need to talk. As drunk as I was, and as late as it was – it was now quarter past two – I'm going to take a chance and say I understood this man perfectly. I suppose that if a shrink should read this, he'd probably say to himself, 'Don't talk bollocks!' But I swear I did feel an empathy with this man.

It wasn't all one-sided. I confessed a lot about myself as well. The fact that I was emotionally abused as a kid, how I was humiliated, demeaned, degraded and all the rest of it. I suppose the amount of alcohol we'd drunk, and the impact and level of intimacy of our conversation, finally took their toll and we both eventually fell silent. It wasn't one of those awkward silences. I suppose we were just reflecting on the seriousness and the implications of what we'd been talking about for the past three hours. By now his bottle was empty. He crossed over to a cupboard and took out this box-like thing and put the empty bottle inside. Attached to the box was a sort of lever, similar to the hand-brake on a car. He placed the box squarely on the floor and knelt on it. Then he pulled the lever down, waited a couple of seconds, and pulled a small drawer out. I couldn't believe what I saw next. There in his hand was his whisky bottle, completely transformed. It had been reduced to a handful of tiny crystals of glass, which he dusted off into the waste paper basket!

He suggested we turned in, and said that he'd enjoyed talking to me. I could stay in the B&B, and he understood and accepted that I had to drink. But what he would ask of me was to understand that if at any time I displayed any outward signs of drunkenness, he would have to ask me to leave. I assured him I understood his reasons, appreciated him understanding me, thanked him for his honesty, and said that I would see him in the morning.

Morning came, and everything seemed the same as usual; I was sick, which was par for the course. I had a bath and went downstairs, admittedly a little apprehensive about the aftermath of the previous evening, and what sort of reception I'd get from The Major. I needn't have worried. I wasn't up to breakfast and went straight into the lounge. I hadn't been in there five minutes when in came Lurcio with a message from Mr Jacks: Would I like a cup of tea? Having been sick, I was ready for one. When he came in a few minutes later, Mr Jacks did look a bit sheepish, but was actually smiling! We exchanged pleasantries and established that we were both fine, thanks, apart from lack of sleep. He admitted to being a bit worried about our nocturnal ramblings, but I reassured him that no-one in the world would know but him and me. There was obvious relief on his face and he believed me.

The Major admitted to a tendency to typecast people, but I must say he was pretty quick to add that he was nearly always right. He called Lurcio and asked him to fetch his tea along with mine. Mr Jacks asked me about my plans for the day. He said he wasn't being nosy, just genuinely interested. 'When will you have your first drink?' he enquired. I told him I already had. He was incredulous, and asked me when.

'Just after I was sick.'

'When was that?'

'As soon as I woke up.'

'How often does that happen?'

'Every single day of my waking life.'

'I'm sorry, I had no idea.'

'I know you don't.'

'What about the people you drink with in the park? Are they the same?' 'You ought to know, you've thrown most of them out at some time or other.' I didn't mean to bully him. I was just answering truthfully. He fell silent for a moment and his face went ashen. He looked at me and said, 'I'm sorry.'

I said, 'don't be, it's got nothing to do with you. You're not the reason they're like they are. With respect, you have no idea how these people have been brought up. I'm not saying this to defend them or excuse their behaviour; some of them are bastards, whether they drink or not. But the over-riding fact is most of them were dealt a bad, bad hand when they were very young. It's not your fault, and it's not mine either, so don't lose any sleep over it.'

Lurcio appeared from nowhere and took my cup away. I told Jacks I was off and I'd see him later. He held his hand out for me to shake. I did, but couldn't help squirming a bit with embarrassment.

1 resumed my morning routine. First to the offy, then go and sit in the park with anyone I could see with a can or a bottle. With this drinking business, you could join someone who was already drinking and, apart

from muttering, "ok mate?" neither of you had to talk if you didn't want to. I'd normally drink until about two, and then go round to Pat's. That's if I wasn't too pissed of course. For some reason, she was becoming more and more affectionate towards me. In fact, at this point, I was sleeping in her bed. Although only in the afternoon of course.

Bizarrely, it was Pat who finally got me thrown out of Jacks' place. My routine was to get back to the B&B about mid-evening, go to my room and drink whatever I could afford at the time, and then go down to the lounge. I don't know how, but he always knew when I came in. I'd been there several weeks by now, and there were about eight or nine residents. But the lounge just wasn't a place where people would gather. I guessed they just stayed in their rooms. I'd never be in there more than 20 minutes when Mr Jacks would pop his head round the door and say, 'Do you fancy a drink, Brian?' Naturally I'd say 'Yes'.

Things were different now. The net curtains that used to shroud the office were now pulled wide part and the spotlights lit up the rockery. It really was quite beautiful. Aware that I had limited funds – and I'm not sure I was that comfortable with this – he always made sure he had a quarter of a bottle of vodka in his drawer to go with my cider. I like to mix the two together. As drunks do, we would sit there for hours talking about anything and everything. We talked about really personal things. But our little soirées were soon to come to an end.

Pat and I had grown closer and closer. Her son was leaving college and had secured a job in London, so she asked me if I'd like to move in permanently. I actually *loved* Pat but, unsure, I said I'd think about it.

And that was my big mistake. From then on, every time I went to the park, someone would say, 'Pat's been looking for you.' It could be first thing in the morning, or last thing in the afternoon. But either way, she was looking for me. It all came to a head one afternoon when I was supposed to meet her at her flat. She was having some furniture delivered, and asked if I would make sure I was there to help her when it arrived. I promised that no-matter what happened, I'd be there.

To this day I don't know what the circumstances were that made me so uncontrollably drunk on that particular day, but drunk I was. I remember being asleep in the Major's lounge; in a stupor, to be more accurate. Pat came storming in and tried to rouse me. None of the other guests wanted to know, although they were naturally curious as to how I could get so drunk in Mr Jacks' place and not get thrown out. Pat was in such a fury that she pulled me off the chair and onto the floor. This was too much for Lurcio and he ran out to the boss's living quarters and told him I was so drunk I was lying on the floor with my wife kicking me! Pat then picked up a nearby coffee table and, as she smashed it over my head, The Major marched in. She'd knocked me unconscious. This was all too much for the man, and he called his wife. Lurcio and the pair of them then bodily threw Pat out the front door. Mr Jacks saw to me, and I remember little more than him asking me if I knew where I was. I came round after a few seconds and the Major sat me on a chair.

'Was that your wife?'

'Yes.'

'Sorry, Brian. I can't have her in here again.'

'I know, sorry.'

'The thing is Brian, I'm really disappointed to be in the position of having to ask you to leave immediately yourself.'

'I understand.'

He asked Lurcio, and the others who had gathered for the show, to leave the room.

'I'm sorry this had to happen, Brian. If you're well enough to get to your room, I'll help you pack.'

I realised I'd made a friend. He didn't ask how or why this happened, just helped me up. He seemed to want to excuse Pat's behaviour by saying he couldn't see how I'd done anything wrong. When I explained how I'd let her down that afternoon, he just nodded.

'Listen, Brian, you've taught me a lot in recent weeks, but I haven't got the guts or the bottle, or whatever language you people use, to let you stay now.' He said the other guests were beside themselves with fear at the violence they'd just witnessed. 'Perhaps this is just the way you live; I hope you understand my position.'

I asked him to explain to the others that Pat and I meant no-one any harm; it was just the way we were.

He said, 'I take it you've got some drink, Brian.'

'No. Actually, I don't even remember coming back here.'

'OK, I'll take your gear to the office. Come down in a minute when you've sorted yourself out and I'll make sure we've got something to drink.' I sat on the bed and thought, what the hell is it about me? I get a room in a totally non-drinking establishment, and within weeks I can sit down with the boss, the governor, the bloke in charge, have a drink with him, and before you know it I'm thrown out. Where am I going wrong?

I went down to the office and, in true regimental style, everything was packed immaculately. The Major passed me a glass of scotch. I think that to him, this was some sort of joke, and I suppose to someone else it might have seemed amusing. In another mood, so might I. But what if Pat wouldn't let me back in? I now had a serious accommodation problem. There's no way I fancied sleeping in the park.

He then said something I would never have expected. Did I have any money? I'd got about £9, and in reply to his enquiry said I had no idea how long it would last. He handed me a £10 note. I was really embarrassed, but the street had taught me to take it.

He seemed to feel uncomfortable when I told him how much respect I had for him. I told him I understood why he felt he had to drink in secret. I didn't necessarily think it was a good thing, but if it suited him then that was OK by me. I'd never forget him, and I thanked him for allowing me to indulge my addiction in his house. We were both getting emotional by now, and sensed it was time to part company. We shook hands and I left.

The grapevine informs me that Mr Jacks is still alive, although widowed. He's gone on to be a warden in an old folks' home and loves it. He also likes to take a drink every day at his local pub. No secrecy! I think of him still, and hope he occasionally thinks of me. Although it was him that made me feel like I needed to hide in a lair, it was also him who made me realise I needed my wife.

Goodbye, Major.

24

Two Suicides

The most violent man I have ever met was Brighton Barry, as he was known (nobody knew his real name). I've always been a bench drinker, though during the latter years of my drinking life I became a more solitary drinker – one or two fellow drinkers was all the company I needed – but in middle to late '80s, I always sought out schools of drinkers; for some reason I felt safer in their company. In those days there were no "no drinking zones".

I'd been in Barry's company on many occasions, although neither of us spoke much to each other. I suppose I was frightened of him, and I was to realise later that I had every reason to be; even big Andy Anderson was wary of him. There was another chap on the scene at about this time, who was called the poison dwarf; I always thought this was rather unkind, for he was very physically disabled, but as I've said ad-nauseam, alcoholism isn't discriminatory. In order for him to walk, this is what he had to do: he would have to put his good leg forward first, and then quite literally with his hand drag his bad leg level with his good leg, then he would have to put his good leg forward again and drag his bad leg level with his good leg; and bear in mind he had to do this wherever he had to walk. This, then, was the poison dwarf.

As incredible as this may sound, the dwarf had two rottweilers. He had them for one reason and one reason only, because with his disability, people were always taking the piss. Before he had the dogs, some people would just simply mug him, but the dogs made them think twice, although the spectacle of the dwarf who had to drag his own leg trying to control these two rottweilers was sad beyond words. I always had a soft spot for him myself, but he was a bench drinker and needed his drink just as much as any of the rest of us alkies.

I'm not sure of the day, and I'm not even certain I've got the year right, but this is what happened: like so many other times in my life, I wish I could say I only remember this vaguely, but I don't; I remember it vividly, and how I wish I didn't.

There was just Brighton Barry and I sitting in the shelter opposite the offy. We each had just one can left, and no money. We were right on the seafront, so we were able to see the whole length of the promenade. We spotted the dwarf walking in our direction with his dogs. Barry was very drunk and, although the dwarf was severely disabled, I was a bit concerned whether Barry might just mug him, dogs or no dogs. I knew Barry had drunk a minimum of a half-bottle of whisky, because I was already sitting on the bench when he arrived. I realised now I should have just left. I was there when he opened it, and now it was gone. He was down to his last can of Special Brew, and he knew I had no money.

As the dwarf got within hearing distance, Barry jumped to his feet and said, 'go and get me a four-pack of Brew.' I felt so sorry for the dwarf, who, like everybody else in this town, was only too aware of how extremely violent this Brighton Barry could be, and there didn't always have to be a reason. The dwarf said feebly, 'Look man. I've only a fiver to my name.' 'Fucking get me some Brew,' was Barry's answer. The dwarf was beaten, and he knew it; he went to pass me the leashes for the dogs to hold while he went over the offy. I didn't want to know, and told him I was just about to leave anyway. Barry said, 'Give me those fucking leads here. I'll hold them.' The dwarf meekly handed the leads over to Barry, and crossed the road to the offy but, just before he entered the offy, Barry jumped up again and shouted out, '– and get me a fucking burger as well.' There was a burger bar right next to the offy.

Five minutes later, the dwarf came back with a four-pack of Brew. Barry, without so much as a thank you, said, 'And where's the fucking burger?' The dwarf said he hadn't got enough money, but Barry again said, 'Get me a fucking burger.' The dwarf went off for the second time, and I don't know how he did it but he came back with a burger. Barry gave me a can, the dwarf a can, and kept two for himself.

The dwarf and I sat there in silence. My heart went out to him, for not only did he have to endure the stares from almost all the general public at his obvious physical disability, he had just been humiliated, demeaned and made to look a fool. Whereas two minutes ago he at least had £5, now, after his encounter with Brighton Barry, all he had was a can of Brew, and he'd almost certainly had to beg an extra 20 or 30 pence to make the money up to buy the burger.

Barry took the burger out of the bag and took a bite. Now it was obvious that both the dwarf's dogs were underweight – one was actually emaciated – because the dwarf couldn't even feed himself properly, let alone two fully grown rottweilers. It was the emaciated one that sat closest to Barry, and as Barry took his first bite, it was too much for the under-fed beast, who began to salivate. Suddenly he made a lunge at Barry's burger, ripped it out of his hand and devoured it in one swallow. For a split

168

second, Barry sat there mortified, and then in less than a split second he became incensed – enraged wouldn't even be close to describing Barry at that particular moment. He was demented – murderous is what he was.

He leapt to his feet, and punched the dog full in the face. Brighton Barry was a very physically powerful man, and for a few seconds the dog was slightly stunned. Barry's hand was bleeding badly, and the dog was now in his element; it was going to kill this man. The dog lunged again at Barry, who was now trying desperately to kick it, kick it to death. The dwarf, in the meantime, and I don't blame him, grabbed the other dog and ran, hobbled, staggered, crawled, as fast as his dysfunctional leg would allow.

Barry by now was bleeding so much you couldn't actually see where the blood was coming from. As it happens, the shelter where we were sitting was one of four along that stretch of promenade, and one by one the council were doing some minor repairs. Whilst they weren't actually working on the one where we were sitting, they had left a bucket of tools at the back of it, and in this bucket was a jemmy.

By now, the rottweiler was tearing Barry to bits. An audience had gathered, not believing what they were witnessing. Barry knew his only chance of survival was to kill the dog outright with the jemmy, or the dog would surely kill him. Its killer instinct was now unstoppable so, although Barry could hardly see for the blood covering his face, he managed to get the jemmy, and with some sort of superhuman strength battered the dog senseless. The dog lay on the concrete promenade, making just the odd slight convulsive movement.

The police arrived, accompanied by a veterinary surgeon. Brighton Barry was arrested, and the dog was taken to the vets. We were later to learn that, within an hour of the vet taking it away, the dog was put to sleep forever by injection.

As the crowd grew, I had slipped round behind the shelter and joined the back of the audience. There's no way I was going to be a part of this, and when the duty doctor was called to the nick to tend Barry, he soon realised he needed to go to hospital. Although rumour had it that he had to have a hundred stitches, in fact he had 27, and we know this because at the time he was sleeping with 'Anne the can'.

Brighton Barry was bailed several hours later for, as he explained to the police, it was a totally unprovoked attack by the dog, whose handler was singularly ill-equipped to cope with such a vicious uncontrollable dog. He then went on to explain how he loved animals, and that he didn't think he would ever get over it. Barry's next job was to go and find the dwarf, and instil enough fear into him to prevent him saying anything different. Up until this point, the police had no idea who the owner was, so time was on Barry's side. It didn't take long for the whole of the drinking fraternity to find out exactly what happened that day and, whilst he was never a popular bloke, he was now despised.

I do believe that if the dwarf hadn't been involved with heavy class A drugs as well as alcohol, he might have got more support. You see, druggies are not all that keen on alkies, and alkies are not all that keen on druggies; we simply don't understand each other. Nobody saw much of the dwarf after that little episode, but I'm very pleased to say that from then on, wherever a little drinking congregation sprang up, and they did all over town at different venues, purely by chance, depending on whose giro day it was, if Brighton Barry appeared we would all make our excuses and disperse. Even the weaker ones of us found strength in the fact that we were all of the same opinion.

Brighton Barry soon became conspicuous by his absence. He had somehow got into a dry house just outside Hastings. Neither Ronny nor I had heard of this place, which was unusual seeing as we had both over the years been in and out of them almost all our lives. Apparently it had a fairly strict regime, and Barry was on what they called a one-to-one – that is, he had two key workers whose job it was to follow him wherever he went, be it the toilet, the bathroom, the smoking room, the library – wherever he went. When he went to bed, they would have to sit outside all night. As I say, there were two of them so they arranged their shifts accordingly, and, if needed, there were two agency nurses available. What they didn't know was that Barry was going to kill himself. You see he wasn't on a one-to-one because he was a suicide risk, he was on a one-to-one because he was violent and may possibly, given the right or wrong situation, inflict injury on others. Obviously nowadays he would be put in a secure unit with locks.

What he was doing, in fact, was stockpiling his medication; this was quite an easy thing to do. I'd done it over 20 years ago when I was scared. You simply put your pills under your tongue, swallowed the water, and that was that. As soon as you got out of the medication room, even with a nurse behind you, it was still polite to put your hand over your mouth when you coughed. The pills went in your hand and your hand went in your pocket; job done.

I know from experience that Barry would have been on some really heavy medication. It would probably have even included Largactil. In prison, it's called the liquid cosh. Now none of us knew exactly how long

170

he'd been in there. We didn't even know how he got a place, but what we did know was that Big Andy Anderson was already in there. Andy was six feet four inches, and psychotic to boot, so you can understand why Barry took to him like a fish to water.

I'm five feet six, and Brighton Barry was shorter than me, so he was about five-five, but even so, despite Big Andy Anderson's psychosis, his massive size and obvious strength, Brighton Barry was still able to instil fear into him. It was because of this fear that Andy agreed to organise for a litre of whisky to be brought in.

From day one, Barry had point blank refused to sign any welfare or social security forms. He was getting a giro every week, and was on top whack; he didn't want this stopped, so every week without fail one of his flunkies would cash it for him and bring him the money. I've tried and tried, but I just can't put myself in the mind of this man; the only thing I could fully understand about him was his total addiction to alcohol. He was consciously stock-piling drugs, had ordered a litre of whisky and was going to kill himself, and yet he wouldn't sign any forms at the dry house. And he would have killed the flunky had he for some reason not brought his giro over! Since his arrival, Barry had shown no signs of aggression or violence, so the rules on him were relaxed; he was now allowed to walk the grounds of the dry house unescorted, with the proviso that he didn't leave the grounds.

The whisky had been dropped off along with his cache of money just outside the main gates. If Andy is to be believed, Barry had accumulated £400. Barry had decided that he had enough drugs, coupled with the whisky, to be able to kill himself, and today was the day. Barry had been there long enough to establish some sort of routine, and part of this routine was to take a stroll after tea at about seven o'clock.

Barry sought Andy in the smoking room, and asked him if he would like to take a stroll with him. Andy was shitting himself because he knew tonight was the night. Andy had been diagnosed as a psycho, and he would have no control over Barry's death. This didn't suit him because a psycho needs to be in charge. They walked around the gardens for a couple of minutes, and then, when they thought it was safe, they went through the main gates.

Andy sat sideways on the kerb so that he could see the house and the road at the same time. Barry went to the designated site for his whisky and his money, and came back; they both sat in silence. It was an awkward silence because I don't think either of them had ever attended a social event before, and after all this was a social event. There was no attempt from Andy to talk Barry out of it, and I rather fancy at this point that Andy was thinking more about the £400 in Barry's pocket.

Barry talked loosely about his wretched life: he was actually a Londoner, but had lived in Brighton for so long that everyone called him Brighton Barry. He had moved to Hastings about three years ago, because some people in Brighton were going to kill him. He'd been a rent boy from the age of about 13, and had been subjected to unmentionable abuse. I was later to learn from Andy that Barry actually cried. I was to talk with Andy only twice after Barry's death because Andy himself committed suicide later that same year.

According to Andy, Barry had something like five week's supply of his medication. Now I've been in and out of detox units for 20-odd years, and I'm telling you that if I were to take one week's supply of my medication in one go, without any booze, it would have killed me. My point is, this man wanted to go. Andy went to say something, and Barry told him to be quiet. He said he was going to take all those pills, drink all the whisky in one go, and then jump in front of a lorry or a car or something, because if they found him they would probably try to give him a stomach pump. He added, 'Andy, if you grass me up, I will kill you. You can have the £400.' He then went on to say that the lorry or car driver would be upset only for a short while, because when he learnt about the way he'd lived, he wouldn't be that sorry.

All Barry's drugs were in an envelope. He took them out, a handful at a time, and swallowed them with the help of a bottle of methadone that had also been smuggled in with the whisky. He then drank the whisky and, according to Andy, it took no more then 15 minutes. Barry got to his feet and leant against the gatepost. Several vehicles passed, but they were too fast for Barry, so he asked Andy to get him nearer to the kerb, which Andy did. Barry saw a lorry, not going too fast, but just fast enough to kill him if he timed it right. He did; the lorry was so close to Barry that he would have no chance of stopping even if he was given prior notice that someone was going to jump out in front of him. Barry lurched in front of the lorry and was killed outright.

Andy left the next day. He simply packed his bags and walked out; after all he was only an informal resident. He had never been so rich; he even got a taxi from the dry house to Hastings. There were just a few lines in the local paper about Barry's death. I think there was some sort of inquiry, although nobody was interested, myself included; nobody knew when the funeral took place, and nobody cared. Andy made his way straight to Bottle Alley, and treated everyone to a drink.

172

Nobody at this point knew about Barry's death but they soon realised that for whatever reason, Andy had some money. Most of the drinkers at this particular gathering were living in a squat in the square, and naturally Andy, with his newfound wealth, was most welcome. They had no idea where he got the money from, and they wouldn't have given a damn anyway. They were mostly druggies, and as Barry was an alkie, they probably wouldn't have known him anyway, at least by name.

They invited Andy back to the squat, and naturally Andy accepted. They knew he was a fool, but they were also aware that they had to be careful how they treated him; one false move, or one wrong word, and he would have, and could have, killed any of them, but their need for money, because of their dependency on drugs, gave them some sort of false brave recklessness.

At this point, they didn't know exactly how much money he had, but they'd seen him pull out several £20 notes. Whatever happened, they knew that for at least the next couple of days, if they treated him right and said the right things, they could eat and, more importantly, have almost as many drugs as they wanted.

When the local paper came out on the Friday, there was a piece in there about Brighton Barry, and they named the dry house he was in. Andy at this point had been in the squat about four or five days and of course, during this time, had told them about Barry. They suddenly all wanted to know what part Andy had played in Barry's suicide. Andy, like Barry, had never really been liked, and now he was some sort of celebrity, so of course he exaggerated every little detail, making himself out to have been some sort of hero. He never mentioned the £400, and he also forgot to mention that, as big as he was, he, like everyone else, was scared witless of Barry.

I cannot believe that Barry's death had anything to do with Andy's death but as you read on, it is certainly a question that's worth thinking about. Don't forget that Andy was a psychopath, and psychopaths are not renowned for their sensitivity towards other people's misfortunes, but having said that, Andy's suicide was so close to Barry's, I have to wonder whether it did actually affect him.

The staple diet of Andy's squat mates was crack cocaine and heroin; naturally everyone smoked dope, but that was neither here nor there. I'm beginning to think I'm the only bloke who doesn't smoke it. Andy very quickly developed a heroin addiction; I say very quickly, because his squat mates knew he could get on prescription methadone. All he had to say was that he was addicted, and that would mean one extra bottle in the squat each week. These people were vile; I don't care about being politically correct, but I know what's right and what's wrong.

Now, Andy wasn't the sharpest knife in the box, but he was a psycho so you had to be careful how you approached him. His squat mates had set up a deal to buy a load of drugs and because of Andy's size and reputation, he was nominated to actually make the transaction; their rationale was that nobody would dare rip him off. Apart from prisons, care homes, dry houses, re-hab centres, and institutions of all types, he had suddenly found himself a social life, with his new found squat mates, so he readily agreed.

I'd been in Andy's company just a couple of times since Barry's death and, drunk or sober, I could never fathom his mood, so I've no idea why he did what he did this particular day. He made the transaction with no problems, and went back to the squat. Not only did he get their drugs, he also picked up his methadone. Now, nobody knows whether he bought extra drugs, or whether he stole some of theirs, but the fact is he had a pocket full of drugs, and he also had with him a full bottle of vodka.

For some reason, Andy had made a decision to kill himself that night. I got this information from a very unreliable source, whose name is C—. She's a crack head and a heroin addict who is so bad she's run out of places to inject the stuff. When I first met this girl, she was so gorgeous I slept with her a couple of times. The drugs took over and C— didn't exist any more; she was not the C— that I had known, but despite the drugs she always had a soft spot for me.

She told me what Andy said while they were sitting on the sofa. He suddenly said to her, 'tonight I'm going to die'. She told me that she asked him if it had anything to do with Barry's death, and his reply was, 'fuck Barry, it's got fuck all to do with him or anyone else.'

C— was the only person I knew who was in that squat when Andy died. I knew the others by sight but didn't actually know their names, but I do know there were six people in there at the time. The conditions and squalor were such that you needed protective clothing to just walk in there. Apparently Andy refused any heroin, and didn't want any crack either. He just lay on the sofa in a world of his own, oblivious to the people around him who were also in a world of their own.

He slowly but surely took his pills over a period of about two hours. What they were, nobody will ever know; even the coroner couldn't pinpoint the exact drug that killed him. He put it down to a cocktail of drink and drugs. One litre of 36% vodka, drunk on its own in less than two hours, would render most people at the very least hospitalised. Andy

174

had downed this, plus the methadone, plus a colossal amount of unknown pills. He wasn't bluffing; he wanted to be dead.

The events that took place immediately after his death were sickening, and almost beyond belief; C— told me that when Andy didn't respond when spoken to, they at first didn't take too much notice. Andy wasn't a particularly intelligent man and also, being psychotic, would sometimes go for long periods of not speaking at all, but after a while one of these pieces of lowlife decided he fancied some of Andy's vodka.

He tried to rouse Andy to ask him if it was all right to have a swig of his vodka, and then realised that not only was Andy's bottle empty, but there was no response at all. He called the others over, and they noticed that Andy's lips were blue. One of the less stoned of them came over to have a look and noticed immediately that he also wasn't breathing; they tried for a pulse and couldn't find one. 'He's fucking dead,' said C—.'

They now panicked, didn't know what to do. The whole flat was littered with drug paraphernalia; nearly everything in the squat was stolen, half of them already had warrants out for their arrests for various misdemeanours, all drug related, so they couldn't just leave him there. We were later to learn from our local paper that he lay there for four hours before they contacted the police.

C— was the sharpest; she relieved him of what money he had left, searched him for any remaining drugs, got rid of anything incriminating and then they all sat down to try to chill out before calling the police. How they could sit there for four hours with a dead man is beyond me; perhaps C— from Eastbourne could do it, but I couldn't. Big Andy had an illness; he was psychotic. Some people have cancer, some people are born with epilepsy; Andy just happened to have psychosis. He obviously wasn't born with it. I know this will cause arguments, but it's more than likely it was caused by environmental association, that is to say, he was abused beyond the limit by everyone who was supposed to have loved him, and having been pushed over that limit, even if he wanted to, he wasn't mentally equipped to get back into society; he was made a psycho.

The people in the squat gathered what belongings they had and fled, including C—. The phone call was made, and the police and the ambulance were on their way. There were only two good things to come out of this little episode: one was we never ever saw the druggies again, and secondly, having got as much information as I could from C—, I never ever spoke to her again. I understand she's still around, and still on heroin (big time). I hope it kills her.

25

Fitting

I've suffered from alcohol-induced fits (seizures) for more than 18 years. It's odd that I don't actually remember the first time it happened to me, because they're so damned frightening. But I'll try to recall and describe the first time I think I had a fit and how I gradually came to realise that I'd probably been experiencing minor fits for something like 25 years prior to this one. I just hadn't realised what was happening to me at the time.

This particularly nasty seizure happened around the mid-80s. I was working for Colin, just about the only person who had the courage and decency to employ me. The bulk of his work consisted of council contracts, but for the past year he'd been doing quite a bit of "association" work for a company based in East Grinstead. It was clean work and the money was good, the cheques regular and consistent. But until this point, Colin hadn't actually met the gaffer, Mr Bolton, so a trip to East Grinstead to put a face to the signature on the cheques seemed timely.

I was asked along for the ride. Bearing in mind that I managed never to combine drink and work, Colin had no reason to be cautious, and in those days I still knew what respect was and I had a lot of respect for Colin. I could do with the day out and Colin was glad of the company. Besides I'd still be paid and as far as the Gaffer was concerned I was Colin's right hand man, apprentice served, painter extraordinaire etc. In other words, he was relying on me to make a good impression.

The office building was impressive, and we were greeted by the attractive friendly smile of the receptionist. I felt chuffed when Colin stated our business using the word "we" instead of just introducing himself. It made me feel as though I amounted to something.

We sat in silence waiting for Mr Bolton, each knowing the other was surveying the crumpet. However, before any decent fantasy could be conjured up for later use, the gaffer appeared. We shook hands and he invited us into his office.

Next thing, I'm laying on the floor staring at a pair of paramedic's boots. I can hear my name being called gently, and at what seems a distance. *Brian, Brian, Brian, can you hear me?* I feel soothed. Then I hear a female voice. *Brian, you've had a fit, are you hurt anywhere?*

I don't know if you've ever woken in the middle of the night with a cramp that's so painful you can hardly bear it. Well that was how my entire body felt right then as I lay with my eyes fixed on this massive pair of boots. 'Yes, you beautiful girl, whoever you are, I hurt everywhere.' I had blood in my mouth and down the front of my shirt. I'd bitten my tongue. I was entwined in computer wires, telephone wires, typewriter wires. I'd even lost a shoe. But as I lay there, inextricably bound by my writhing and thrashing about, these gentle people freed my body piece by piece, and somehow got me on to a stretcher and off to hospital.

Most of the association work we'd been doing for this company consisted of paper-hanging which was my forte. Up until this meeting, Colin had heaped praise upon my work, so it doesn't take too much imagination to work out the depth of my embarrassment when I finally came round. Seconds after our very first meeting with our contractor, this number one paper-hanger was writhing around on his office floor in the full throes of an alcoholic seizure, if he had but known it. Colin simply explained that I was an epileptic, had been for years but had only had a fit every six or seven years and was normally able to keep things under control.

A couple of days later I received a card from all the girls in the office. I was so moved by the kindness and the lovely things they'd written, and I even got my shoe back. Several hours later, when I came to in a hospital bed, I took a while to work out what had happened. A nurse sat near the bed doing some paperwork, and I asked her where my mate was. She replied that he'd left a message that he'd be back at four o'clock to pick me up. Apparently he'd been told that I'd be OK by then. Well I didn't know what time it was then, but I did know I wanted a drink.

Up until then I'd been doing pretty well working for Colin. It had only been a matter of weeks, but I'd been fairly reliable and turned up for work as regular as clockwork. But I was crushed to have to face that I'd blown it now. I managed to get off the bed, but my muscles were so taut that I could barely walk. I told the nurse that I needed some fresh air, so she gave me a couple of crutches and told me not to go too far. I asked if there was anywhere I could get hold of some cigarettes, and she said there was a Londis just around the corner. That's exactly what I needed to hear.

I told her to tell Colin I'd be sitting outside having a fag. But I wanted a drink, and that's what I intended to have. When she'd told me the shop was just outside, I thought she meant next door. I could see the sign swinging in the wind, but it was so far away that I could only just make it out. I knew there was no way I could reach it, not with what I'd just been through. But all I wanted was a couple of cans of Special Brew. I did have a smoke on me though, so that was something to console me. I spotted a bus shelter just opposite, and after about five minutes a couple of lads sat themselves down and lo and behold, they opened a bottle of cider. Well. I thought if I could just get to that shelter, I could send them on a mercy mission to buy my cans for me. I had about 20 quid on me and was prepared for the deed to cost me: what the hell. I'd have my cans.

I tottered lamely over and plonked myself down next to them. 'Can you spare us a fag mate?' was the greeting. This meant I was in luck. They were obviously skint, and I immediately took advantage of the situation. I passed round my fags and asked if they'd mind shooting up to the offy for me. 'Get me a four-pack of Special Brew and I'll treat you to a bottle of cider.' Just to cover myself, I asked them to be careful how they delivered the goods because one of the security guys at the hospital was my brother and he would be watching me like a hawk. I alerted them to the likelihood that they too were under surveillance, which seemed to secure their loyalty.

Within minutes, one of my new young friends returned with my four cans and a bottle of cider as a reward for services to a desperate man. My ploy of the fictional security guard ensured they hadn't done a runner, because in my embattled condition I could have done nothing about it.

I sat and chatted with them for about an hour. I hadn't a clue where Colin had got to, but for that time I just didn't care. I'd drunk two cans and, apart for a slight ache, my muscles had limbered up considerably. My drinking pals left and I decided to make my way back to the hospital entrance so that Colin would be able to spot me on his return. If I wasn't there when he arrived, he would naturally assume that Brian had gone off on one of his benders again, and leave.

I don't know what time it was when he arrived, but I was drunk. What absolutely slaughters me is that for the past few days I'd been in control. I would drink a few cans every night when we finished work, and be able to maintain a routine. Colin had given me that routine. I'd had a fit, and the constraints of that routine were broken. I was lost again. As I write this, I fully appreciate that these don't read like the words of a fully-grown man. They sound pathetic. But being in control of my drinking was a joke, and I'll always be fully aware of how much I've constantly kidded myself and clutched desperately at those in that other, "sober", world who have at times thrown me a line and shored up my fantasy of being able to live in their world.

Colin heaved me bodily into the van, and we drove home pretty much in silence. There really wasn't much to talk about. I was so drunk again, and didn't want to be. What a contrast to first thing this morning. We'd been so full of we'll get this contract or that contract, and there we were, eight or nine hours later, and Brian's reverted to type. Same old story.

Do you know, I'd reached a stage, a kind of paranoia of uncertain origins, where I was convinced that there was a conspiracy against me but I also knew I was the only conspirator in my life. The only time I'm safe from having a fit is when I've got a certain amount of alcohol inside my body. The danger point is when my blood alcohol level drops to such a level that the withdrawal syndrome begins, and a seizure becomes likely.

My question is: Am I the cause of this? Am I doing this on purpose? As I write now. I'm safe in the knowledge that there are at least two litres of chemical cider left in my room. I'm hungry, my stomach is swollen, and I have severe heartburn, but in spite of that, and against my better reasoning, I will drink as much cider as I can until I can no longer stand the pain, then I shall go to bed. Every time I wake up, I shall be in just as much pain, but the cycle will start again. And I don't know why.

I've written about the fit at Mr Bolton's office because it was so embarrassing. There have been so many others, and memories of them are naturally hazy, but this one left me reeling with the social impact it had had. People look at us alkies and only see the mess; the state we're in. But trust me, we know the shame of it. We squirm in our filth and smell.

One other fit also had a profound impact on me, and was so terrifying that I have nightmares about it to this day. I was living in a basement flat at the time. I remember going through the front door into my living room. I was alone, I was dirty. I don't know where I'd just come from. I had no idea of the time or the day, nor did I care. But I clearly remembered where I lived and, by some miracle of navigation, I'd got there.

1 honestly believed that this was the day I'd die. I didn't care. This wasn't bravery; drinking held more power than the desire to live. I lay prostrate on the floor. I'd reached a stage in my drinking where I didn't even know if I had any of the stuff in the house. I didn't know if I had any money. I looked up at the ceiling I had artexed two years previously, and wondered why God had rendered me incapable of doing any sort of work now. Self-pity and denial meant that it didn't enter my head that it was the drink and not God that had brought me so low. I could see the lighting rose, and could reflect on how neatly I had cut around it without getting artex on it. What happened next is unbelievable, inexplicable and impossible.

I'm now lying in the foetal position. On the ceiling. My foot is inches from the ceiling rose but I can't move. Now we all know that I should have come crashing to the floor, but I was up there looking down on myself. I felt sad and ashamed at how dirty and old I looked. I could see myself so very clearly. I had a bottle of vodka in my hand, which had fallen onto one side and was seeping out onto the carpet. I remember thinking, *what a waste*. I could feel the sharp stipple of the ceiling where the back of my head lay, and while I lay there I was overwhelmed with a deep shame for what I had put my family through. How could I do this to them? Why was I so filthy? Why couldn't I get up? I just simply lay on the ceiling, helpless. I couldn't get down. I was defying the laws of gravity. I didn't take drugs, and never have. But my mind was blown.

I heard someone knock on my door. I heard voices and laughter coming from outside. I recognised the laugh as belonging to a drinking friend of mine, Helene. I heard the knocking again, and then, 'Brian, it's Helene. Are you in?' I managed to get to my feet and answer the door. Helene took one look at me and said, 'Fucking hell, Brian, who's been giving you drugs?' She knew that wasn't my scene, but I must have looked so awful. I told I hadn't touched anything, but just didn't feel right. Now no-one who knew Helene would call her an alarmist; she just wasn't into histrionics, but she thought it best to call a doctor. I just wanted her to sit with me for a while. I was certain I'd be all right soon.

As usual, Helene was drunk. Neither of us had known the other in any other state. But she was straight enough for me to be able to explain to her that I'd just been lying on the ceiling for a couple of hours, looking down on myself. She was completely unfazed, and diagnosed that I'd just had an "out of body experience". I'd never heard of such a thing, but the remedy she recommended was to knock the vodka on the head for a while or, she predicted, I'd end up dead.

She then noticed a wet patch on the carpet and asked me if I'd pissed myself. I explained that my vodka had leaked out while I was lying on the ceiling. She went to the kitchen and returned with a spatula and an open-ended tin tray. She then proceeded to try and scoop the vodka out of the carpet pile up into the tray, but this salvage operation proved unsuccessful. No matter, she'd brought her own drink with her, which in the spirit of an alkie's approach to first aid, we proceeded to share.

We drank until we both fell unconscious. Then, having slept for a couple of hours, we roused ourselves and did a stock-take; how much money, how much drink, what time was it, what time did the offy close etc. A couple of glasses of what cider was left, and Helene left to catch up

180

with her partner and domestic duties. It was an understanding between us that we were never to be more than drinking buddies.

I was still too frightened to go to bed, so I slept as best I could on the sofa. What the hell had happened to me? Even Harry Houdini couldn't lie on a ceiling without falling off, but I had.

One more seizure warrants some explaining. Luckily I remember very little about it, otherwise it would haunt me, too. I was still living in the basement flat and, by my standards, it was a fairly normal evening. I was no more drunk than usual. In fact, for some reason, I'd probably had less than I normally would have. Pat and I were sitting in the lounge watching telly, and the only indication that everything was not as it should be was that Pat asked me a couple of times if I felt OK. I told her I felt fine. She asked me what we'd been watching. I hadn't noticed. I knew it was a soap of some sort and I recognised some of the faces. But I couldn't remember what I'd seen. I began to feel detached. I couldn't connect the faces with the programme I was watching.

This is so difficult for me to explain. Once more I was having to try to feel normal by association. I looked at the clock. The time meant nothing to me. I asked Pat who the bad guy was in this particular episode. She looked at me and mouthed the words of her reply to me. Her mouth was moving but I couldn't hear the words.

I knew I didn't feel right in the head, and I was frightened. I got up and started to walk around the lounge. I walked along the hall; I walked into the bedroom. It seemed so small. I wandered into the bathroom. It was so cold. I was cold. I went back into the lounge and walked around with my hands in my pockets, completely oblivious to Pat.

I was completely alone in this weird state. I felt totally isolated. I believed I was losing my mind, and the most frightening thing was that I was aware of it. Again I tried to regain my sanity by association. I checked the washing up had been done. I made sure the rubbish was in the right place for the dustman to collect the following morning.

I made all these familiar moves to try and regain my normal consciousness. I knew that people take drugs to alter their state of consciousness, but I wanted mine intact. I needed to regain the damaged state of mind that was familiar to me. I know that sounds contradictory for an alcoholic. We too look to altering our moods and consciousness, but I was so familiar with where alcohol took me, and this was different. Alcohol had been my drug of choice for so long that the places it took me were by now the fabric of my mind.

Suddenly my bowels were moving. I had to get to the loo sharpish. Pat had turned the telly off and she just got up without me needing to ask and guided me towards the bathroom. Then I knew I was going to have a fit, and the seizure and bowel movement collided.

Pat ran and fetched an attractive young nurse who lived in the flat upstairs. When she arrived I was lying on the floor with my tracksuit bottoms around my ankles, and I was convulsing violently. She put me in the recovery position, and Pat called the ambulance.

Pat later told me that they had given me an injection immediately, and put an oxygen mask on my face before taking me to hospital. When you have a fit they usually keep you in until they're sure you're all right. Sometimes it's just a few hours, sometimes overnight. They kept me in for seven days. I had to be detoxed, and for that I was grateful.

Isn't vanity a funny thing? Do you know, after a few days, once I was compos mentis, and despite what I'd just been through, I had one major concern and one major regret. Had the nurse who tended me at home, and who I'd always fancied, seen me covered in my own mess? That was my concern. My regret was that she had apparently arrived in her nightie, and one of the paramedics later told me that it had been see through.

26

Dehydration and Near-Death

As I've said earlier in my book, I married my first wife, Pat, in April 1984. By August of the same year we decided to sell what meagre possessions we had, move out of my wife's two-bedroom flat in Hastings and move to Eastbourne. My rationale at the time was that I would leave all my old drinking cronies behind and start a new life with my new wife in Eastbourne. How bloody stupid and naive was that?!

Because of course, when you move you necessarily take yourself with you. I hope you realise the insanity of my actions at that particular time. Please understand that when I say we sold what meagre possessions we had, we only had meagre possessions because I had already sold anything and everything I could get my hands on to buy drink with.

I don't know what Pat's thoughts were at the time, but she was more than willing to come along with me. She was an extremely attractive woman, but she was also was extremely shy. It occurs to me now that at that age, I had the ability to attract people, not only females but males also. Looking back, I now realise that people in general did tend to gravitate towards me, and I suppose Pat's thinking at that particular time, was that despite my by-now obvious drinking problem, that this "Brian Harding" was going to make it somehow.

If that was Pat's theory, she was soon to be proved wrong. At least in Hastings I knew everybody who drank. I also knew everybody who was on the dry, just coming off the dry, or just about to go on the dry. I knew everybody who was having a residential detox, or had just come out from a residential detox; in short, I knew every hardcore drinker in Hastings. Here in Eastbourne, I was lost. Sure, I could find the hardcore drinkers, but I wasn't accepted. I had to resort to petty theft, cons, scams and hard-luck stories to get credit from off-licences.

We finally moved into some grotty B&B. There were two single beds in our room, and the central heating didn't work. For breakfast, we got one fried slice, one sausage, one bacon rasher, one egg, and a pot of tea for two. We got £7 between us for the week's pocket money, and for this the DSS paid the landlord £90 per week.

Earlier in this book, I said that a charge was brought against me, and that I was found guilty. The charge was making off without paying rent, and extracting electricity. Now I realise that what I did was wrong, but please try to understand that at the time, it did seem to be the only option.

It was while we were living at this B&B that Pat and I decided it might be a good idea for Pat to get the train over to Hastings to see if her mum might lend us some money. I was totally incapable of doing a day's work and, like Pat, was undernourished. I was despondent, angry, frustrated, depressed and, quite simply, felt like a second-class citizen.

The only reason Pat had a problem with going over there was that her mum was a paranoid schizophrenic. And so she was a bit apprehensive as to how she might react. We weighed up all the pros and cons, and decided it was worth a chance. We managed to put the fare together, and off Pat went. That was my mistake.

I knew there was a squat somewhere by Eastbourne station, and I also knew that there would always be about a dozen hardcore drinkers there. Now, the only entry fee to this squat would be that you had your own bottle and that you could stand up for yourself. I could do both. Now, I've been a street/bench drinker all my life, but I must admit I was a bit shocked. The weakest drink anyone had there was some sort of 9% chemical cider. Everybody else (and their ages ranged from about 12 to about 75) had vodka, whisky, rum, tequila.

We all know that in any community, sect, cult, gathering of any kind, under any conditions, there is by nature a pecking order. And this little gathering was no different. Here was a Glaswegian, nothing exceptional in stature. He was drinking a bottle of tequila and had another one in his pocket. I put him at about five foot ten, and about 70 years of age. His first words to me were, 'What the fuck you doing here, you cockney bastard? Have you no home to go to, or are you just here because you've heard that when Dixie's drinking tequila, he'll let you fuck his arse? Well, you're out of luck because last night I had a hysterectomy.' This made everyone roar with laughter.

It occurred to me that the young lad I noticed when I first came in might be Dixie's toy boy but, after sitting on the floor talking with Dixie and sharing his tequila and drinking my chemical cider, I realised there was no way that could ever be. You see, Dixie had no desire. He had no love for man, woman or beast. He had no conception of beauty. Even his laughter was maniacal.

For Dixie this was a normal conversation. And, while at first I thought it was bizarre, as the tequila and cider flowed it became more

184

normal. Dixie told me, quite matter of factly in his broad Glaswegian accent, that he'd only ever had two erections in his entire life. And on both occasions, he raped someone. They were both totally unrelated incidences. The first victim was a 62-year-old Salvation Army lady, and the other victim was a 19-year-old boy. He got eight and 12 years respectively.

As I sat there chatting to Dixie, people came and went. There were two girls in particular that I was interested in. They were the first two people I noticed when I arrived. They were laughing and joking and drinking whisky but, having by now spent a couple of hours there, I realised they were lesbians.

People were now beginning to fall in and out of drunken stupors, as I was myself. I thought of Pat, and wondered how she had got on with her mum. I'd worked out that I must have been there a couple of days, so I decided to leave and take with me a bottle of something. I knew I was at Eastbourne station because I could see the sign, but where the B&B was from there, I had absolutely no clue. My next recollection is very vague. I was half on and half off a paramedic's stretcher; I think they were trying to put an oxygen mask over my face and, as far as I know, I was trying to take it off. The insanity.

Somehow the police became involved. They gave me every opportunity but I was having none of it. They handcuffed me with my hands behind my back and took me to Eastbourne station. They took the cuffs off and threw me in a cell. I will not exaggerate in any way but, had there not been a toilet bowl in that cell, I would be dead today. There is absolutely no question of that at all; there is dehydration and there's dehydration.

It later transpired that I'd first entered Dixie's Den about midday Friday, and came out of there Tuesday morning. Despite drinking, for just on four days, vast amounts of excessively strong alcohol, not one morsel of food went into my mouth. Plus, I didn't drink any liquid that wasn't very high in alcohol content. I was now lying in a cell in Eastbourne, unconscious.

I don't know at what time I came round, but I was more frightened than I ever remember being. My breathing was so shallow, I thought this must be death, and my legs, feet and hands were numb. I think this was probably peripheral neural... something to do with the nervous system. I was so dehydrated that my tongue had fused with the top of my mouth, and because I hadn't eaten for so long, and also hadn't cleaned my teeth, the bacteria had built up on my tongue so much it had caused it to fur up, so when it came into contact with the roof of my mouth, they naturally fused together. This is so unbelievable, but let me assure you it's absolutely true. The only way I could separate them was to very gently put my little finger into the corner of my mouth, try to find a gap between my tongue and my palate, and prise my tongue from the roof of my mouth. But even after I'd done that, I just couldn't salivate at all. This was dehydration like I've never known before.

Now I told you there was a lavatory bowl in this cell, and it was putrid. The flusher for this toilet was on the wall away from the actual toilet. So what I had to do, if I didn't want to die, was flush the flusher and then get to the toilet bowl as quickly as I could to scoop up handfuls of water. I did this about six times, but then became just too weak to move. The jailer, hearing the flusher going every five minutes, opened the flap to see what was going on. He took one look at me and opened the door. He asked me if I'd been taking drugs, and I told him I hadn't. He told me not to move and came back with a beaker of water and two pillows. He propped me up on the pillows and fed me the water. He then called the custody sergeant. They had a conflab, and then told me they were taking me to the Eastbourne County Hospital. On the journey there, although they spoke in hushed tones, I got the general gist of the conversation. They considered themselves lucky I hadn't died in their cell.

I stayed in that hospital for two days and then went back to the grotty B&B. The following week, Pat and I kept the landlord's giro for £90, went back to Hastings and moved into another grotty B&B. This was the one mentioned earlier in this book, where there was just one paraffin heater for the whole house, and just two other residents. One was a prescription drug addict who was very violent, and the other one was to be sectioned under the '68 Health Act for continuously flashing at young girls.

Some game, this alcoholism – some game, this dehydration.

27

Another Memory Loss

This incident took place shortly after my first and last drink of methylated spirits. There was no direct link between my loss of memory and my one-off drink of methylated spirits, it was born out of a lifetime of alcohol abuse, and this is how it happened. Again I woke up in the spare room of the woman I was living with at the time. I looked at the clock; it was ten to seven. I still had my trousers and sweat top on. I panicked.

At this point I still managed to have a social life, and the pub I was using at the time was what we called a serious drinkers' pub. There was a hard core of serious drinkers that needed alcohol. Before, people came in and pretended to enjoy themselves, so the landlord would open his doors 20 minutes before the lawful and official opening time, especially for us alcoholics. You would be amazed at how many people needed and took advantage of this facility. I knew if I didn't look sharp, sensible and acceptable drinkers would already be in the pub, and if I couldn't get a drink in me I would feel inferior and intimidated.

On this occasion, I splashed some cold water on my face, picked up my money and tobacco, and walked down the hall. My girlfriend came out of the lounge. Before she could launch herself into a tirade of verbal abuse at me, I said, 'I'm going down the pub. I have my own money and it's my life; leave me alone.' She just smiled and told me to carry on. Whilst I didn't understand her response at the time, it wouldn't be long before I did.

I walked down to my pub. I worked out that I had woken up at ten to seven, so the time now would be just after seven. I peered through the semi-glazed translucent door. I saw the wall lights were on but there was nobody in the pub. I couldn't understand it. I was at this point already shaking and I was becoming agitated; I wanted a drink.

After about five minutes I began to feel conspicuous. I crossed over to the other side of the road and positioned myself in the doorway of a chemist. I could see directly into the public bar. I didn't have my watch on and could only guess the time, but had probably been there about five minutes. However, with my need for alcohol, it was an interminable time.

1 noticed a friend of mine walking towards me. As always Nigel, a meticulous man, had his newspapers tucked neatly under his arm. He was a keen chess player, and that's how we became friends. I always had the impression that he was wary of me, and that made me feel uncomfortable but I also think he had a sneaking respect for me. Nigel had had a good education and I hadn't but, more often than not I could beat him at chess. His religious and political beliefs were always beyond me, so apart from our mutual love of chess we had nothing in common.

I asked Nigel the time; he looked at his watch and told me it was exactly 14 minutes and 22 seconds past seven. I asked him if there was anything wrong with Jane and Ben as the pub wasn't open. He laughed, checked his watch again, took the newspapers from under his arm and told me it was 14 minutes and 50 seconds past seven on the morning of Monday, February 3rd, Greenwich mean time.

I was stunned. He could tell by my face I was in shock. Nigel never got anything wrong. When I had woken up in the spare room, to me it was ten to seven Sunday evening; it couldn't possibly be any other time, let alone another day. As Nigel was talking to me, I suddenly realised I was very frightened. I squatted down on my haunches. I couldn't get my head round the fact it was Monday morning and not Sunday evening.

Nigel could see I needed a drink. He asked me if I would like to walk down to his flat. He said he needed to talk to me, and thought it was a good time to do so. I nodded obsequiously and we walked down to his flat. Nigel poured me a large whisky, and made himself a cup of tea. He asked me if I had noticed a change in the attitude towards me in the company we both kept; I told him I hadn't.

He then went on to tell me that he had, and he asked me why I hadn't noticed that for the last three Sundays I hadn't been able to get a lift from our local pub down to the club that, on Sundays, had an extension of 30 minutes drinking time. I knew in the back of my mind what he was getting at, but I didn't want to admit it. He told me that as I entered a social group, so the people would dissolve away from me. He had been witness to this for some time; people didn't want to know me.

He also told me that the last time he had seen me was in the local park with a bottle of vodka, I was so drunk that it was pointless talking to me. That was Saturday morning two days ago, and here I was on Monday morning totally convinced it was Sunday evening. I was in a mess. Nigel told me that when I first went in his local pub, everyone, including himself, liked me, but as the months went by they realised this drinking business was turning me into something that none of them liked.

188

Alcohol is a thief: it steals your brain; it steals your tongue; it takes your morals away; you become unprincipled; you lose your self respect; you have no dignity; it turns your friends away from you; your attitude becomes irrationally distorted; you are unable to respond in a time-honoured acceptable proper manner, and you cannot be intimate with anybody other than a drunk. It lays your innermost secrets bare for all to see, and you become a fool, somebody to be laughed at, somebody not to be trusted. You don't know or understand what inhibition means; you have no concept of this at all; you're transparent, with no secrets to conceal; you don't know what a secret is because it would be pointless for anyone to confide in you; you become empty; you become lonely; you know something is missing but you don't know what it is; you reach a point where you have no concept of what a friend is; to you at this point a friend is somebody with a bottle who will listen to the same bollocks that he or she is talking about themselves. That's alcoholism.

Nigel and I talked for about an hour; it did him good and, I was later to realise, it had also done me good. He offered to walk me home. I was beaten, and accepted. I knew my girlfriend started work at 9am, and it was now 20 to. I needed her; I was desperate; I had just mislaid 12 hours of my life. I had just been counselled by a man much younger than myself, and once again I felt liked a whipped cur.

Nigel rang the doorbell, and my girlfriend answered. She liked Nigel. Nigel was a gentleman, and Nigel didn't get drunk. I walked straight through to the lounge; Nigel and my girlfriend stayed in the hallway talking. My girlfriend came into the lounge and told me to get into her bed; she tucked me in, told me she would be back at lunchtime, and that she would make me some broth.

I was again back in my wilderness of pain; I was still a conspirator; nobody was forcing me to drink alcohol, but I felt powerless to stop. I fell into some sort of catatonic state, dreaming of clowns with black circles round their eyes, and they weren't smiling.

28

The Probation Officer

I was on probation, for what I've no idea, and was assigned to a Mr Tiller (not his real name). I was dossing at the corner café because I'd been thrown out of this girl's house for some misdemeanour, probably drunkenness. I received a letter from Mr Tiller, asking me to attend the police station at a certain time on a certain date. I was due in court about three weeks after receiving this letter, and it was his job to write a report about me. He knew nothing about me, as I knew nothing about him.

I attended the police station on time and took my place in the queue; my name was called and I went through to where I saw a door marked Mr Tiller. I knocked and walked in; that was my mistake. I should have waited until he said come in; never mind. Then I sat down before he asked me to take a chair. Neither of us had ever met before, but we took an instant dislike to each other. He asked me about the quarrel I'd had with my former girlfriend, and I told him it was none of his business and if all he wanted was smutty talk, then he should buy a girly mag. He said he needed the details for the court report, and I said, 'no you don't, you just tell them I'm an alcoholic. I was pissed, I regret it, and that I'm sorry.' The truth is I have not a clue what it was about, but you can bet your life it was my fault.

He could see I'd done this a hundred times before and just couldn't be intimidated. He asked me about my education. I told him secondary modern, plus four years at the West Kent technical college. I was on what they called in those days, day release, plus I had to attend two nights a week. It was all part of my apprenticeship as a painter and decorator.

He suddenly threw his pen down and said, 'You've never done an apprenticeship, have you? Where's your indentures?' I told him my mother had them. You see, as I'd never settled down properly my mother kept all the things that we thought I might need in the future, or at the least might like to have a look at in the future.

I asked him if he thought I was lying, and if so why? He said, 'look, I know you feel you haven't achieved much in life, but if you've served an apprenticeship then surely you must have some paperwork to back this up.' I told him again that my mother had them. He said, 'Yeah sure, according to the reports I have here of you, you've done a number of painting jobs. Well, how did you get them?' I told him I would go on a site, tell them I was a painter and at the end of the day they would know I wasn't talking bollocks. They could see by my work. I had to say to him that if they all had his attitude I would be out of work. I knew he was furious with me, and I didn't know why. He knew that he was just a "jobsworth", and more painfully for him, he knew that I was aware of this, so he then went on to remind me that I wasn't to go anywhere near my latest girlfriend's house – as if I wanted to – and that any correspondence that was addressed to me would be forwarded to his office, and that I would be duly notified and was free to pick it up any time between nine and five. He asked if I understood. I said, 'No, could you repeat that all again?' No response.

I left his office and went to the main desk, and asked if I could speak with the manager. Two minutes later, the manageress came down and I told her I had just spoken to Mr Tiller, and that there was no way I wanted that man to write a report about me. I said that while I accepted I was on probation, I wanted my probationer changed. This conversation was taking place in the foyer. You must know, reader, that if I had chosen not to have a report made available to the courts by my probationer, it would have been construed as negative behaviour and an unwillingness to comply with my probationer's requests designed to keep me out of trouble.

These people have got a way with words, haven't they? The manageress said that if I was being unreasonable with Mr Tiller, then a change of probation officer would be better all round. It was while we were having this conversation that Mr Tiller came through, and I asked him point blank, with the manageress as witness, 'Do you think I'm a liar, and do you think that I actually didn't serve an apprenticeship?' Mr Tiller didn't answer my question. He just bade the manageress goodnight, and left.

I was furious. I rang my mum and asked her to send down my indentures. A letter arrived about three days later asking me to go to the probation service to pick up some mail. Now, since my meeting with Mr Tiller and the manageress. I'd been drunk pretty much 24/7, so I was in a hell of a state. Anyway, I managed to get myself up there; the manageress recognised me and said Mr Tiller had some mail for me. At that point he was still my probation officer. I walked along to his office, didn't knock, on purpose, and just walked straight in. He handed me some letters, one of which was a big manila envelope. He tried to tell me that it was always polite to knock before entering. I told him I couldn't act and that I had no respect for him. There was a letter from my ex-girlfriend which I just tore up, some bumph about poll tax, and there was this big manila envelope. My brain was addled, but I did recognise my mum's handwriting.

I emptied the contents on to Mr Tiller's desk, and there before us were my indentures in pristine condition, just as my mum had kept them.

It was rock solid proof that I had indeed served an apprenticeship. I also had two City and Guilds certificates, cert A part one and cert A part two. While all this was going on, Mr Tiller said nothing at all. I said to Mr Tiller, 'Do you remember saying to me, "You haven't done an apprenticeship, have you?" Do you remember saying that?' He said, 'I misunderstood you.' I put it to him that you can't misunderstand *I HAVE SERVED AN APPRENTICESHIP.*

He didn't know what to say; he had openly called me a liar, and just couldn't admit it. The manageress told me that she would have to make a report of what went on at this particular meeting, and that she didn't think I was doing myself any favours by acting this way. I repeated to her that he had called me a liar. I had proved him wrong and he wasn't man enough to admit it. Her response was to remind me about my court hearing and that there would be another probation officer to take care of things on the day. I was furious that I was not worthy of a simple apology.

About a week later I received a letter from the probation service, apologising for any misunderstanding on my last visit, and asking if it would be possible for me to at least understand Mr Tiller's doubts, bearing in mind he'd never seen me before, my attire, the alcohol on my breath and my past record. I couldn't make out the signature, but I rang the probation service anyway, and asked who had sent me this letter. They told me she was on leave, and asked if I would like to leave a message. I said 'Bollocks', and hung up. I realised nobody was going to take responsibility for this.

I appeared in court on the due date, half an hour early. I made sure I was early because that would give me time to get acquainted with my new probation officer. I had a flat bottle in my inside pocket, and took a seat in the waiting room. After sitting there for about ten minutes, I went into the gents' for a couple of swigs of my vodka.

When I came out, I had a shock; there was this stunning blonde. She could have only been about 20 years of age, and she came towards me, arm outstretched to shake my hand. 'Mr Harding?' 'Yes,' I replied. 'Ms Smith, I'm your new probation officer. Shall we take a seat?' 'Certainly,'

I replied. 'Let's see if they've got a more private room,' she said, and I followed her like a sheep, wallowing in her fragrance.

Just as we were about to sit down, there was a slight tap on the door, and who should walk in? Mr Tiller. 'Ah,' he said, 'You've found him; don't worry, Brian and I are old adversaries.' 'Old adversaries?' I said, 'You're just a liar.' Ms Smith asked me to just give her two minutes with Mr Tiller. Two minutes later, she re-entered the room, apologised and said she wasn't expecting him either.

I said when I first saw this girl I thought she was about 20 years of age, the youngest probation officer I've ever met. She talked openly and candidly about herself, which in turn made me talk the same way about myself. In fact I couldn't believe how openly I was talking to her. I don't know what the probation profession would think of her approach towards me, in that she told me she had very limited experience with people like me, but we discussed in detail my relationship with alcohol. I was amazed at how much she knew at such a young age. I forget what the charges were, but she assured me that I wouldn't be going down.

She then said, 'I'm afraid we're going to have to discuss accommodation. There's no way I'm letting you back out on the streets.' 'Well that's heartening,' I replied. But she said, 'Wait until you hear what I have in mind; have you ever been to a rehabilitation centre?' I said I hadn't. She said, 'This is what we will do; you're not allowed back into your parents house, right? So, when we come out of court, I will drive you to Sevenoaks to pick up whatever it is you have to collect. Then I'll get you a travel warrant down to Sittingbourne rehabilitation centre, and we will take it from there.'

My name was called: *Harding, court two.* I quickly said to Jo, Ms Smith, that I must go to the loo, and I couldn't believe what she said to me. She was totally expressionless, and she simply said, 'Vodka smells just the same as any other booze, you know,' and with that she went to court two to wait for me while I drank the remaining vodka.

I don't recall what my heinous crime was, but I was bound over for one year, in the sum of £100, to be of good behaviour. I thanked the magistrate, and left with Jo. We drove to Sevenoaks, where Jo went in to my mum's house and brought out clean shorts, vest, socks and that was it. We then drove to Sevenoaks Station where Jo got me a travel warrant to Sittingbourne and a cheese sandwich.

My train wasn't leaving for 20 minutes, so it gave Jo and me a short while to talk. I told her a little bit about my short life at sea, and she in turn told me a little bit about her training and why she wanted to be a probation officer. She said she felt she had something to offer. It turned out that she was in fact 23, and not 20 as I had thought. She confided that she had only seen one rehabilitation centre, and according to her it was just what I needed at that time in my life.

She was very excited about it, and she told me how it would help me integrate with other people. Her enthusiasm was beginning to rub off on me, and I asked her quite innocently how she had gained so much knowledge at such a young age. The reason I asked her was that, as I'd been mixing with drinkers all my life, I had never heard a good word spoken about them, and yet here she was telling me that this move could be my saviour, and what's more I was believing her.

She told me about a place in Hertfordshire, which was immaculate, and that she had been to a place in Southampton; the people were friendly, they cooked for themselves, cleaned for themselves, and they even had a mini gym. While I didn't know it at the time, it would only be a couple of hours before I was to realise that this poor girl had been hoodwinked like all the other would-be do-gooders.

You see, this poor girl, in her innocence and her gullibility because of her young age, was shown purpose-built rehab centres. She attended the opening of these places, with officials and the dignitaries, where even the inmates were almost hand picked so as not to upset anybody. She actually knew nothing about the real world; she wasn't even aware of it, and I felt sorry for her. I swear I'm not patronising her; she wasn't selling me a line, she believed what she was saying, she really did.

I arrived at the Sittingbourne rehabilitation centre with one pair of shorts, one vest, one pair of socks and the clothes I was standing up in. Within 30 minutes, my underwear was stolen, and when I went to complain, the bloke at the desk said, 'If you don't like it here, then you can fuck off.'

29

The Eyes That Betray An Alcoholic

This is a subject I was initially reluctant to broach. You see, I wouldn't want an elderly lady or gentleman to think that if they had the odd glass of sherry, their friends might look at them and say, 'Oh yes, we can see you're an alcoholic.' I'm anxious to draw a clear distinction between how I drink and how the majority of people drink, and how that gulf will always be visible.

One incident, eight or nine years ago, brought this home to me. It was during one of the few times that my alcoholism allowed me to work. My boss, Colin, and I were working somewhere in Bexhill. He gave me a lift, and on the way he happened to spot a nice-looking table in an antique shop, which he thought would look great in his lounge. He said, 'If we finish work on time I'll pop in and see how much they want for it.'

Our routine at the time was, as soon as we had finished work, to buy three cans of Special Brew and park up somewhere in the High Street where we could see all the girls leaving their shops and offices. Drinking at work didn't happen. Far too dangerous. After work though, I would have two cans, and Colin would have one.

We parked up in front of the antique shop and, as it was my shout, Colin said for me to get the beers in while he popped in to check out the table. When I returned with the cans, Colin had his back turned to me talking to this bloke, obviously about the table. Now when Colin's in a talkative mood, he can talk for England, plus tax! Both the van doors were locked so, expecting him to natter on a bit, I thought I might as well open a can now. I had quite literally only had two mouthfuls when Colin came out of the shop. He opened his door and leant over to open mine. I hadn't even climbed into the van when he looked straight at me and grinned. 'You've had a drink already, haven't you?' I wasn't close enough for him to smell it on me, so how the hell could he tell? He laughed. 'It's in your eyes, Brian.' 'But I've only had two mouthfuls.' 'I know, mate, but you've reached that stage where even the slightest drink changes you completely, and with you, the first thing to go is your eyes.'

Colin wasn't judging me. He was, as my friend, simply telling me the truth. Someone else would probably have pretended there was nothing wrong and ignored the change in me.

I suppose that this is a reminder to fellow alkies that your closest friends, the people that really care about you, will tell you those things you refuse to recognise in yourself.

I can sit at home with my drink and stay comfortable, blind to these things. To me. I'm normal!

Say I have an appointment at 10am. By the time I've done my puppet trick, cleaned my mouth and probably drunk three litres of 7% cider, the only differences I see in the mirror are that I'm possibly six inches taller, have less grey hair, no paunch, I am witty, intelligent and miraculously possessed of a staggering intellect!

This is where, as an alcoholic, I "fall down". When I go out drunk, I think I'm OK. But we don't fool anyone. Don't think people don't notice. Believe me, they do.

30

Reunited with Lydia

I've previously mentioned a very special girl called Lydia who I'd met during one of the periods when I was sleeping rough on the streets. I was actually sleeping under the arches at the time with about 39 other blokes. She was a lovely girl and always looked after me, and would tell me each day where I could find fresh cardboard for use as a mattress. We had an affinity; a real bond between us. She was a prostitute and I was an alcoholic, but neither of us had chosen our occupations as a career move, and they didn't preclude us from having the same kind of feelings as so called ordinary people.

Her uncle, she had confided in me, used to rape her when she was 11. He would have anal sex with her and force her to perform oral sex on him. She was 11 years old! Her father had abandoned her and left her with his brother who swore he would look after her no matter what happened.

Although she was a working girl, Lydia and I made the time to be together as often as possible. We were both "fucked" in our own way, but she taught me a lot. Lydia held the respect of the people we knocked around with, but I didn't; alkies generally don't. It had nothing to do with our "dress code". It had nothing to do with the way we spoke. I think it was simply because people looked at Lydia and instinctively knew that she'd had few choices in life; that she didn't deserve to be making her living this way. It was just the way the cards were dealt.

Although she had a boyfriend – not a pimp, but a genuine boyfriend – he was powerless to do anything about what she was doing, although he hated it. She was too deeply involved in the trade and dependant on its murky rewards.

Lydia could never understand my alcoholism. She told me that she thought I was a good-looking bloke and that I should have a girlfriend of my own. I tried to convince her that I'd had loads of girlfriends, but I was lying. I didn't have a friend to my name. I had no-one to talk to that I didn't drink with.

Although an alcoholic, I was still a man. I could still fancy a girl. The impotence hadn't fully set in yet, and I could still get turned on. And if I'm honest, Lydia did it for me, but I really don't think she realised it at the time. It's hard for me to put into words how I felt back then, but it began when I was sitting on Charing Cross station one day and I saw Lydia twice trying to ply her trade. At first glance, I thought why the hell would any girl want to do that? I watched her for about an hour. She was attractive, pretty even, and well turned out. Eventually she walked over to where I was sitting on my own on one of the benches and plonked herself down.

'Excuse me mate,' she said, 'have you got a fag?'

'I've got a roll-up if you can roll them.'

'Cheers,' she said, and helped herself to my baccy.

Now I don't know what happened from that moment. Up until then I hadn't known what love meant. But whoever this was sitting next to me, I loved. As I looked at her beautiful face, I suddenly realised she was the girl who had asked me if I was looking for business just a couple of weeks previously. I remember it because we had both laughed. She'd launched into her spiel, and I'd just looked gobsmacked, not knowing what she was talking about, and then we both just fell about laughing. There was me looking like Coco the Clown, hadn't had a bath since God knows when, and obviously begging for money. I couldn't have looked less like a punter if I'd tried.

In my own way I loved Lydia. Not the kind of love a more secure and well-heeled couple could enjoy, but I loved her none the less. I loved her because she'd been abused and she allowed me to confide in her about my own abuse. I felt as though we were fused together. Wouldn't it be wonderful to be able to say that from then on we lived happily ever after? But people like me and Lydia will never be able to pledge our undying love for anyone. My father, and her uncle, made sure of that the day they made the decision to sexually abuse us.

Prostitution, drug-taking, solvent abuse, alcoholism, self-mutilation; none of these behaviours develop out of a need to amuse ourselves. I would like those who judge us to sit and think for a moment, and ask themselves where we went wrong. I'm a fully-grown man and yet I'm still unable to come to terms with my life and the way I've been compelled to live it.

16 or 17 years passed, and I never forgot Lydia. I was married to my second wife, Indra, when I received a letter from the borough treasurer inviting me to attend their office. There had apparently been a mix-up with my rent.

As I expected, there was a queue, but I had my drink with me, and a chair was available, so I was quite content to wait. There were about 12 or

198

15 people ahead of me, some faces I knew but if they recognised me, they automatically averted their gaze. They'd probably seen me around somewhere drinking in the town centre. I spent my time trying to be invisible; looking at the floor or glancing at the information pamphlets pinned around the walls, taking occasional sips from my drink disguised in a coke bottle. Slowly, names were called and we went to the window to be interrogated about our rent.

The only thing Lydia ever told me about her father was the unusual name she'd inherited from him. Funnily enough, I can remember it quite clearly. It was while I was busy studying the floor that suddenly this unusual name was called. A few moments passed and the name was called again. This time a woman stood up and walked towards the protective glass panel. I was stunned. I stood up suddenly and dropped my drink (I was mortified at the waste even at such a moment). If people hadn't sussed I'd been drinking alcohol up until then, they certainly knew now as the precious liquid seeped across the carpet and stunk the place out. I didn't care. Not three feet away from me was Lydia.

She turned and I knew she still recognised me after all these years. She lay down the paperwork she was holding and walked over to me. She put her arms around me and we kissed right there in the middle of that unfriendly, uncomfortable waiting room. It didn't matter. Nothing did. We broke apart and arranged to meet outside when we'd finished. The housing officer was becoming impatient.

I sat back down in shock. The drink I'd dropped had made quite a mess, but it didn't bother me. Nothing did. Lydia was here and that's all I could think about. The woman sitting beside me asked if I was going to clean up my mess and I said, 'Lady, I think I already have.'

When my name was called, I just sat dazed. The woman behind her protective glass window went on and on about percentages, government cut-backs, the old, the infirm, you name it she talked about it as though it was all my fault. All this because they couldn't decide whether or not to pay my full rent or only part of it. In the end I just said. 'Look lady, do you want me to give you a sub?' She was furious, and dismissed me with the assurance that I would have their decision by the end of the week.

Lydia was waiting on a bench on the other side of the road. This was all like a dream to me. I sat down beside her and we just held on to each other, kissing, for about five minutes. We talked about what had been happening in our lives since we said goodbye all those years ago. She was on her own now and that's how she wanted it to be. I told her I'd married again, and she told me how pleased she was for me. She wasn't at all surprised that someone had snapped me up, which was quite a compliment for someone who thinks as little of himself as I do. She also told me that she'd never forgotten me, and that hardly a day had passed without her thinking about me and wondering how my life was going.

Something strange was happening to me. It confuses me still. As Lydia and I sat there we both felt a powerful bond between us. We both knew that either one of us would have given our lives for each other right then. I don't know why or where those feelings came from. I just know we both felt the same. I'd never felt it before, and I've never felt it since.

But beneath all of this ran a current of deep sadness. We both knew that within the hour we would part and never see each other again. We'd never made love, but we knew that the love we shared couldn't be matched by anyone else's on earth. God knows why we were put on this planet. We were both decent people. We just couldn't deal with our demons.

Why the hell was I drinking myself stupid?

Why was I drinking to the point where I made myself look a fool?

Why was Lydia a prostitute?

Did she entice her uncle to abuse her when she was 11?

Did she ask him to force her into having anal sex?

Did she solicit him in any way?

Why?

Why?

Why?

Just give us a clue as to where we went wrong as children, and we'll both promise to make amends.

We'll both promise to try and be just like you.

It turned out that Lydia had unexpectedly come into some money and, as she'd always dreamt of living in Hastings, she decided to make the move. She'd been here just on three months.

Lydia barely remembered her father. He'd been a Polish seaman and had never married her mother. In fact, it seems he didn't marry at all and Lydia was his only living relative. She'd been receiving solicitor's letters for the last three months asking her to contact them. But, in common with most disenfranchised people who tend to live on the edges of society and, therefore, the law, she had a deep distrust of solicitors and so hadn't bothered to get in touch with them. Had they told her what it was all about she would obviously have been round there like a flash. Apparently her father had died and had left her a hefty sum of money in spite of abandoning her all those years ago. Now, whilst it wasn't anywhere near six figures, it was certainly a small fortune to Lydia.

Her mistake was to have rented a flat when she arrived in Hastings and, when the authorities asked if she had any savings, she maintained that she hadn't and so the council paid her rent. But they somehow got wind that in reality she did have money, and quite a lot of it.

Lydia offered to pay it all back but the borough treasurer was having none of it. Too many Londoners, he considered, were coming into the town and taking advantage of the system. He was determined to make an example of her and take her to court.

That's the last place Lydia wanted to be seen. She had a three-year-old son and was naturally terrified that the authorities would take him from her. After a childhood like hers, there wasn't a force on the planet that could part her from that little boy. There were so many outstanding matters against her waiting to be dealt with by the courts, and she couldn't risk being taken into custody. If it hadn't been for the boy, she'd have taken a chance and paid her dues, but he was the only thing in her life that meant everything to her. He kept her alive and her heart beating. She had no alternative but to do all she could to keep out of prison.

She began by giving quite a lot of the money away to friends, such was her nature. Then she planned to write a cheque out to the borough treasurer to cover any money owed, and then just keep her fingers crossed that that would be an end of it. Her thinking allowed that even if this official was an out and out bastard, a real jobsworth, if she made every effort to pay, they wouldn't bother following up her case. In spite of what she'd endured over the years, she still managed to keep a faith in fair play.

There was no-one else in her life, she assured me, only the lad, and she lived for him and him alone. She planned to go back to London to tidy a few things up, and then to move away. She couldn't tell me where, because she hadn't worked that out herself. I asked her if she would at least come for a drink with me before she left. I desperately wanted to snatch as much time with her as I could. I would have loved her to come and see my flat and meet Indra, to see the two things in my life I was most proud of, so she could see that something good had happened to me. But she wouldn't.

'If I don't leave you now, Brian, I'll never be able to,' she told me. 'You have your new wife, and I have my son. Neither of us has led a good life. We can blame our parents, the government, neighbours or any other scapegoat you'd like to name, but the bottom line is we have to accept that we can't have a normal life. People don't accept us. So let's put a brave face on it and let's make the lives of the two people most important people – Indra and my lad – happy. Let's do it for them.'

All the time she was talking, during every syllable she uttered, I didn't once take my eyes off hers. She was like some sort of angel, sitting there in Wellington Square, telling me the truth.

I damn nearly cried.

We kissed and wished each other well. She left and I've never heard from, or of, Lydia from that day to this.

31

The Funnel Run

Ronnie and I called this our funnel run, and this is why: we would meet up every Saturday and Sunday, and sometimes Monday mornings, at about 5am. We would have with us a funnel, a small kitchen-type plastic funnel, plus two empty two-litre bottles. We would meet in Bottle Alley and drink whatever we had left over from the night before.

We would then cross over to the other side of the road where all the hotels, pubs, clubs, bars, restaurants and any other establishment that sold alcohol late at night were. We would then walk very slowly past each and every one of these establishments, each armed with our empty two-litre bottle and our plastic funnel.

These clubs and bars were all open until the early hours, and invariably there would be at least a half-empty glass of drink of some sort or another. If not a glass, there would be a can or a bottle, but there would always be something left in them. Sometimes we were extra lucky and would find a full bottle or a full can, but either way we got a drink.

We would start our journey at St Leonards and walk right along to the old town, then come back on a route that would take us past the backs of all these clubs, pubs etc. If I found a can, Ronnie would help me pour it into the bottle via the funnel, and I would help Ron if he found a can.

Pouring a glass or a bottle wasn't too much of a problem because you could see the contents, but pouring a can had its drawbacks as you couldn't see the actual content until it disappeared down the funnel into your two-litre bottle, and for some strange reason people had a nasty habit of putting their dog-ends in the can. On the occasions that this did happen, we tried to pick them out with our fingers, but if we couldn't we just took a chance, and when we came across a dog-end or two, we just spat them out.

When Ron and I had filled our bottles, we would head back to Bottle Alley and drink our fill. I am aware it was a filthy, nasty, disgusting habit but needs must, and when you're rattling for a drink you'll do almost anything to get it. What we called our funnel run took place round about the mid-80s, and I'm pleased to say we've never done it since.

As I'm married now and there's some sort of semblance of order in my life, I don't see that much of Ron, but on the few occasions when we do bump into each other, we always have a lot to talk about. Our lives are so different now; we're that much older and our tolerance level, because of our ill-health, has dropped dramatically compared to what it was. Both of us have severe liver damage, and seem to be prone to almost anything that's going.

This is Ron Milligan on the left, and me on the right, sometime in the middle to late 80s. Ron and I had one common bond; we are both entirely dependent on alcohol.

Ron and I both became solitary drinkers, neither of us trusting the company of drinkers when they were drinking en masse. We 'ere both very serious drinkers and couldn't afford to waste our time snapping and snarling which is what drinkers en masse nearly always do; also drinkers en masse always seemed to attract the attention of the police, and that too was a waste of time.

Ron and I have often in the past, purely by coincidence, found ourselves in the same detox unit together. Ron, like me, is a qualified tradesman, a plasterer, but also, like me, is unable to work.

Bless you, Ron.

32

Newspaper Cuttings

SELLY Ring (01424) 854242   Fax (01424) 853850   Hastings & St Leonards Obs

BRIAN Harding has been spat upon, insulted and beaten up - and his only crime is that he likes to drink on the street.

'I've been spat at by half-wits for just sitting drinking'

DOMINIC PONSFORD talks to alcoholic and street drinker Brian Harding

The newspaper cutting above was an interview given by me to Dominic Ponsford from our local *Hastings and St Leonards Observer* dated June 2001. The reason I gave the interview was that, completely covering the "letters to the editor page" for something like three or four consecutive weeks, there were letters from members of our local community complaining about the disgusting, insulting and foul behaviour of us street drinkers. I felt the public might want to know about the abuse I have suffered from them. The headlines speak for themselves. This is the entire interview as given to journalist and writer Dominic Ponsford by me:

> *Brian Harding has been spat upon, insulted and beaten up, and his only crime is that he likes to drink on the street. Brian, 53, is a street drinker and alcoholic and, perhaps surprisingly, he backs the Council's plans to ban drinking from certain public areas, but he*

says there is a danger that all drinkers are being tarred with the same brush.

He said, 'I don't ever imagine anybody respecting me, but I would like some sort of acceptance.' On Tuesday morning last week, Brian was sitting on the sea front with a can of beer and a newspaper when, he said, he was subjected to a verbal attack from a "respectable" couple whom he described as in their 60s. He said 'They looked down at me and said, "look at the state of him, he can't even wait for the pubs to open, he's disgusting." I wish I were the type of bloke to say, "who are you talking to? You're insulting me and you don't even know me."'

Brian says verbal abuse is common but, more disturbingly, he says he has also been physically attacked: 'I was in Warrior Square Gardens and it was evening; I had a bottle and there was a gang of people, the oldest couldn't have been more than 15; they started throwing dirt and rocks at me. When I got up, they chased me and cornered me and gave me a right kicking. They called me a pervert, a wanker, a drinker. I tried to get away with my drink and they threw it all over me.'

He said, 'I've been spat at by young half-wits for just sitting there drinking.' Brian is below average height and weight, but still manages to drink around five litres of strong seven and a half per cent cider a day. He starts drinking as soon as he wakes up in the morning, often sitting on the seafront near his flat off Warrior Square, St Leonards. He said, 'I have people that walk past me and comment on the weather and that makes me feel part of it, but only yesterday someone said, "you piece of shit". You have to just say 'well all right have a nice day.'

'If you get a bit depressed in the early hours of the morning you think about these things that people say. It does hurt you, especially when you get a bit low with yourself.' He added, 'I understand the anger of people who see drinkers en masse, they give people like me a bad name.' But he said, 'there's so many negative things about street drinkers and I have to agree with most of it, but at the same time there are drinkers out there who haven't got much choice. They are not very strong characters but they are certainly not doing any harm.'

End of interview.

Alcoholic's five minute court penalty for being disorderly

ALCOHOLIC Brian Harding, 55, was sentenced to sit at the back of Hastings magistrates' court for five minutes instead of paying a £50 fine.

Harding, of Cornwallis Gardens, pleaded guilty to a charge of being drunk and disorderly in a local shop.

Alison Avard, prosecuting, told the court Harding took off clothing and stood naked from the waist up shouting abuse.

She said he was in breach of a conditional discharge imposed by the court for a similar offence last October.

Harding appeared in court well dressed and spoke articulately about his problem.

He told magistrates, "I am an alcoholic. I am steeped in drink most of my waking hours. I have been like this for about 20 years.

"For the most part I am not disorderly but on occasions I get caught out and become disorderly. It's not because I have no respect for anybody. It overtakes me."

Harding, who also suffers from depression, said he had been given med-ication by his doctor so he could cope with the court appearance.

He said, "It's a vicious circle I know I won't get out of."

Harding told the court he had been to a detox unit but he could not explain why he started drinking again as soon as he came out.

Presiding magistrate Andy Burrage told him: "An alcoholic is the only person who can address their alcohol abuse. I strongly urge you to take some action to try to stem your alcoholism."

Mr Burrage said the court would allow the conditional discharge to continue running until next October.

He ordered Harding to remain in court for about 50 minutes until the lunch break instead of paying a £50 fine for the latest offence.

But Harding said he could not wait that long without a drink and the court reduced the 50 minutes to five minutes.

Mr Burrage warned Harding: "If you come before this court again for a similar offence you will not be treated so leniently."

The above newspaper cutting is also taken from the *Hastings and St Leonards Observer*, our local paper, and it was a result of my appearance in Hastings Magistrates court on February 4th 2003 for being drunk and disorderly. The headlines speak for themselves, but here is the complete transcript:

Alcoholic Brian Harding, 55, was sentenced to sit at the back of Hastings Magistrates court for five minutes instead of paying a £50 fine. Harding, of Cornwallis Gardens, pleaded guilty to a charge of being drunk and disorderly in a local shop. Alison Avard, prosecuting, told the court Harding took off clothing and stood naked from the waist up shouting abuse. She said he was in breach of a conditional discharge imposed by the court for a similar offence last October.

Harding appeared in court well-dressed and spoke articulately about his problem. He told magistrates: 'I am an alcoholic. I am steeped in drink most of my waking hours. I have been like this for about 20 years. For the most part I am not disorderly, it's not because I have no respect for anybody, it just that sometimes it overtakes me.'

Harding, who suffers from depression, said he had been given medication by his doctor so he could cope with the court appearance. He said, 'It's a vicious circle, I know I won't get out of.' Harding told the court he had been to a detox unit but he could not explain why he had been drinking again as soon as he came out.

Presiding Magistrate Andy Burrage told him, 'An alcoholic is the only person who can address their abuse, I strongly urge you to take some action to try to stem your alcoholism.' Mr Burrage said the court would allow the conditional discharge to continue running until next October.

207

He ordered Harding to remain in court for about 50 minutes until the lunch break, instead of paying a £50 fine for the latest offence. But Harding said he could not wait that long without a drink, and so the court reduced the 50 minutes to 5 minutes. Mr Burrage warned Harding: 'If you come before this court again for a similar offence you will not be treated so leniently.'

End Of Transcript

As you can see from the leniency the magistrate showed me in court that day, he must have come from the same school as the custody sergeant who, all those years ago, dropped the drunk charge against me. As did the two officers who found me drunk in the road and, instead of arresting me, helped me into my mate's van and told him to take me home. As did also our very own Community Officer, John Hearn, when he found me with my drink hidden under my hat in an alcohol-free zone and told me to put it in my pocket and make myself scarce. So I will ask you again to forgive me my ridiculous theory about people in uniforms having flawed characters. The only point I would like to make is that I feel I ought to share the shame and guilt of my abusers. The only difference being that if they hadn't started it all those years ago, I wouldn't have felt the need to carry it on right up to this present day. By ruining my life, that automatically affects others and that makes me an abuser also.

33

The GP's Dilemma

For something like 35 years I've been presenting myself at doctors' surgeries, and every illness or ailment I've ever suffered during that time has been in one sense or another, alcohol related. Of course, over time this becomes more and more apparent to those GPs, and they eventually feel compelled to "give me the sack". Each time, the NHS allocates me another doctor and the whole process starts again. Here's how:

Have you ever drunk for say, something like 24 hours non-stop? Has it ever gone on for longer? I'm talking about alcohol of course. Has it ever gone on for perhaps three, or even four, days? If so, you'll know what it's like to wake up rattling; clucking for a drink. I don't mean water. I mean a *DRINK*.

And of those who have experienced this, there will be very few who will ever admit to it. Those of you who have drunk for more than 48 hours without solid food will know that desperate need to sleep for at least five or six hours. And this isn't the sleep of a naturally tired man after a day living as a productive citizen.

Now, when you wake up you'll be dehydrated, so you'll naturally need a drink of water or juice, anything but alcohol. That's what *YOU* would do. But put yourself in the mind of an alkie: me. I won't get a glass of water. I won't get a glass of orange. I want a drink. I need a drink. I will die for a drink. *I WANT ALCOHOL.*

Like those of you who know – those who admit it – after your three- or four-day bender, I'm just as dehydrated as you. Those of you who haven't gone to this particular hell-hole of a desert, just imagine four days in the Sahara without water, and that's how much I want alcohol.

I'm fully aware of how revolting I feel, and how repulsive I look, first thing in the morning after a bender. But now imagine on your return from the Sahara, waking up a squat or a worse place and you can't get a drink of water. In fact, you can't get a glass of anything unless it's some alcohol left lying around. There's nowhere to wash and you have to be at your doctor's in 15 minutes. You realise that all you need to get you to the doctor's and to be able to speak coherently to the receptionist, take a seat, and perhaps engage in a little light banter with one of the kids off school sick, is alcohol. I've described this scene for two reasons.

Firstly, of the millions of people out there, there must be a good percentage who have fallen into this category at some time in their life; who have come a bit closer than just nodding terms with too much booze.

Secondly, by talking about three- or four-day benders. I'm trying to get across the extremes inherent in this lifestyle. How ingrained are the patterns and behaviours, and how inseparable the person eventually becomes from the substance.

Is it possible for you to imagine living and drinking like this, year in and year out, not always in squats, but more often than not in places not dissimilar? Accommodation that your local council deems habitable and worthy of charging an astronomical rent for? Do you get the picture? Some of the local councillors own some of this property themselves, too. Funny old world, isn't it? Anyway, to get back to the doctor's surgery:

So, you've had your three- or four-day bender and you feel terrible but, ideally, if your sleeping quarters allowed, you've managed to clean your teeth, had a shower or bath, managed to drink something other than alcohol and so you feel reasonably OK.

Now, multiply that little bender of yours by say, 100. Put yourself in the doctor's surgery by about 8am; you haven't cleaned your mouth, and you haven't had a wash. You're sweating, you're paranoid and the pleasantries you've just exchanged with the receptionist are hallucinatory. Your eyes and mouth twitch involuntarily and you can't sit still, you can't stand still, and you can't even crouch down on your haunches against the wall to steady yourself.

I've always believed the old dictum, *When the drink's in, the wit's out*. However, in place of those wits, we do have an in-built radar system. In the past, I have crouched down in a doctor's surgery and I've noticed that people who have been sitting quietly minding their own business for anything up to an hour have eventually got up and gone over to the reception desk. Something is said under their breath and they sit down again. During this whispered exchange, the receptionist will steal a sneaky glance in my direction. My name will then be called, and I'll fumble my way towards a sign saying Dr –.

The usual routine. They treat me for any signs and symptoms I present, tell me to cut down on my drinking, and wish me well. Two days later I get a letter through the door telling me they are no longer able to treat me as a patient. It is their right not to give me a reason why, as it is equally my right not to wish to be seen by a certain GP.

You see, the physical symptoms of a man whose body's systems are craving alcohol can be a very frightening thing to watch, no matter how often you've witnessed it. It's particularly horrific if you've never seen it before. Now, I can fully understand fellow patients being more than just a little alarmed at the spectacle, but it's a hard and fast rule that you do not drink on the morning of your appointment, or the doctor simply will not see you. So you will obviously be rattling.

Now, if they allowed you, say, one can before going into the waiting room, you would be able to sit quietly, not look nervous, probably be able to control any eye movements and mouth twitches, and therefore avoid upsetting the other patients.

In the past when I've been given my marching orders. I've actually gone back to the surgery and asked the receptionist for a reason. Occasionally, out of sheer decency, one of them, "Of course, in the strictest confidence," has told me that my very presence, manner and demeanour had upset them so much that they didn't feel safe in my company and would have to think twice before giving me another appointment.

So you can see the predicament an alcoholic finds himself in when he needs to visit his doctor. And you can clearly see his doctor's dilemma.

Believe me, I fully understand that dilemma, but I also ask you to believe me when I say I mean nobody any harm, and I would also be grateful if you would accept the way I look and not stare at me. That would be a tremendous help. I'm sorry for causing so much offence and fear by the involuntary movements of my mouth, eyes, arms and legs... And anything else that moves when it shouldn't.

211

34

Witness Statement

The statement (reproduced on pages 215-6), given to PC John Hearn, our local community police officer, by me, is as a result of another example of insults and abuse I have had to endure as a street drinker and alcoholic. The shelter where I used to sit at the time, where I had to suffer this bloke's abuse was actually the furthest shelter from the beginning of Bottle Alley, where all the drinkers used to sit en masse. It was there I felt the safest, but it was where, funnily enough, I was to become the most vulnerable, not because of my fellow drinkers but more from the supposedly respectable members of our community who, whilst I would sit there very quietly and peacefully, were still unable to hide their resentment and disgust of me.

Whilst I felt reluctant to go to the police to lodge a formal complaint, as I didn't feel I had any rights in our society, I still felt something ought to be done, so I went to our local community police office. It was here I was to meet PC John Hearn. As soon as I saw John I realised we had met before; but the last time we met, whilst he knew my name, I had no idea who he was. I suddenly felt confident about making this complaint.

Whilst my last meeting with John is a bit vague, I still remember the general gist of it. I was sitting in the local precinct, an alcohol-free zone. So while I sat there watching the world go by, I had my can hidden under my hat. Unless you knew it was there, it couldn't possibly be seen. I noticed the security guards talking to a policeman; it was John Hearn.

Quite suddenly, John appeared. He reached over, lifted my hat up, exposed my can, and said, 'Thank you very much. I'll take that'. I was gutted. He pointed to one of the many alcohol-free zone signs, and said, 'You know the rules'. John then mentioned the name of his colleague, PC Howard, who was now a sergeant, and asked me if my name was Brian Harding. I told him it was. He asked me if his colleague's name rang any bells; I said it didn't.

He then reminded me of a little incident that happened in 1989, 14 years ago. I was asleep, and very obviously drunk, in one of our parks. Howard thought that, for my own safety, he would arrest me; parks can be very dangerous places. He was to regret it, because not only did he have to carry me, with the help of an over-zealous senior citizen, to his car, but when he got me to the station, he had to get one of his fellow officers to help carry me to the cells. He said to his mates in the station, 'I don't know who this bloke is that we just put in the cells, but I hope to God he's not going to make a career out of drinking because I don't fancy carrying him all over the place.'

14 years later, as John was telling me about this incident, we were both able to laugh. On a more serious note, he told me that he wouldn't confiscate my drink provided I made myself scarce and tried to observe the rules. I thanked him, and left feeling grateful. This then was the man I was to ask about making an official complaint about harassment of my wife, my in-laws, me and anybody who chose to sit with me while I was drinking.

The complaint that I made in my official statement to the police is word for word exactly how it happened. I asked John whether this would just be logged, filed and forgotten about, but he assured me that, while I might be an alcoholic, I still had the same rights as anybody else, and that he would make a point of paying this man a visit personally as John was, after all, our local community officer.

I was a bit apprehensive about any repercussions that might follow this official complaint, but I needn't have worried. John contacted me the following week and told me they had found the bloke and taken him to the police station, where he admitted he didn't like nigger-lovers, gays, lesbians and especially alcoholics who had probably never done an honest day's work in their lives. He was released after five hours, with a formal caution that should he ever be brought to the attention of the police again for any complaint made against him of a similar nature, from any section of the general public, he would be arrested and brought before the court, and the statement that I had made against him would be taken into consideration along with any new charge.

I am very relieved and pleased to say that, since PC John Hearn not only took my complaint seriously, but also took the trouble to follow it up, this man, whilst I've passed him many times on the street, no longer looks in my direction. In fact, he averts his gaze from me in an almost exaggerated way, and for this I have to be grateful to our community policing policy.

I said earlier in my book that people in uniforms, who have an urge to police other people, must have some sort of basic fundamental flaw in their own character. I now know this to be absolute rubbish. It might possibly be true in some areas of security work, but to apply this concept to the work that the community police do in our town simply isn't true.

SUSSEX POLICE   **WITNESS STATEMENT**   MG 11(T)

(CJ Act 1967, s.9, MC Act 1980, ss.5A(3) (a) and 5B; MC Rules 1981, r.70)

Statement of: BRIAN CHARLES HARDING

Age if under 18:   0 18   (if over 18 insert over 18)   Occupation: UNEMPLOYED

This statement (consisting of   page(s) each signed by me) is true to the best of my knowledge
and belief and I make it knowing that, if it is tendered in evidence, I shall be liable to prosecution if I have
wilfully stated anything in it, which I know to be false or do not believe to be true.

Signature. [signature: Harding]   Date 26TH JANUARY 2003

I have lived in Hastings since September 1978. In 1981 I became a registered Alcoholic. I have been in a

number of Detox accommodations. The majority of people that I know and associate with are alcoholics. I

still regard myself as a sensible person and still have my wits about me. I married Indra in 1993. She is an

Indian lady with dual nationality. She is the most supportive person in my life. The house is tidy and warm.

Although my life style is some what different to what people perceive as normal I keep myself clean and tidy.

In the summer of 2000 I can not remember the exact date but this incident sticks in my mind. Indra's sister

Sabil and her husband Gary had gone to the bus shelter at the front of the pier intending to meet me. This is

where I normally sat and they knew I would be there at some time. I was about 20 feet away from the shelter

when my attention was drawn to a male towering in front of them gesticulating with his finger. I could see my

wife and relatives sitting there. I could hear voices but I could not hear what he was saying. None of us are of

very big stature and seeing this male who was at least 6 feet tall and quite muscular in build was quite

frightening. I did not know what was happening but it was quite clear that he was menacing. I had seen this

male before but never spoken to him. He is the sort of male that you did not want to know. His overall

demeanour was that of an agitated man who was unpredictable. I can further describe this man as white,

with thick black hair, not short but I would say collar length. He always had a 'donkey' jacket either on or in

the hot weather carried over his arm. I have never seen him in company of any one else.

When I got closer to my wife I enquired if she was alright. Gary referred to the man as the ' Niger lover'. This

was so that I identified this male as a person who had been both verbally and racist to Gary on a previous

incident and had referred to Gary as a ' Niger Lover'. When he saw me trying to console my wife he said

" Is this another Niger lover". I had no dealings with this male before. This remark I found offensive . How

dare he make such a remark. He made several other remarks to us all as " shit" and why didn't we get a job.

I did not believe I would have stood a chance had I tried to physically deal with this man and tried to use

verbal reasoning with him. I could see that he was getting wound up as his face was beginning to contort and

his veins were becoming obvious. He was also starting to raise his fists. He got his face as close to mine as

Signature: Signature witnessed by

214

Continuation of statement of   B.C. Harding

he could. So close that I could smell his breath. He did not actually touch me which I found unbelievable because he was so beside himself with rage I was expecting some sort of physical assault. He said in a clear and loud voice

" I will cut your fucking throat down a dark alley". I made a comment to the effect that it would have to be dark and in an alley because unlike him I had friends. It was a stupid thing to say but I was frightened and my wife was there. I felt that I needed to be protective to not only my wife but also my In-Laws.

I think it was the same summer by chance when I again was walking towards the same shelter when I saw the same man walking towards me. I did not want to make contact with him but as he approached me he said

" you are a fucking cunt" I had seen him after the first incident a number of times but had made every effort to avoid him. Again he towered over me and put his face as close to mine as he could. There was no way I was going to get into a fight with him although his actions I could only describe as if he was trying to goad me into one. I tried my normal tact of verbal reasoning and I simply carried on walking. I am aware that this same male has had a number of confrontations with my in-laws and associates.

I believe it was Saturday 18th January 2003. I was in Priory Meadow shopping centre in Hastings with my friend MATT and my wife. He is not a drinker but has had a number of operations on his legs and is currently on crutches. We were directly outside Marks and Spencer's. I could not believe it when I caught sight of the male with his donkey jacket coming towards me. I suggested to Matt that he talk to me in order that it would give the appearance that I was engrossed in conversation and there be no need for the man to talk to me. For what ever reason he went out of his way to come up to me and as with all other occasions he started to swear at me. He called me a cunt and asked why we did not get a job. He made reference to Matt as a wino which he is not. We had both been sitting there peacefully and this man was causing a disturbance. There were lots of people around who must have heard what was going on.

Again as with previous incidents he got more and more wound up. He threatened to cut my throat down a dark alley but this time he pulled what appeared to be a biro which he held in his hand and with an outstretched arm pointed it directly at Matt as if he were holding a knife. Matt challenged him verbally but as with all the other meetings he went on his way in a bad mood. I have had enough of trying to avoid this male who I believe has the surname of ████ He goes out of his way to confront me and verbally insults me and any one with me. He would appear to be unstable and I am afraid of what he may do hence the reason I am making this complaint. At 0955hours on Sunday 26th January 2003 I showed PC Hearn the address at which

Signature   Signature witnessed by:

215

I recall the custody sergeant who came to my cell, all those years ago when I was waiting to appear in court on a drunk charge. I'd just spent the previous night in one of his cells, and before the court opened he came and told me that if I gave him my word that I would go immediately to Hellingly Psychiatric Hospital for a detox, where he knew there was a bed waiting for me, then he would make some excuse to the court and drop the charge. Which is what he did. That wasn't the act of a man with a flawed character; if there was a flaw, then that flaw was compassion, as with my friend PC John Hearn and his colleagues. Whilst they were street-wise, with a first hand understanding of all our social ills, they also had compassion, so please accept my apologies for my theory on people in uniform.

Ten years prior to my making my statement to the police about the harassment, an incident happened that couldn't help but give me conflicting views on our police force. I had managed to do a few weeks' work, and had actually got a little bit of money in the bank. I decided to draw some money out and buy some clothes. I walked down to the bank in the town centre and, for some reason, couldn't draw any money out until after midday. This threw me out a bit, for as long as I had a routine I was reasonably safe from getting too drunk.

I knew if I sat on a bench anywhere for any length of time, a fellow alkie would want to sit and have a drink with me. Nearly all the alkies I drank with were street drinkers, and for various reasons would never use pubs; these reasons included being too scruffy, that they couldn't afford it, were barred, or simply too paranoid to socialise with normal people who didn't know what it was like to have to drink. On this occasion, I decided it would be safer for me to go to a pub myself, and that was my mistake.

I was quite smartly dressed, and there was nothing about me to suggest I was a street drinking alcoholic. In fact, the bar staff were very pleasant and friendly towards me. The problem was, I realised, it had been so long since I had been in a pub, I didn't really know what to order. The cider they sold was nothing like the strength I was used to drinking on the street. I ordered half a pint of bitter in a pint glass and a Gold Label with the top off. I poured the Gold Label into the pint glass with the bitter. The barmaid told me she couldn't see how I could drink Gold Label and bitter mixed at that time of morning; she had no idea.

I drank several more of these, then went to the bank. It was 12.30, so I drew £100 out and went over to the off-licence and bought a bottle of vodka. I sat on a bench near the public toilets in case I had an accident. I knew I wasn't going to buy any clothes, and couldn't think why I should want to anyway. That's what drink always did to me. It simply takes away any sense of responsibility or respect that you may have for yourself or others.

I finished my bottle of vodka, and was by now very, very drunk. I knew I had to get home. I didn't want to be sitting here drunk with almost £100 in my pocket. I plotted the best route I could take where I would be least likely to encounter any of my fellow street drinkers. I managed to get about halfway home when I collapsed face down on the pavement. I was vaguely aware that a small crowd had gathered. A few people prodded and poked me and asked if I was all right. Suddenly a police car arrived, then another one. I was aware of a policeman asking me my name, and did I know where I lived?

Someone in the crowd said, I've seen him before; there's nothing wrong with him. He's just drunk and should be locked up. I remember the officer telling him that if he didn't have anything helpful to say, then would he please be quiet. It was obvious that this officer was of the same ilk as the custody sergeant who helped me all those years ago, and of that of PC John Hearn who, whilst I didn't know at the time, was also to help me at a later date.

The officer managed to get me to my feet, and said if I couldn't manage to get myself home he would have to arrest me for my own safety. He had already done a CRO [Criminal Records Order] on me, and had found that the police didn't want me for anything. It was while all this was going on that the chap I had been doing a bit of work for came along. He said he had known me for over ten years, and assured the officer that if they could just help to get me in his van he would guarantee to get me home safely, where I would sleep it off and not come out of my house again that day.

The two officers walked over to their cars and spoke to someone over their radio. They had confirmed where I lived, and asked to check my mate's ID. Satisfied with that, they told me I was lucky to have such a good friend and put me in my mate's van. They also told me to try and get some sort of treatment, and said they hoped they wouldn't see me again.

They weren't to see me again, but in less than an hour one of their colleagues would, and he was to be a totally different kettle of fish. The contrast in the attitudes of these officers was so great I couldn't believe they were members of the same force. My mate drove me to my flat, made sure I got in safely, and said he didn't think I would be up to work for at least a couple of days, so he would see me soon. As soon as he left, I hid my money under the carpet – street mentality – went in to the kitchen and got a bottle of cider. I walked up to the putting green opposite my flat. The putting green was closed so it was nice and quiet. I sat on a bench and slowly drank my cider.

The only way you could be seen in the putting green from the road was if you stopped directly in front of the entrance that was down a path about a hundred yards away, and it was here that a squad car pulled up. They didn't sit there for any length of time, nor did they even look in my direction. They simply pulled up, got out of their car, and came storming straight towards me. Neither of them spoke one word; one grabbed me with one hand round my throat, threw me to the ground face down, and smashed my bottle into the litter bin, whilst the other one manacled me with my hands behind my back. At this point I was sick. I knew that if I couldn't control my breathing, there was every chance I could die of vomit inhalation.

At this point, the police and council policy of introducing "no drinking zones" hadn't even been agreed upon, so as far as I was aware I wasn't breaking any law. Sure I was drunk, but I certainly wasn't in any way disorderly, loud, insulting, abusive, or a nuisance of any kind. In fact, what I was doing was taking this opportunity to actually wallow in self-pity and depression. The attitude and actions of those two officers in those few minutes had simply reinforced what I had just been thinking about myself; I was worthless. It's interesting to note that, as soon as I was able to speak and I had given them my name and address, they didn't even bother to do a CRO on me.

We drove to the station in silence. They took the handcuffs off me, and took me straight to the cells. They didn't even bother to stop at the custody desk. This seemed a bit odd to me, as they didn't seem to be interested in asking me for any details, or giving me any details. They put me in a cell, locked the door, and closed the flap up. All I heard was the sound of their footsteps disappearing down the corridor. The cell was cold, and I had no blanket. I lay down in the foetal position and dreamt of clowns with black rings round their eyes. By something like midnight, I was beginning to suffer bad withdrawal symptoms.

They opened my cell door at 3am, and I was told to follow them to the processing room. At this point I hadn't eaten for about 72 hours, and my blood sugar was at an all-time low. I was dehydrated, and was frightened that I would just collapse. As my fingerprints were being taken, by the same officer who had arrested me the previous afternoon, I couldn't understand how he could still be on duty.

218

I had a fit. It was sudden and without warning. I recall writhing on the floor and knocking things over. The officer who was fingerprinting me grabbed me by the scruff of my neck, hauled me to my feet, slammed me down in a chair and said, 'If you don't fucking well behave. I'll stick you back in the cells and keep you there until the magistrate's ready to see you. And the way things are going, that will probably be about three days.'

I sat there motionless. I'd lived rough on the streets; I had been in numerous detox units and rehab centres, and yet here I was in a police station and had never been more frightened. They talked amongst themselves for a while, and then just turned to me and said quite casually, 'C'mon we'll bail you.' We went to the custody desk where I was bailed to appear at a later date, and they handed me my custody sheet. My custody sheet read:

> *Brian Charles Harding was arrested at the White Rock Putting Green at 4pm whilst being drunk and acting in a disorderly manner. He was held in custody until the duty sergeant* [no name] *thought he was sober enough to be released 3.30am.*

There was no mention of me having a fit, and there was also no signature on the custody sheet.

35

My Most Recent Home Detox With No Medication

It's Saturday morning, 7.15 April 5th 2003.

My last drink was 7pm Wednesday 3rd April 2003. I was just about to finish my eighth can of the day. It was a weak lager. 4.1% volume – my tolerance level had dropped. I went through to the kitchen to get my ninth can, opened it and put in on my table ready to drink. I realised I wasn't actually sitting on my chair, but was actually perched right on the edge of it.

I had got up that morning, come through to the lounge, and opened a tin of my high nutritional food supplement. It was in liquid form and therefore should have been easy to digest, but although it's a small 250ml tin, I could only manage about a quarter of it before my puppet trick set in; I managed to bring it up, but I was in agony.

I had been shivering and shaking for the last two hours; this was every drinker's worst nightmare, to suffer the after-effects and withdrawal symptoms of alcohol, whilst still drinking. It is at this point that you need medical attention or risk an alcoholic seizure – a "fit". It's frightening. I put the can back in the kitchen, just in case I accidentally knocked it over and wasted it, and I came back and sat down.

I was covered in sweat; it wasn't pouring from my body; I was too dehydrated for that to happen, it was just like a thin film of some sort of moisture that covered my entire body. It also gave off a sickly smell, a smell I was familiar with. I had first noticed it over 20 years ago when I started going into detox units and dry houses. At the time I didn't know what it was, but it always repulsed me.

This film of sweat causes you to scratch constantly; it itches to the point of distraction, and is also painful. It feels like something is alive and crawling just below the surface of your skin, and coupled with this you have involuntary twitches of the eyes and mouth. My wife is quietly spoken, but if she were to suddenly say something, I would jump out of my skin.

My mind would be miles away, and I would be back in my wilderness of pain. My puppet trick set in for the second time that day. My blood sugar level dropped dangerously low, my heart was pounding, and yet I felt as if I was just ticking over, almost as if I was about to expire. I knew it was going to be some time before this spectacle would stop, and the most frightening thing is that at this point, even if I was able to get some alcohol down me, it still wouldn't stabilize me. I needed medical treatment, and knew I couldn't get it even if I was somehow to manage to get to my doctor's surgery. I would probably be asked to leave the surgery. My presence, with the involuntary twitches of my limbs, my eyes, my mouth, my inability to sit or stand still anywhere – at this point I always felt the need to rock to and fro – would have caused too much distress to the other patients.

My wife helped me into bed, and I lay there in the foetal position trying not to be scared. I felt so much guilt – for my wife, it was unbearable. I tried to think of Alex One, a specialist alcohol detox unit in London. I was so fit and well for the last 14 days I was in there. I was in there for 28 days, and my detox worked after just 14. When I was discharged, I came out and got drunk on my first day out, and this all took place just a little over three months ago. I actually came out of there December 20th 2002; it's now just April 2003.

During the course of the night, I'd drifted in and out of some sort of fitful and hallucinatory sleep. Whether my eyes were closed or open, I would see things that weren't there. At some point during the night I realised, and it wasn't for the first time either, that if it wasn't for my wife being there for me, I would have to be put in a nursing home or a permanent dry house. Many of the people I've drunk with over the years have to live like this.

Somehow morning came. I walked through to the lounge and got a tin of my milky baby food, which I managed to drink without bringing it up. It was then 12 hours after my last drink of alcohol, and 24 hours since I last tried to drink my baby food. I just had at this point what we call the normal shakes; I still had a few twitches and the occasional involuntary limb movement, but apart from that I was able to sit fairly still. I didn't want to evoke my puppet trick by any sudden movement. I thought about the last dream I had just before I woke up; the one about a clown with black circles round his eyes. I always seem to have this dream when I'm coming off the drink.

My main goal now was to get to seven o'clock tonight without having a drink. I was absolutely desperate for a bath and I knew if I could sit quietly without having a drink for the next couple of hours, I should be able to do this. My wife wouldn't be going out until four that afternoon, when she would have to go to work, so I should be fairly safe. I never had a bath unless my wife was at least somewhere in the flat with me, in case I had a funny turn, a "fit".

If I could get to seven o'clock, that would be 24 hours without a drink. I knew that having a bath and sorting myself out with fresh clothes would take the best part of a couple of hours, and that would be another two hours without drinking. When you reach the stage I was at as an alcoholic, you quite literally have to take this battle one hour at a time, but one false move and you end up dreaming about clowns again. It's part of the AA's 12 steps, to take it one day at a time, but you do reach a point where you have to narrow that down to one hour at a time.

I sat as still as possible, with my clothes clinging to my clammy, smelly body, and while I was sitting there, with my wife busy around me, I realised that I needed to feel the hurt and the fear because, as long as I could feel it, it would help prevent me from picking up that can.

I did manage to get in the bath, and I did manage to kill a couple of hours; anybody who has ever tried to come off the drink – it doesn't matter for how short or long a time that is – they will tell you that every hour that goes by without a drink makes it that teeny bit easier for the next hour.

My wife had put all sorts of smelly oils and lotions in the bath for me, and I had a really long soak and a good scrub. I left the bathroom door wide open so my wife could keep an eye on me. When I finished in the bath, I had a lukewarm shower, put my clean clothes on and went back to my chair. I thought about doing some writing but knowing the state I was in, it would be out of the question. My wife had to leave for work at four o'clock and she would be back at 6.30pm. This would be a very dangerous two-and-a-half-hour period.

Although I was now clean, and had clean clothes on, I just couldn't do anything other than sit there looking at the floor. I would like to say I was brain-dead; but I wasn't. My mind was racing. I was quite literally filled with terror. Every little noise I heard, although I might not have known where the noise had come from, or even what it was, filled me with dread.

I would like the reader to bear in mind at this point that it wasn't hard drugs I was coming off, but alcohol. This was the effect it had on me. Do you know, as frightened as I was, I knew in the murky depths of my tortured mind that if I were still alive in, say, ten years from the time of this home detox, despite the fear and the pain, I would and will do it all again. It's called alcoholism.

As I sat there, rocking to and fro just staring at the floor, I couldn't help but notice the little pin-pricks of blood gradually beginning to appear on my forearms. This was caused by my liver impairment – alcohol abuse over a very long period. Now, this didn't particularly faze me as I'd had it so many times before, but as I watched the tiny droplets of blood drip onto the carpet below me and, being so small, disappear altogether, never to be seen again, it made me think: why am I so scared? There I was, sitting in my own flat, with my rent fully paid up, security locks on all my doors and windows, no unpaid debts and yet there I sat, rocking to and fro, scared witless by anything that I thought I saw or heard, simply because I wanted and needed to drink alcohol.

Medication from my GP, remember, was out of the question. If I were able to get to the surgery, I would probably have frightened the other patients.

I stopped dabbing the blood from my arms and sat there, fascinated at my lifeblood freely falling to the floor. I rather fancy, in fact I'm certain, I let this happen purposely, just so that I could go to the fridge and get my cider. For, after all, with bleeding arms you must be entitled to a drink.

My wife left me at 4 o'clock to go to work. It was now 6.30 and I was drunk. That was the end of my home detox with no medication. My arms had stopped bleeding and I was frightened of nobody. Just before I had my bath, and my puppet trick was at its worst, there was a workman working outside, putting up a new gatepost. And, because I hadn't had a drink at the time, I was so frightened that he might knock at my door and ask me for some water or something, that I actually hid under the bed. I knew, without alcohol in me, I just simply wouldn't be able to speak to him. But as I lay there thinking to myself that I had just been sitting in my chair with blood dripping from my forearms for about 30 minutes, and that had no fear for me, why on earth am I frightened of drinking my alcohol to make me feel as normal as the workman outside? That's when I got my bottle from the fridge, and that's also when I chatted to the workman like we were old friends.

End of home detox.

36

A Letter From Alcoholism

Dear Reader,

I am the disease that my friend and victim Brian has been writing about. Allow me to introduce myself: I am Alcoholism.

I am your disease, and to all who come into contact with me, I wish you death. Although it's always a bonus if you suffer first.

I am the disease of alcoholism. Cunning, baffling and powerful, that's me. I've killed millions, and will continue to do so. I've given you comfort. I was there for you when you were lonely. When you felt like dying, you called to me.

I love to make you hurt. I love to make you cry. Better still, I love it when I make you so numb you can neither hurt nor cry. That, to me, is true glory. I will give you instant gratification, and all I ask in return is long-term suffering.

When things were going right in your life, you invited me in. When things were going wrong in your life, you invited me in. I was the only one that could console you, and that consolation was your invitation. You weren't inspired or influenced by anything other than the fact that you simply wanted to feel my manifestation. Together we were able to destroy all the good things in your life.

People don't take me seriously. They take strokes seriously, and heart attacks; diabetes they take seriously. But fools that they are, they do not realise that without my help, these things, for the most part, would not be possible. I am such a hated disease, and yet I still can't be present unless YOU invite me in. It still amazes me how many people choose me over reality and peace.

I absolutely love and adore people who, even to this very day, still will not accept that I, alcoholism, am a disease. For how would I flourish without these fools? Not only would I not be able to kill people, I wouldn't be able to hurt their loved ones either.

You may very well meet me one day. And do you know? By the time you recognise me, you will obviously be suffering. But far more importantly, and unbeknown to you, your family, whoever they might be, will be suffering just as much, and you won't even know it.

Yours faithfully

ALCOHOLISM

37

Conclusion

It was time for Indra to take a holiday. She is Trinidadian, and, while her father could neither read nor write, he did manage to build his own house, which still stands today. He had managed somehow, with sheer hard work and guts, to buy a piece of land which, with the help of local labour, he farmed. Her father and mother have long since died but the house remains, so it was there that Indra decided to go for her holiday for one month.

Indra's biggest concern was whether I would be able to look after myself for a month on my own. I assured her I would, so she made all the arrangements and off she went. In truth I was scared witless; my biggest worry was what would happen if I had a fit and Indra wasn't there. Then I thought of all the people I drank with; probably about 80% of these people lived on their own so, I thought, if they can do it, so can I.

Something strange was to happen to me for the next four weeks. I neither knew how or why. It just did. I can only imagine it came about because of my fear of suddenly being on my own, but I cut my drinking down by about 50% and, instead of going down the seafront to where I knew all my drinking friends would be, I went in the opposite direction, right down to the old town purposely to be on my own. I didn't want to be among my fellow drinkers; I didn't want to be influenced by them; I didn't want to be in the Bottle Alley environment.

I kept this up for two consecutive weeks, and managed to save up quite a considerable amount of money. Now, I knew Indra was desperate to move out of our damp basement flat, but in the past there were three things that wouldn't allow me to do this, they were: no confidence, no guts and no money. Now, all of a sudden, with Indra gone and the knowledge that I could sit down the old town on my own and cut my drinking down by 50%, save money and not feel the need to sit with fellow drinkers, it gave me a lot of confidence. If I could do this for the next two weeks as well, there should be no reason for me not to try for another flat. After all, I knew that's what Indra wanted and deserved.

When I walked home that day, I was a very happy, confident, focussed man. I would do it; I would sit down the old town for another week, just for that little bit of extra money, and then the fourth and last week of Indra's holiday I would look for a flat. As far as the benefit system and the medical profession were concerned, I was what they termed "lifed off". I was on permanent disability living allowance for chronic alcoholism. My rent was paid and I didn't have to pay council tax. I started visiting estate agents and, because I had cut my drinking down by half, I was at that point bathing on a daily basis. I know normal people do that all the time, but I wasn't normal. I finally found a flat that I liked; the rent was much higher than I had expected, but it was a ground floor flat with a garden, two bedrooms and our own entrance. There was a chance that I might have to pay some sort of top-up rent, because the council only pays X amount, but I didn't mind; in fact I was ecstatic.

For Indra and I to be able to move in, we would need the following: a month's rent in advance, the same amount as a deposit, plus references. I had all three. I filled out the necessary forms and took them straight round to the borough treasurer who ultimately paid our rent. After they had checked that the place was habitable, they then confirmed with the estate agent that they were happy to pay the rent. I was in.

Indra was due home on the Tuesday, and I had arranged with the removal people to move us on the Friday. I was so excited. I had lived in that basement flat for no less then 17 years. I just hadn't had the bottle to move but, with Indra gone for four weeks out of my life, I'd realised I didn't want to lose her. Apart from when I had to see the estate agent, I still spent my time on my own down the old town away from my fellow drinkers. I felt so proud as I walked down the old town on the Monday, just one day prior to my wife coming home. I had a job to settle; I was on tenterhooks. It was exactly 27 days since I had seen my wife and, in all that time, I hadn't been drunk. Please God, let this be the end of my wretchedness and the beginning of some sort of pleasure in my life where I could actually make other people happy for, as I knew from experience, when you feel wretched and worthless with next to no self-esteem, it automatically rubs off onto others.

Indra arrived home the next day, tired, jet-lagged and shattered. I told her not to unpack anything as we were moving in three days time. She just couldn't believe it. She'd had a marvellous holiday, I was sober and looking well, and I'd finally managed to find us a new flat; and not only that but I had organised everything on my own. She was over the moon. My sister-in-law was just as excited, and helped us pack. We moved on the Friday, and we were happy; happy that is until I started, for whatever reason, to drink heavily again. My puppeteer was starting to play up again, simply because I was drinking too much. I would drink in the morning up until about midday, then wander over to the park just opposite to where we now lived. I would drink until the early evening and then wander back home. This routine went on constantly for about two months; it reached a point where I could no longer even get myself over to the park. India contacted CAT for me, and told them that I was once again out of control. My CPN visited me and we spoke for a couple of hours. A couple of days later, I received a phone call from CAT telling me they were trying to get me a bed at Alex One, specialist detox unit. Two weeks later I received a letter telling me they had a bed available; the programme was to last one month. I was pleased and relieved, as was my wife.

It was a good detox and, after just eight days, I was allowed to walk the grounds on my own unescorted. I completed the course, and Indra came and picked me up. The only stipulation they made was that I wasn't to leave the unit until Indra had actually arrived in the unit itself. This wasn't unusual; it was a policy they had for long-term drinkers. Indra and I walked the short distance to the town centre where we would get a bus into Croydon, and from there we would get the train down to Hastings. Just behind the bus stop was an off-licence; I walked in there and bought a six-pack of Stella lager. I opened my first can and had drunk it before the bus arrived. We got to Croydon station, boarded the train and off we went, and by the time we had reached Hastings I was drunk. I neither understood why, nor cared.

This is alcoholism, so don't try to understand it; after all I'm an expert and even I don't know the answer. Indra and I muddled through and then one day, I had a brainstorm. I do not know what came over me. Naturally I was drunk: very, very drunk. I don't know whether I did this out of guilt or self-hate, or because perhaps I knew in my heart that what I was doing to Indra was wrong. I don't want to launch myself into some sort of tirade of psychobabble, but I can only think that somewhere in my subconscious, I felt that I'd probably hurt India so much that she didn't know how to leave me. There was never ever any question that mentally and emotionally I was in great pain, and always had been, and while I think she could see it, over the years I'd always made a point of telling her I was like this long before she ever came on the scene. I didn't want her to think that she was somehow responsible for my condition, which obviously she wasn't.

This is how my brainstorm (insanity) came about. One of my wife's nieces was having a christening. It was her first child. My wife had told me earlier that day that she would be going, and asked if I would be all right. I told her I would be fine. When she told me, my puppeteer had only just finished with me so I was in a bit of a state, but was perfectly happy for her to go along. They would christen the baby and then go back to my sister-in-law's for a bit of food and of course a drink.

I took my drink over to the park, just opposite, sat down and started drinking. God knows why, but the more I drank the more maudlin I became. I remembered all those years ago when I was excluded from the family holiday; I remembered having to position myself so that my father didn't have to look at me; I remembered my uncle Bob hating me, and here I was sitting in a park while my wife was with her family who, in effect, were also my family, albeit not immediate family. Again I got this overwhelming feeling of being outcast; someone who had committed a crime and yet didn't know what it was. I remembered the bloke at the first re-hab I was in who said, when I told him my underwear had been stolen, that if I didn't like it then I could fuck off. And the lady at a B&B where I once stayed, who, when I asked her why we had to be so cold, said if I didn't like it then I could fuck off. I really was fast becoming paranoid.

Suddenly, in my drunken stupor, it made totally good sense that, as I had never done any of these people any harm, why on earth shouldn't I just ring them up and say I'm going to pop down for a while. I walked back home and rang Rajeer, my sister-in-law. After I had dealt with my puppeteer that morning, I had had a bath, shaved, and also had clean clothes on, so I was quite respectable looking. Rajeer answered the phone, and I said I would like to pop down. She said she'd rather I didn't, and hung up. I dropped the phone and slumped down in the chair like I had done a million times before. I wasn't paranoid; people really did hate me.

I picked the phone up again, and nobody answered. I let it ring for 30 minutes and still nobody answered. They knew it would be me, and Rajeer had probably told them not to answer the phone. I phoned one of Indra's nephews and explained I couldn't get through to Rajeer. He said, 'Look Brian, they don't want you there, so don't bother ringing anymore.' I hung up, totally dejected as I had been all my life. I then did something that I've never done before in my life. I did something spiteful, malicious and totally out of character. I gathered all my wife's personal letters, cards, photos, books, pictures, personal papers, everything and anything to do with my wife's family, put them all in a bin liner, dragged them out to the bottom of my garden and set light to them.

I flaked out next to the fire, still with my bottle in my hand. The next thing I knew was a policeman standing over me asking me if I was all right. It was dusk; he asked me if I was able to stand up. I said, 'Yes, officer,' and stood up immediately. He said, 'Only we had a call that you might be drunk, and that to light a fire at this time of night is illegal.' I pointed out to him that this was the furthest spot from the building, and therefore couldn't possibly be of any danger to anyone. He said to me, 'You haven't long been out of Alex One, have you, Brian?' I said, 'How on earth did you know my name, and how on God's earth could you have possibly known about Alex One?' He said, 'One of your neighbours told us,' and then he added, 'They only told us because they were concerned about your welfare. Shall we go inside?'

We talked at some length. He told me there was no charge against me, but to be careful in the future. I thanked him and he left. Indra knew nothing of this until the morning. To say she was distraught would be an understatement, she was beside herself with grief at how I could do such a thing. Don't ask me how, but we did get over it.

The following week, I got a notice of eviction. Indra and I had to move. We did find another flat, but unfortunately it was back in the St Leonards area – walking distance from Bottle Alley.

I needn't have worried about Bottle Alley as, where we were situated, our new flat was so awkward in that it was halfway up one of the steepest hills in St Leonards, and I was in such a state health-wise that while I could make it down there all right, it was almost impossible for me to get back up. I virtually became a recluse, doing all my drinking indoors.

Indra could see I was becoming more and more depressed; our only plus now was that if we did find another flat, at least we had the necessary funds to move, because we could just transfer our month's rent in advance plus our deposit into another flat. It was just a question of finding the right place as near to Hastings town as possible. We'd reached a stage whereby whenever Indra came home, either from shopping or from one of her part-time jobs, she would find me drunk, and while I was never a nuisance to her, it has to be said that I was no use to her. My alcoholism was now beginning to make her depressed; she became sullen, withdrawn, and we would sit there in the evening with really nothing to say. There were never any rows; in fact we were always polite with one another, but it was a politeness normally associated with working colleagues, not that of man and wife.

Indra had many friends and was well liked in our community. It did made me wonder how many of these friendships were born out of sympathy for her, simply for living with me, but I had to put that out of my mind because I just couldn't deal with it. Indra came home one day very, very excited; her sister – my sister-in-law – had told her there was a flat directly above hers that had just become vacant. My sister-in-law was friendly with the landlord, and she had recommended Indra and myself as good, responsible tenants. All we had to do was contact him and almost certainly the flat would be ours. We didn't hesitate; we contacted him and took the place over the phone without even looking at it.

We gave proper notice to our present landlord in order to get our full deposit back, plus our month's rent in advance, and moved into our new flat three weeks later. I was now back in town and, when the weather was fine, was able to wander down there, find a bench right in the centre of town, and do what I've always enjoyed doing, people-watch.

Indra became my official registered care-worker, and was paid for this accordingly. This did actually bring with it one small problem, in that if I were to comply with this arrangement to the letter, it meant I would have to be escorted wherever I went. I contacted the powers-that-be and explained that both Indra and I had mobile phones, and I would always carry my emphysema pump and my medication to stop me fitting, and that I would never leave the spot where Indra left me, plus they must appreciate that Indra couldn't take me into every shop she went in, so they told me they were happy with that, and then went on to remind me that the rules and regulations were only designed for my benefit, and for people like me.

I've told my story in my own way, through my own eyes, possibly self-indulgently at times, but it is a true account of my life as I've lived it. You see, I still hurt – and regardless of whose fault it was or wasn't, I have become an abuser, an abuser in that anyone who gets anywhere near me is pushed away. I really am very frightened that I've inherited some of my father's traits, and for that I'm ashamed.

Nowadays, you'll find me in the town centre – when my health allows – on a bench somewhere with my drink secreted about my person. Nowadays, 57 is a relatively young age but, in my embattled state, I not only feel 20 years older, I look it. When I first started writing this book, I was going to give such a clear message to young people not to drink whatever the circumstances, but I don't feel I'm qualified enough. You can look at me and see the end result, but I still didn't have the guts not to drink; hopefully the way I look, and the state of my health, will be enough to put people off drinking.

For me, the future is uncertain, and the end is always near.

Alex One
Clinical Treatment Contract

Treatment Offered

Welcome to Alex 1 Ward, inpatient alcohol treatment unit at Bethlem Royal Hospital. Your treatment here will consist of the following components:

1. A medically assisted withdrawal programme using sedative medication and vitamin supplements.
2. A medical assessment, including blood tests, to investigate your physical condition.
3. A structured programme of group work helping you to prevent relapse.
4. You will be required to undergo a risk assessment on admission which may be reviewed during your stay on Alex1.

Conditions of Treatment

In return for this we expect patients to agree to certain conditions of treatment, in order to ensure the best therapeutic environment for all patients on the Ward. These conditions are as follows:

1. You are normally expected to stay on the ward for the first 5 days of treatment. After this period leave from the ward is negotiated with your keyworker. Initially it may be decided that it is best for you to only leave the ward with an escort. You are expected to comply properly with the agreed leave arrangements.

2. You will not drink any alcohol or use any illicit substances or medication not prescribed on Alex 1 while receiving treatment here, even if on leave. You will not bring such items on to hospital property or organise someone else to do so.

3. You are expected to comply with regular breathalyser tests and give urine samples when requested.

4. You will comply with the Trust's requirements and rules regarding the reasonable conduct of clients while on the ward. A copy of these rules can be obtained from the nursing staff. They are designed to protect other patients and staff. Please note that any violence towards staff will normally result in prosecution.

Consent

I agree to comply fully with the treatment programme as outlined above and I agree to the above conditions of treatment. I understand that this consent represents a contract between myself and the staff and breaking this contract may lead directly to discharge from the Unit. I agree that Alex 1 staff may give information to and liaise with other involved agencies as necessary and appropriate to my care and treatment.

GP Yes/no	Referrer yes/no	CPN yes/no	Other relevant services yes/no	Legal services yes/no

Client's Name: ....
Witnessed by: ....
Signature: ....
Signature: ....
Date: ....

232

South London and Maudsley

NHS Trust

ADDICTIONS DIVISION
ALEX ONE
PART TWO & DISCHARGE SUMMARY

Name:	Brian Harding	**Address:**	
Date of birth:	20.10.47	First floor flat 18 Cornwallis Terrace Hastings	
Hospital No:	2002013585	East Sussex TN34 1EB	
Consultant:	Dr Jane Marshall	**Date of admission:**	2.12.04
Keyworker:	Peter Musgrove	**Date of discharge:**	20.12.04
Associate Worker:	Paul Pinn		

Type of discharge: Self

Address on discharge: As above

Discharge plans: Back to home/referrer

Prescribed medication taken on discharge:	**Hepatitis B injection:** YES
Multivitamins 1 tablet daily Vit B Complex 1 tablet tds	1st injection given on 17.12.04
Other medication: Serevent, Combivent 2 Salbutamol inhaler	**Due date for next injection:** 17.01.05

Diagnosis:

Axis I   **Clinical Condition:**   F102   Alcohol dependence syndrome
Axis II   **Personality, Mental Retardation:**
Axis III **General Medical Condition:**
Axis IV   **Psychosocial Stressors:**
Axis V   **Global Assessment of Functioning:**

Investigations Undertaken: as @ 16.12.04

FBC	-	Abnormal MCV:	101.2
		Abnormal WBC:	11.3
U&E	-	Abnormal K:	5.1
LFT's	-	Abnormal GGT:	169

Appendices:

Left, **Treatment Contract**, above and overleaf, **Discharge Summary**, both from Brian's detox visit at the end of 2004. There follows (pp235) a series of excerpts from a local authorities' partnership report on alcohol abuse strategies.

233

Medical Report & Complications of Treatment

Completed Detoxification	YES	
Medically assisted detox with:	**Commenced:**	**Terminated:**
Chlordiazepoxide	2.12.04	11.12.04
Pabrinex (10 days)	2.12.04	11.12.04

Vit B complex√
Multivitamins√

Other medical treatment during admission: He was referred to the Dermatology Dept. at Mayday for assessment of his skin irritation, confluent over trunk and extremities. However, Brian discharged himself prior to this assessment. We suggested to him that the deterioration in his eczema was related to his withdrawal from alcohol and that with abstinence it will improve. Topical standard remedies were of little help. I would be grateful if you could monitor this. Please find enclosed a copy of his normal chest X-ray.

Contractor: Hastings and St Leonards PCT

Group work:
Brian attended all group activities on the ward. He was an active participant and gave his peers positive feedback about their progress on the unit. He always answered questions ask in group about the complication of alcohol.

1 x 1 work:
Brian used 1x1 where he expressed his fear of relapse and his skin irritation.

Overall Impression of admission and recommendations for follow-up:
Brian successfully completed his assisted withdrawal from alcohol. During his stay he was a very active member of the unit, socialising with peers and giving advice on how to manage high-risk situations. He expressed his difficulties in remaining sober during his stay. After stress management he decided to self-discharge.

Follow up:
1. Copy of discharge summary to GP and referrer
2. Engage with Action for Change, Hastings

Signed: Dr. B Arroyo	Date:	Signed: Angela Raven	Date:
SHO to Dr Jane Marshall	24.02.05	Nurse	20.12.04

GP's address:	Referrer's address:
Dr. E A Furley-Smith	Ms Jo Dutson
Carisbrooke Surgery	Action for Change
Marlborough House	46 Cambridge Road
19-21 Warrior Square	Hastings
St Leonards-on-Sea	East Sussex TN34 1DT
East Sussex TN37 6BG	

Other interested parties:	Copy to client: (Does client wish to receive copies of correspondence written about him/her?) YES

If you require any further information regarding this admission, please contact: Alex One, Bethlem Royal Hospital, Monks Orchard, Beckenham, BR3 3BX, Tel No: 020 8776 4654. Fax No: 020 8776 4659

234

Local Authorities Partnership
Report on Alcohol Abuse Strategies

My own affair with drink has rendered me for the most part incontinent, Impotent and without any real place in society. There are so many negative things about street drinkers and I have to agree with most of it. But at the same time there are drinkers out there who haven't got much choice. – Brian Harding, service user, Community Alcohol Team Projects (South East Ltd).

Brian Harding is 55 although he looks at least ten years older due to 40 years of alcohol abuse. Brian still starts every morning with a drink, has been in and out of detoxification programs I6 times in the last 20 years and has "lost count of" the number of times he has been arrested for being drunk and disorderly. Brian is representative of the one in 13 adults who are so addicted to alcohol that they are unable to gel through the day without drink according to the charity Alcohol Concern's State of the Nation report 2002. The report also reveals that the South East has the largest number of people who misuse alcohol of any region in the UK with almost half a million people dependent on alcohol.

The effects of alcohol

Alcohol is a mood altering substance that, if taken excessively, can cause psychological and physical harm. It can cause harm in a variety of ways including:

- Aggression
- Anxiety
- Depression
- Heart and Liver damage
- High blood pressure
- Sexual difficulties

Although the Government is committed to producing a National Alcohol Strategy, it is unlikely to be implemented until early 2004. In the absence of national guidance, Hastings and St Leonards Primary Care Trust, together with neighbouring Bexhill and Rother Primary Care Trust, have produced a local alcohol strategy.

Why write a strategy?

Alcohol misuse has a significant impact on three key areas: social problems, crime costs and health costs.

Social problems

235

- Street drinking
- Family breakdown
- Child protection
- Domestic violence
- Work absence
- Truancy – 20% of excluded pupils were suspended for alcohol misuse, 16% of excluded pupils drink alcohol daily compared to 3% among other pupils
- Unplanned pregnancy & sexually transmitted disease – 40% of 13 & 14 year olds were drunk when they first experienced sexual intercourse.

Crime costs

> *"If anti-social behaviour caused by alcohol related violence is not effectively tackled, then the future regeneration of Hasting and St Leonards could be at risk." – Inspector Mike Fagan, Sussex Police.*

- In 41% of contact crime, either the offender or the victim had been drinking.
- 40% domestic violence incidents have alcohol as significant factor.

Sussex Police have a vested interest in improving the health of the population of Hastings and St Leonards as poor health has a direct impact on crime through anti-social behaviour. Alcohol abuse is a larger problem for Sussex Police in Hastings and St Leonards than drug crime. The majority of drug crime is acquisitive, eg; burglary, unlike crimes caused by people under the influence of alcohol such as violent assaults caused during binge drinking. This has a significant impact on police resources.

Health costs

- The cost to the NHS of Britain's drinking habits is as high as £3bn a year.
- Nationally, one in six people attending A&E have alcohol-related injuries or problems.
- Locally, one in four admissions to the Conquest Hospital in Hastings are as a result of violence related to alcohol.
- 65% suicide attempts linked to alcohol misuse.
- 1 in 7 traffic deaths alcohol related.
- Cirrhosis of the liver now kills more women than cervical cancer.
- Over 28,000 people are admitted to hospital every year in England and Wales because they are dependent on alcohol or have been poisoned by it.

Any strategy, to be successful, needs to target all three areas in partnership with other local agencies as well as implementing national initiatives.

236

"Alcohol misuse is one of the main causes of inequality in Hastings and St Leonards. The Community Alcohol Team is a strong believer in the joined up approach to finding solutions. This approach has strong support throughout the community in Hastings. Sitting down and finding solutions with groups as diverse as community and neighbourhood groups, Sussex Police, Hastings Borough Council, the Primary Care Trust. East Sussex County Council, East Sussex County Healthcare NHS Trust, and a range of colleagues from the voluntary sector make the problem solving so much more likely to succeed. We have real problems to tackle in this town but we will succeed because of the commitment to find answers."
– John Reading. Chief Executive. Community Alcohol Team Projects.

Although Hastings and St Leonards Primary Care Trust focuses on the health aspect of alcohol abuse it also targets young people before they become a problem. It takes a multi-disciplinary approach and its focus is on joint initiatives with other agencies, particularly the voluntary sector. The core principles at the heart of the local strategy are:

- focusing on all those affected by alcohol misuse, including the wider community
- the promotion of social justice and equality of access to services
- the use of a range of measures to maximise the potential to reduce harm
- the creation of an accountable structure with a long-term, consistent approach.

To achieve this Hastings and St Leonards Primary Care Trust has formed a strong working relationship with the local Community Alcohol Team.

Community Alcohol Team Project

The Community Alcohol Team Projects (South East) was established in 1991 with Section 64 grant funding and matched funding from Hastings Borough Council in order to plug the gap in provision for services for people with alcohol problems. As John Reading, Chief Executive of CAT explains; "Although Hastings and St Leonards isn't unique in having problem drinkers, the area does have a deep rooted cultural tradition of drinking. Hastings is a geographically isolated community and most social activities are based around drinking. Drinking is learned behaviour, so if people meet socially around pubs they will drink."

CAT provides a dedicated service for people with substance misuse problems, particularly problem drinkers, their relatives and partners. The service offers a range of educative, preventative, counselling and treatment services both directly through a professional staff team of paid and voluntary members, including staff seconded from the NHS and Social Services, and in collaboration with other voluntary and statutory organisations.

CAT gradually expanded from its Hastings base in late 1998 to provide services for the rest of East Sussex. CAT's budget is a combination of funding from a number of sources including the NHS, East Sussex County Council, the Probation Service, Hastings Regeneration Partnership and other sources. Recognition of CAT's positive impact on local communities was confirmed with funding from the Neighbourhood Renewal Fund. "Although we are based in the voluntary sector, I believe CAT is part of core NHS service delivery. We are really a statutory sector service based within the voluntary sector," says John.

Hastings and St Leonards – the way forward

We are not in the business of stopping people from drinking but helping them to conduct their lives more healthily by drinking more safety." – Frances McCarron, Hastings and St Leonards Primary Care Trust

The population of Hastings and St Leonards is not drinking any more than the national average, but there is a perception that there is not much to do in the town centre at night in terms of entertainment but drink. Anecdotal evidence suggests that many local people go out of the area to Eastbourne for theatre or cinema and older people consider the town centre a "no go" area at night. There are over 800 licensed premises in Hastings and St Leonards and the majority of entertainment activity in Hastings town centre is based around drinking. The result is that the only evening activity is around pubs/bars attracting predominantly young binge drinkers.

Both voluntary and statutory sectors are aware of this problem because of high visibility. Nationally more young people are drinking more often than previous generations and this is reflected locally in Hastings. Agencies are now seeing alcohol dependent 17 and 18 year olds who started drinking as young as 10 or 11 years of age.

There has also been recognition by planners that in years gone by the Council had allowed the area to get run down. Certainly the cheaper accommodation in the St Leonards area in particular has attracted people who are less likely to cope with life experiences and therefore may lead to alcohol related problems.

This is reflected in the fact that the ambulance callout peak days for Hastings town centre is Friday to Sunday and the peak day for central St. Leonards is Wednesday, which is benefits day.

"Historically there has been an absence of diverse leisure activities in Hastings and St Leonards which has led to the majority of entertainment activity being geared towards bars and pubs. Hastings Borough Council can help tackle alcohol related violence in our town in two ways. Firstly, the change in licensing laws will permit the Council to restrict the number of licenced premises or ensure that licensed premises are spread more evenly throughout the community. Secondly, we can work to facilitate more diverse leisure activities that are not based around alcohol consumption and would help attract a broader age range into our town centre in the evening and at weekends." – Jeremy Birch, Leader, Hastings Borough Council.

One innovation that the Community Alcohol Team is in favour of establishing, which is supported by partners including the PCT, Hastings Borough Council and Sussex Police, is a wet centre in Hastings. However, it is recognised by all partners that such a step could prove contentious locally. John Reading admits that a wet centre could be viewed as just a containment strategy to keep street drinkers out

238

of sight form the public but believes that there are good reasons for curbing nuisance drinkers who are at risk of harming themselves and others. "Street drinkers are a very difficult group with which to engage. A wet centre would help us identify their health problems, provide them with access to medical and care services, and hopefully provide a point of stability in their lives."

Hastings and St Leonards PCT has always placed alcohol at the centre of our agenda to tackle inequalities in health, particularly due to the significant impact alcohol has on other services such as mental health and teenage pregnancy. However, alcohol abuse has a far wider negative impact than on the health of individuals and can damage relationships, families and the wider community. Because the PCT has effective relationships with our key strategic partners in local government and Sussex Police, we have been able to influence the agenda so that all agencies are taking an holistic approach to tackling alcohol abuse in Hastings and St Leonards." – Toni Wilkinson, Chief Executive, Hastings and St Leonards PCT.

In latter years, Brian was a familiar figure in Hastings town centre, selling his book and talking about alcohol abuse and the realities of life for street drinkers.